Honored Citizens
of Barcelona

James S. Amelang

Honored Citizens of Barcelona: Patrician Culture and Class Relations, 1490-1714

PRINCETON UNIVERSITY PRESS

Copyright © 1986 by Princeton University Press
Published by Princeton University Press,
41 William Street, Princeton, New Jersey 08540
In the United Kingdom: Princeton University Press,
Guildford, Surrey

Library of Congress Cataloging in Publication Data will be found
on the last printed page of this book

ISBN 0-691-05461-4

Publication of this book has been aided by a grant
from the Publications Program of
the National Endowment for the Humanities,
an independent Federal agency

This book has been composed in Linotron Janson

Clothbound editions of Princeton University Press books
are printed on acid-free paper, and binding materials
are chosen for strength and durability

Printed in the United States of America
by Princeton University Press
Princeton, New Jersey

TO MY FATHER, JEAN, AND ELENA,
IN MEMORY OF MY MOTHER

TABLE OF CONTENTS

CONTENTS

TABLES

GRAPHS

MAPS

ILLUSTRATIONS

NOTE

I have modernized the spelling and punctuation of citations from original sources; all translations are my own unless otherwise noted. Catalan renderings are given for place names in the absence of more familiar equivalents (e.g., Saragossa for Zaragoza, or Perpignan for Perpinyà). I have tried to minimize the use of foreign terms and to make their meaning consistently clear. Readers seeking further information should consult the comprehensive glossary and appendices in J. H. Elliott's *The Revolt of the Catalans: A Study in the Decline of Spain, 1598-1640* (Cambridge, 1963), 553-78.

Full references are given at the first citation of all documents and manuscripts. Printed works are referred to by the author's last name and short title; more complete information can be found in the bibliography at the end of the book.

The term "oligarchy" designates the ruling group of honored citizens prior to 1510. "Nobility" and "aristocracy" refer to the traditional Catalan second estate of predominantly rural origins. "Ruling," "governing," or "upper class"; "patriciate"; "notables"; and "elite" all denote the composite group created by the merger during the sixteenth and seventeenth centuries of the urban oligarchy and traditional nobility that is the subject of this book.

ABBREVIATIONS

A.H.M.B.	Arxiu Històric Municipal de Barcelona (Municipal Archive, Barcelona)
A.H.P.B.	Arxiu Històric de Protocols de Barcelona (Notarial Archive, Barcelona)
A.C.A.	Arxiu de la Corona d'Aragó (Archive of the Crown of Aragon, Barcelona)
Can.	Cancelleria (Chancery)
Gen.	Generalitat
C.A.	Consell d'Aragó (Council of Aragon)
A.E.B.	Arxiu Episcopal de Barcelona (Diocesan Archive, Barcelona)
B.U.B.	Biblioteca Universitària de Barcelona (University Library, Barcelona)
B.C.	Biblioteca de Catalunya (Catalan Library, Barcelona)
F. Bon.	Fullets Bonsoms (Bonsoms Pamphlet Collection)
B.P.T.	Biblioteca Pública de Tarragona (Public Library, Tarragona)
A.G.S.	Archivo General de Simancas (National Archive, Simancas)
A.H.N.	Archivo Histórico Nacional (National Archive, Madrid)
B.N.	Biblioteca Nacional (National Library, Madrid)
A.R.S.I.	Archivum Romanum Societatis Iesu (Jesuit Archive, Rome)

A.S.V.   Archivio Segreto Vaticano (Vatican Archive, Rome)

Dietari   *Manual de Novells Ardits: Vulgarment Apel.lat Dietari del Antich Consell Barceloní* (Barcelona, 1892-1975), 28 vols. (minutes of the Barcelona City Council)

leg./llig.   *legajo/lligall*

ACKNOWLEDGMENTS

This book owes more acknowledgments than it deserves. Various institutions have provided grants for study in Spain, beginning with my first doctoral research in 1977. They include the: Council of European Studies; Committee on European Cultural Studies, History Department, and Graduate School of Princeton University; Social Science Research Council; Whiting Foundation; Danforth Foundation; American Philosophical Society (Penrose Fund); American Council of Learned Societies; National Endowment for the Humanities; and the History Department, Division for Sponsored Research, and Graduate School of the University of Florida. I am grateful to all these organizations for their support and encouragement. I am especially indebted to Professor John H. Elliott and the Directors of the Institute for Advanced Study, and to the History Department of Princeton University for the assistantship (1980-1981) and postdoctoral appointment (1983-1984) that provided the tranquility needed for writing this work. The generous support (and tolerant good humor) of my colleagues at the University of Florida also contributed vitally to the finishing of such a lengthy project. Finally, I am obliged to Steven Boyett, Adrienne Turner, and Tina Slick for typing endless versions of the text with exemplary speed and surprising cheerfulness.

I gratefully acknowledge the *American Historical Review*, the University Presses of Florida, and the *Journal of European Economic History* (published by the Banco di Roma) for permission to reproduce excerpts from previously published essays and articles. Similar thanks are due to the Institut Municipal d'Història, the Museu d'Història de la Ciutat, and the Museu de Ceràmica of Barcelona for permission to reproduce materials from their collections. I am also indebted to Michelle Mannering, editorial assistant to the *American Historical Review*, and Marjorie

Niblack of the Office of Instructional Resources of the University of Florida for their expert assistance in preparing the graphs and maps. I consider myself particularly fortunate to have had as editors and designer Miriam Brokaw, Joanna Hitchcock, and Peter Andersen of Princeton University Press. Their patient forebearance and good humor have been much appreciated.

Many teachers and colleagues have made my task easier by criticizing this book at several of its stages. Natalie Zemon Davis, Felix Gilbert, Temma Kaplan, Peter Sahlins, John Sommerville, and Stanley Stein all read chapters and provided helpful comments. Cheryll Cody overcame her initial horror at my manhandling of quantitative data to suggest ways in which their presentation might be improved. The late Allan Sharlin also read portions of this work; I join others in missing his dry humor and generous criticism. I owe a special debt to my graduate adviser, Theodore K. Rabb, and to Anthony Grafton, john Elliott, and Lawrence Stone, the other readers of the thesis upon which this study was based. Needless to say, the indulgence all these scholars have shown toward my work does not oblige them to share responsibility for its conclusions.

I take pleasure in acknowledging two other longstanding debts at Princeton University. Like all other history graduate students, I am grateful to Leona Halvorsen, Alice Lustig, Charlotte Skillman, and other members of the departmental staff for their many kindnesses. I also owe an irrevocable debt to those from whom I learned the most while in school—my fellow students. I feel privileged to have been able to live for years in an atmosphere marked by the free and lively exchange of ideas and criticisms among friends. I need not mention them by name, as they know all too well who they are.

"I went openly to the city of Barcelona, the archive of courtesy, refuge of foreigners, hospital of the poor, country of the valiant, avenger of the offended, and abode of firm and reciprocal friendships." How true the words of Miguel de Cervantes still ring! Throughout my stay in Catalonia I enjoyed the good fortune of coming into contact with historians whose selflessness and generosity can only be described as exemplary. While limitations of space prevent my listing all those who have helped with the research and writing of this book, I could not fail to mention certain individuals. First, I would like to thank the personnel of the archives and libraries where I carried out my research. I am especially indebted to Laureà Pagarola and Ariana Ruiz of the local Notarial Archive for their cheerful assistance. Special mention should also be made of Sr. Jaume Martorell, an exceptionally informed bookseller and a valued friend. To Josep Fontana I am indebted for criticism as constructive as it was forthright. I am similarly grateful to Manuel Arranz, Josep M. Fradera, Ricard García Cárcel, Xavier Gil, Carlos Martínez Shaw, Eva Serra, Jaume Torras, and Jordi Vidal. All the above-mentioned have lent forms of assistance far transcending mere professional courtesy. To each of them I extend my thanks for their help and, above all, their friendship.

Special mention should also be made of other friends who have contributed to the unfolding of this study. Bill Christian, Temma Kaplan, Gianna Pomata, Peter Sahlins, and Mike Seidman did their best to focus my attention on the larger issues of social and cultural history. Lorraine Daston and Richard Kagan offered words of encouragement at crucial moments. Gary McDonogh has been present since the creation of this book. Only he can be aware of the extent to which his suggestions and remarks have shaped it. And I am deeply grateful to John Elliott for the consistent support he has shown for my work. I have found this confidence a dependable source of intellectual stimulus and personal help, and wish to register, once again, my thanks.

It almost——but not quite——goes without saying that I have incurred the greatest debt with kith and kin on both sides of the waters. My warmest memories are of Pep and Carme, Ana and Maria, the two Xaviers, and other *companys* who would doubtless prefer to remain nameless. Because of them I recall with pleasure days at the archives, and nights spent far away from the seventeenth century.

Gainesville, March 1985

PREFACE

This book is a study in the formation of class consciousness. It analyzes the world-view of an early modern urban patriciate, especially in relation to questions of class identity and political dominance. In particular I focus on the ways in which the emergence of a new, unified ruling class transformed elite perceptions of socio-political organization and hierarchy. The links between patterns of social change and the cultural expressions of class relations constitute the principal subject of this inquiry. I also seek to provide a case-study in the consolidation of elite hegemony during a crucial period in the evolution of Mediterranean cities. While concentrating on Barcelona, I have tried to frame my arguments with a comparative perspective in mind. I hope the reader will thus gain a sense of the extent to which the evolution of a single city can serve as a model against which one can test the urban history of early modern Europe as a whole.

My more specific aim is to locate the socio-political matrix of the term "culture" itself by tracing its expanding role in both the perception and reality of early modern class relations. The word *cultura* and its cognates loom large in our everyday vocabulary of description and assessment. Yet how, when, and above all why this came about is a problem historians have yet to explore. "Culture" is, to be sure, a notoriously imprecise concept; like the apostle, it is all things to all men. In the eyes of many it denotes the last, beleaguered redoubt of humane letters. Matthew Arnold, to cite but one example, penned one of the most eloquent statements of this view. In his hands, "culture" served as an emotive rallying cry for the defense of class privileges threatened by a rising tide of social change. Beginning in the same period, however, anthropologists and others among the more relatively minded fashioned and diffused a strikingly different interpretation. To them "culture"—or more properly "cultures"—refers to the plurality of values, beliefs, and patterns of behavior of human beings within a much wider range of social and ethnic groupings. Needless to say, this broader definition has yet to find more general acceptance. The colloquial, almost normative usage of the term still evokes a highly static notion of refinement, learning, and/or good taste. For most members of our society, "culture" is a mark of distinction, an alien symbol of rank and privilege. Its deprivation constitutes one of the many "hidden injuries of class."

The following investigation into the pre-history and subsequent evolution of the vocabulary and beliefs of a ruling class is an exercise in what is known, for better or worse, as the "history of mentalities." While I share with others certain reservations about this term, I fully agree with those who argue that economic, social, and political realities cannot be understood without reference to mental structures. I have analyzed these latter constructs, however, as a historian, and can only hope that my relentlessly unliterary approach to literature will not prove too suspect to neighbors in other disciplines.

Any study of the fortunes of an entire class should devote equal attention to economic, social, and political factors. Its goal must be to capture the elusive quarry of "total history." Such brave words, however, afford scarce comfort to the practicing historian, who in the course of archival work is obliged to impose certain limitations upon the scope of research. The choices shaping the contours of these simple annals of the powerful deserve brief mention here. First, I am aware of the need for more extensive discussion of the economic basis of class relations. This book had, in fact, its distant origins in a proposed thesis on economic ideologies in seventeenth-century Barcelona. However, I arrived there to find serious problems regarding local economic documentation. Barcelona lacked reliable tax-lists or estimates of wealth prior to the eighteenth century. There were few private archives for the study of early modern elite families, while similar documents within the notarial archive were much too dispersed for efficient use. Finally, few secondary studies on the Catalan urban economy existed to guide my undertaking. It became immediately apparent that the sort of patient, methodical reconstruction that the study of the Barcelona economy deserved was not a realistic possibility for anyone with fewer than a dozen years to spend in the archives. I therefore narrowed my focus to a single social class—hardly a small enterprise in itself—and limited my economic research to the rentier patrimony of the elite. I cannot pretend that this choice was out of harmony with my original interest in the study of mentalities. I nevertheless regret the deficiency, and hope that future studies on Barcelona's economy will appear to confirm or contradict my findings.

The case of the political activities of the urban elite, which are dealt with only in passing in this book, presented a similar problem. Clearly the manipulation of power constitutes an important issue for anyone writing the history of a ruling class. However, here too a dearth of documentation hampers analysis of municipal administration. Both of the leading sources for the study of early modern civic politics—the detailed internal deliberations of government bodies (traditionally the principal source of historians of the Florentine regime) and the diaries of participants in the local political system (used effectively by Robert Finlay and Edward Muir in recent studies of Venice)—are generally lacking in the case of Barcelona. With patience and effort someday a thorough study of early modern Catalan urban politics may be written. Unfortunately, if my experience is any guide, much patience will be needed.

Rather different conditions influenced my decision not to undertake a prosopography of the Barcelona elite. An abundance of notarial records permits reconstruction of the family structures, inheritance patterns, and material culture of the local ruling class. However, the haphazard commission and organization of this archival embarrassment of riches prevented my obtaining a statistically significant sample. I quickly found myself facing an all-or-nothing proposition: either to undertake an exhaustive prosopographical analysis involving years of research, or to avoid lines of argumentation whose full verification depended on such a study. I opted for the latter, in the belief that the travail required to produce a collective biography of these dimensions simply was not worth it. Although I wound up reconstructing more genealogies than I care to remember, I remain convinced that this decision was the correct one.

So much for past choices; what of the future? This book represents the initial contribution to a more general study of the history of the social and political functions of "culture." Like a Golden Age play, the script is divided into three acts, and uses a Spanish city for its backdrop. At the beginning of the piece, the lights come up on a stage crowded with many masters and few servants; rich costumes and elaborate posturing betray the players' membership in the elite. At this point the appearance of other citizens is more fleeting; their voices, to the extent that they are heard, sound from offstage. At the beginning of the second act, however, the noble protagonists slip into the wings after a seventeenth-century artisan steals the show by writing a chronicle of his own life. The diary of the tanner Miquel Parets—the theme of my next book—contains precious (and sobering) insights into how members of the "lower" class viewed the elite pretensions to cultural superiority portrayed in the opening scenes. Following his tragicomic soliloquy, the chorus returns to the fore-stage. The final act explores the ambivalent stance toward *cultura* among anarchists and other working-class militants from the later nineteenth century to the Spanish Civil War. In short, I have written the present book as a prolegomenon to a more extensive project of research and revision. As with other first acts, its purpose is to set the stage by introducing the characters and getting the action underway. The sympathetic onlooker may choose to withhold judgment until the lights come up again.

Honored Citizens
of Barcelona

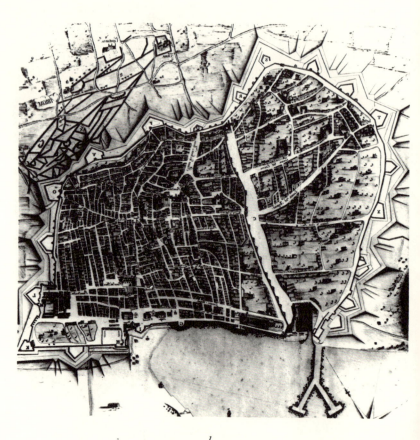

1

Anonymous Plan of Barcelona (1696). Detail from the
original in the Museu d'Història de la Ciutat, Barcelona.

I

A MEDITERRANEAN
CITY

"*Barcelona* measures in circumference 8,300 paces. I myself have walked them off." It is hard to imagine a tiresome university professor stirring himself to trudge along the nearly five miles of the city's outer walls. However, one cannot impugn the rest of Jeroni de Jorba's enthusiastic description of Barcelona as "singularly illustrious, ancient, rich, and powerful." Virtually all early modern visitors to the capital of the Principality of Catalonia echoed Jorba's flattering depiction of its beauty and wealth. Even the youthful Guicciardini—not one to waste words in praise of any city apart from his own native Florence—grudgingly admitted that Barcelona was "a lovely city, large and well-populated. While there do not seem to be any particularly notable or excellent private buildings, houses throughout the entire city are generally quite beautiful. For, as its inhabitants say, it is a city for everyone. This, in my judgment, is its most striking feature, one in which it overshadows even Florence."[1]

Early modern plans and views of Barcelona reveal a city huddled in a sweeping arc around the Mediterranean (see Illustration 1). Until the mid-sixteenth century, the maritime esplanade extended directly from the beach to a row of unprotected

[1] Jorba, *Descripción*, 1r.-v. and 8v.; Guicciardini, *Diario*, 51. Guicciardini visited Barcelona in 1512.

3

frontal buildings. These included, from north to south, the municipal granary, customs-house, a huge Franciscan monastery, and the *Dressanes* or royal shipyards. Fears of attack by Moorish pirates, however, prompted the town's authorities to construct a sea wall. Completion of this lengthy project, begun in 1529, finally enclosed the city's entire perimeter behind an impressive ring of fortified walls, towers, and bastions.[2]

The sea played a prominent role in the everyday lives of Barcelona's inhabitants. Yet the city's true center—geographical, political, and religious—lay, not in its port, but rather inland within the original Roman settlement of Barcino, known today as the "Gothic Quarter" (see Map 1). This area, with its narrow streets and busy shops, housed the leading public institutions of the municipality.[3] These included: the vice-regal Palace, shared by the Viceroy, Inquisition, and the *Audiència*, or high court of appeals; the City Hall; the palace of the *Generalitat*, or permanent commission of the Catalan parliamentary Estates; and the complex tangle of buildings—cathedral, episcopal palace, and almshouse—containing the local ecclesiastical hierarchy. The area's remarkable density merely highlighted one of the more crucial factors affecting the urban organization of Barcelona: its lack of a well-defined spatial center. To be sure, local magistrates made several attempts during the sixteenth and seventeenth centuries to widen and embellish the Plaça de St. Jaume, the small square housing the City Hall and the palace of the *Generalitat*.[4] Nevertheless, the lack of spacious open areas in its center deprived Barcelona of a recognizable urban focus along the lines of Florence's Piazza della Signoria or the Piazza San Marco in Venice.

[2] Galera et al., *Atlas de Barcelona*; Vilar, "Un Moment Crític en el Creixement de Barcelona: 1774-1787," in his *Assaigs*, 43-53; Amich, *Historia del Puerto de Barcelona*.

[3] Platter, *Journal of a Younger Brother*, 201; Ainaud et al., *Catálogo Monumental*; Duran, *Barcelona i la seva Història*, I; Mas, *Notícies Històriques*, I.

[4] Carreras Candi, *Geografia General*, unnumbered map of the Plaça de St. Jaume.

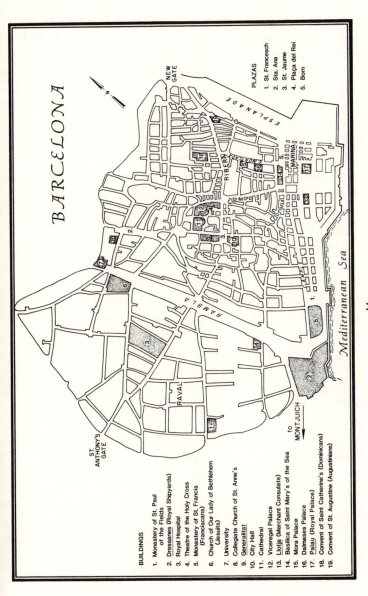

Map 1

Plan of Early Modern Barcelona

BUILDINGS

1. Monastery of St. Paul of the Fields
2. Dressanes (Royal Shipyards)
3. Royal Hospital
4. Theatre of the Holy Cross
5. Monastery of St. Francis (Franciscans)
6. Church of Our Lady of Bethlehem (Jesuits)
7. University
8. Collegiate Church of St. Anne's
9. Generalitat
10. City Hall
11. Cathedral
12. Viceregal Palace
13. Llotja (Merchant Consulate)
14. Basilica of Saint Mary's of the Sea
15. Mora Palace
16. Dalmases Palace
17. Palau (Royal Palace)
18. Convent of Saint Catherine's (Dominicans)
19. Convent of St. Augustine (Augustinians)

PLAZAS

1. St. Francesch
2. Sta. Ana
3. St. Jaume
4. Plaça del Rei
5. Born

Local ceremonial and festive life thus gravitated toward less-encumbered areas on the city's periphery. Prominent among these were the *Born*, or colorful market square at the northeastern end of the stately avenue known as the Carrer de Montcada; the beach, where in a mythical encounter the Knight of the White Moon vanquished Don Quijote; the nearby Plaça de St. Francesch, traditional site of the guild parades following the swearing of the royal oath to the Catalan constitution; and the *Rambla*, a lively thoroughfare which originally lay outside the second set of walls built in the thirteenth century.[5]

The *Rambla* served as an axis dividing the city's center from the newer settlement to the south known as the *Raval*. The outermost ring of walls erected during the fourteenth century enclosed the latter area. The *Raval* (literally, a "suburb") was a large if thinly-populated quarter, famous for its *horts* or garden plots. Its abundant open space encouraged the new clerical foundations of the sixteenth and seventeenth centuries to locate their churches and convents within its walls. The *Raval* also contained the poorest inhabitants of the city, and thus included a large proportion of the town's apprentices and clothworkers.[6]

The relatively low population density of the southern *barri* contrasted sharply with the high concentration of inhabitants in the rest of the city. The northernmost quarter was known colloquially as the *Ribera*.[7] This commercial and artisan district housed many of the city's specialized craft guilds and merchants' palaces. Its principal buildings included the large Dominican and Augustinian convents, and the opulent basilica of Santa Maria del Mar. The latter lay alongside the *Born* and the Carrer de

---

[5] Vila, "Orígens i Evolució de la Rambla"; Casas Homs, "Les *Llaors* de Barcelona," 251.

[6] In his 1716 tax declaration, the physician Josep Pomada claimed he earned practically no income as he lived in "the *raval*, whose inhabitants are almost all impoverished"; A.H.M.B./Cadastre, vol. 15, "Denuncias Particulares," no. 382.

[7] Sanpere Miquel, *Topografía Antigua*; Ros Torner, *Ribera*.

Montcada, where many of its wealthier parishioners resided. Equally prominent was the notorious *Marina*, a row of ramshackle tenements which gave shelter to a transient population of sailors, fishermen, dockworkers, and other casual laborers. During the early seventeenth century, the volatile *gent de Ribera* showed a troublesome penchant for sudden and violent riots—a crowd license which did little to enhance their reputation among members of the urban elite.[8]

Neither the physical dimensions nor the architectural styles and typologies of Barcelona changed significantly from 1490 to 1714. True, certain reforms sought to embellish the city along the lines of the classical urbanistic aesthetic prevailing in Renaissance and Baroque Italy. These projects included the construction in the 1590s of the new facade of the Palace of the *Generalitat*, and the demolition in 1598 for aesthetic reasons of the old fish market.[9] Nevertheless, such alterations were mostly sporadic, incremental endeavors—a far cry from the sustained initiatives launched by the great urban reformers of seventeenth-century Paris or Rome. The handful of aristocratic mansions built in this period proved quite modest alongside contemporary Italian *palazzi*. In fact, with few exceptions they modelled themselves directly upon the standard local artisan residence of the later Middle Ages. Slightly more numerous were the new churches and convents of the Counterreformation orders, such as the Jesuits, Discalced Carmelites, and Minims.[10] Yet, on the whole, early modern Barcelona witnessed surprisingly little transformation of the organization of its urban space or the architectural features of its buildings. Fundamental change of this sort would have to await the dramatically altered political and

---

[8] Bassegoda, *Santa Maria del Mar*; Amelang, "Carrer de Montcada"; Parets, "Sucesos," vol. 20, 43.

[9] Ràfols, *Pere Blay*; B.C./Ms. 505, under the year 1598.

[10] Barraquer, *Casas de Religiosos*.

economic circumstances of the later eighteenth and nineteenth centuries.

The absence of change in the city's physical and architectural fabric was closely linked to stability in the demographic sphere. The overall population of Barcelona increased only slightly during the two centuries under review. According to the census of 1516, Barcelona contained 6,388 hearths housing some 30,000-35,000 permanent residents. The *catastro* or tax-registry of 1716-1717 listed a total of 7,717 *veïns*, or heads of households, which represented a secular increase of approximately one-fifth.[11] This modest expansion did not take the form of a tranquil, uninterrupted rise. Epidemic disease and warfare caused sharp fluctuations in the city's population throughout the early modern period. An especially grave incidence of the former was the plague of 1589-1590, which claimed some 11,000 casualties. The years 1651-1652 proved even more disastrous, as siege, famine, and plague combined to wipe out over one-third of the city's population.[12] Still, comparatively rapid recuperation of earlier population levels usually made up for such demographic catastrophes. A mere generation following the plague of 1589-1590, Barcelona's population totalled some 40,000-50,000 inhabitants—the highest level since the early fourteenth century. This demographic resilience rested largely upon the city's success in assuring regular provisions of wheat and other staples. Security of food supplies—based upon the importation of grains from Sicily, Sardinia, and southern France—helped account for the relative

[11] Nadal and Giralt, *Population Catalane*; Nadal, "Contribution des Historiens Catalans"; Iglésies, *Estadìstiques de Població de Catalunya*; Elliott, *Revolt*, 27-28. Unfortunately, no complete census of Barcelona was taken from 1516 to 1716.

[12] *Dietari*, VI, 136-165; Smith, "Barcelona Bills of Mortality"; Parets, "Sucesos," vol. 24, 396-462; Viñas Cusí, *Glànola a Barcelona*.

absence of the severe subsistence crises which plagued many other cities in early modern Europe.[13]

The rapid replenishment of Barcelona's demographic resources also depended upon the constant flow of immigrants into the city. A sample of over 500 marriage contracts from the seventeenth century affords a glimpse into patterns of inter-generational geographic mobility.[14] Of the 529 families surveyed, some 241 or 46 percent of grooms and their fathers lived in the same place, as opposed to the 288 or 54 percent who lived apart. Of the latter portion, a plurality of 93 (32 percent of this group) were sons of peasants who had left the family farm to take up non-agricultural work in the city. A full one-fifth of this category (60) comprised immigrants from southern France whose families still resided north of the Pyrenees. In short, these figures reveal a substantial amount of "horizontal" change in residence between the two generations of fathers and sons. Over one-half of the grooms had migrated from their parents' home to take up a new trade within the city or in the neighboring countryside. This regular pattern of turnover highlights Barcelona's role as a catchment area for rural immigrants. Their contribution to replacing the city's human resources proved crucial in maintaining the overall stability of the urban population.[15]

The constant influx of migrants from the countryside provided merely one point of contact between Barcelona and its hinterland. The municipal government's need to ensure urban food supplies led it to seize control over many neighboring villages. Direct administration by the city of adjacent towns like

[13] Font Llagostera, "Problema Triguero en Barcelona."
[14] A.H.P.B./Pedro Llunell, *Libro Primero de Capítulos Matrimoniales* (1604-1610); Antonio Roure, *Libros Tercero y Quarto de Capítulos Matrimoniales* (1610-1622); Joseph Galcem, *Manual de Capítulos Matrimoniales* (1649-1660) and *Pliego de Capítulos Matrimoniales Sueltos* (1661-1685); Jaume Rondó, *Llibre de Capítols Matrimonials* (1660-1674); Francesch Llauder, *Libro de Capítulos Matrimoniales* (1665-1712); Juan Romeu, *Llibre dels Capítols Matrimonials* (1679-1692).
[15] For similar trends in the rest of Europe, see Clark, "Migration in England," and Sharlin, "Natural Decrease in Early Modern Cities."

Montcada, Caldes de Montbuy, and Martorell earned the latter
the colloquial sobriquet of *carrers* or "streets" of Barcelona—a
clear testimony to their feudal subordination to the capital (see
Map 2).[16] Ownership by Barcelona's citizens of nearby landhold-
ings also guaranteed urban domination over the surrounding
countryside. Investment in these small estates fostered the emer-

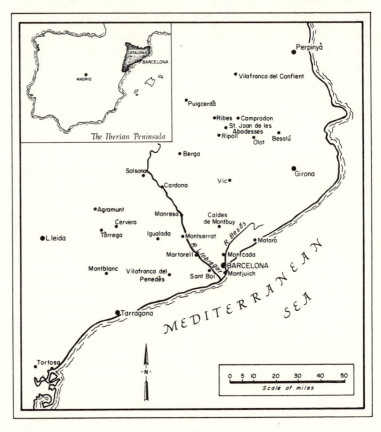

Map 2
Barcelona and Its Environs

[16] Plantada, "Concejo Catalán."

gence of a fairly brisk local land market during the sixteenth and seventeenth centuries, especially in the Llobregat valley south of the city.[17] Lists of properties in inventories *post mortem* reveal that the purchase of small plots and houses in the immediate environs of Barcelona was not limited to members of the city's clerical establishment, nobility, or merchant community. The more prosperous guild masters also invested substantially in rural real estate. The presence of artisans within the ranks of local landowners suggests that direct urban control over rural property was relatively small and individual in character. The reduced scale of this participation distinguished investment in the Catalan *contado* from similar developments in the rest of Europe. The comparatively modest initiatives of Barcelona's citizens bore little resemblance to the massive outflow of urban (especially aristocratic) capital directed toward the agricultural improvement of, say, the Venetian hinterland during the same period.[18]

Barcelona's involvement in the rural sphere was not limited to its control over neighboring villages and tracts of land. The life of the countryside reached up to and even penetrated the very walls of the city. The produce supplying the thriving fruit and vegetable market of the *Born* was cultivated in fields immediately outside the city gates. In 1626 the tanner Miquel Parets noted in this diary that the crowd waiting for the king to enter the city was so large that "people were forced off the roads, thus destroying the harvest in many of the fields near the city's gate."[19] Truck crops were also grown in the many small plots within the city itself. Barcelona even boasted the existence of two separate guilds of *hortolans*, or urban gardeners. Members of the larger corporation, that "attached to St. Anthony's Gate," tended the bulk of the city's plots located near the Benedictine monastery of St. Paul of the Fields in the *Raval*. The other con-

---

[17] Codina, *Delta de Llobregat i Barcelona*.
[18] Woolf, "Venice and the Terraferma"; Pullan, "Occupations and Investments of the Venetian Nobility."
[19] Parets, "Sucesos," vol. 20, 4.

fraternity, the *hortolans* of the *Portal Nou* (New Gate), grouped together those agricultural laborers who worked in the fields to the north and east of the city beyond the *Ribera*.[20]

A symbiotic if unequal relationship thus bound the city to the countryside. As a result, contact with outlying rural areas was normally quite close. Tensions did of course arise as a result of the city's domineering attitude toward its hinterland. For example, resentment of Barcelona's authoritarian control underlay the apocalyptic warnings against the sin and corruption of its citizens in manifestoes issued during the peasant revolt of 1640.[21] There is also evidence to suggest that urban dwellers felt increasingly isolated from "country matters." The condescending description by an eighteenth-century urban lawyer of rural dwellers as "men of another world, living in another century" reflected a widening distance between town and country—one that conferred a renewed sense of cultural superiority upon the inhabitants of the city.[22]

The sense of the urban area as a "world apart" derived in large measure from the existence of separate patterns of work and production. Specifically urban economic sectors like long-distance trade and craft manufactures first arose during the high Middle Ages as a result of increased division of labor and economic specialization. By the fourteenth century Barcelona had distinguished itself as one of the leading Iberian producers of cloth, silk, and ceramics.[23] It exported these wares within an extensive trading area which included the Balearic Islands, Sardinia, Sicily, and southern Italy. The later Middle Ages saw the apogee of Catalan domination within the western Mediterra-

[20] Tintó, *Gremis*, 55; Bofarull i de Sartorio, *Gremios y Cofradías de la Antigua Corona de Aragón*, vol. 40, 324-335.

[21] *Memorial del Capità General del Exèrcit Christià* (1640), B.C./F. Bon. 6139.

[22] Vilar, "Els Barbà: Una Família Il.lustrada de Vilafranca del Penedès," in his *Assaigs*, 63.

[23] Capmany, *Memorias Históricas*; Carrère, *Barcelona 1380-1462*; Sayous, *Mètodes Comercials*.

nean.[24] Beginning in the mid-fourteenth century, however, sharp demographic reversals combined with the faltering competitiveness of local products and heavy military expenditures to diminish the economic strength of the Principality. The capital city was particularly hard-hit by the depression. In the early fifteenth century, representatives of urban cloth guilds began to call for protection against cheaper foreign imports. The increasingly bitter debate between advocates of protectionism versus free trade polarized local society into rival blocs of artisans and lesser merchants against importers and the urban oligarchy. This opposition finally erupted in armed conflict in the Catalan civil wars of the 1460s. The widespread destruction caused by the prolonged struggle merely furthered the decline of the local economy. Despite a return to tranquility beginning in the late 1470s, economic and demographic recovery proved excruciatingly slow.[25]

The sixteenth century witnessed modest growth in most sectors of the Catalan economy. Certain urban crafts even enjoyed bursts of relative prosperity. Shipbuilding in particular flourished in the wake of important royal contracts, like those for the outfitting of the Tunis and Lepanto expeditions of 1535 and 1571. The cloth industry benefitted through participation (if largely indirect) in markets opening up in the New World.[26] Overseas trade also began to recover from the depression of the later Middle Ages, especially during the second half of the century, when the crown rerouted its money and troop transfers to Genoa through the port of Barcelona. Yet, on the whole, the urban economy suffered from grave structural weaknesses. The slow decline in the competitiveness of its products allowed Gen-

[24] Giunta, *Aragonesi i Catalani nel Mediterraneo*; Dufourcq, *L'Espagne Catalane et le Maghrib*; Del Treppo, *Mercaders Catalans*; Watson, "Catalans in the Markets of Northern Europe."

[25] Vilar, *Catalogne*, I; Vicens Vives, *Ferran II*; Peláez, *Catalunya Després de la Guerra Civil*.

[26] Madurell Marimon, *Antiguo Comercio*; Otte, "Comienzos del Comercio Catalán."

oese and southern French merchants to take over the Mediterranean island markets hitherto dominated by the Catalans. The Genoese in particular steadily increased their control over raw materials and international exchange (including the lucrative trade in indulgences).[27] Especially menacing was their growing monopolization of the unfinished wool of Aragon, the principal source of supply for the Catalan cloth industry. It was thus hardly surprising that by the end of the sixteenth century Genoese merchants had emerged as predictable targets of popular wrath, which culminated in an attempt to expel them from the city in 1591.[28]

The turning-point in this modest demographic and economic recovery coincided with the general Mediterranean trading crisis of the 1620s.[29] The economic downswing fed a growing chorus of calls for protection of local industries through taxes on imports and a ban on exports of raw materials.[30] Meanwhile, a sharp rise in urban unemployment led to a perceptible increase in vagabondage and lower-class unrest. The trade crisis also fostered structural changes within the local economy. For example, during this decade urban cloth entrepreneurs shifted production from the city to the countryside, where the absence of guilds rendered labor costs substantially cheaper.[31] The 1630s saw an abrupt worsening of local economic conditions, as war with France halted maritime trade.[32] The revolt of the Principality against Castilian rule in 1640 did little to improve the situation.

[27] Melis, *Mercaderes Italianos en España.*

[28] *Dietari*, V, 18-22, 30, 212, 261, and 386; A.G.S./Estado, Genoa, leg. 1423 (36).

[29] Romano, "Tra XVI e XVII Secolo."

[30] Dalmau, *Memorial Sobre lo Mayor Dret*; Peralta, *Memorial en Favor de la Ordinación; Parer de Jaume Damians*; A.C.A./Generalitat, Procesos de Corts, vol. 1058, 245.

[31] Women textile workers occupied the City Hall in March 1628 to protest the putting-out of cloth outside the city limits; A.H.M.B./Consell de Cent, II, *Deliberacions*, vol. 138, 49-51.

[32] Giralt, "Comercio Marítimo," 206-210.

Its more detrimental consequences included a sharp rise in taxation to offset increased spending on the war effort, along with Barcelona's newfound isolation from traditional markets and sources of supply in southern and western Catalonia. Severe demographic losses at mid-century through plague, famine, and the siege of 1651-1652 reduced the economic fortunes of the city to their lowest point since the later Middle Ages.

The closing years of the seventeenth century witnessed a gradual revival of the local economy. Figures for overseas commerce reveal a substantial increase in port activity beginning in the 1670s.[33] The following decade also saw the launching of the ambitious economic projects of the lawyer Narcís Feliu de la Penya, whose call for a reorientation of Catalan trade away from traditional Mediterranean markets toward the New World reflected growing involvement in colonial trade.[34] Yet commercial expansion could not conceal ongoing weaknesses in the urban economic order. The recovery of the Catalan economy rested less upon the manufacturing capabilities of Barcelona than on the initiatives of the more flexible spheres of the countryside and the smaller coastal towns. The Principality's economic expansion during the later seventeenth and eighteenth centuries was, as Pierre Vilar has pointed out, essentially a product of the rural environment, not of its capital.[35]

The ossified, rigid character of production in seventeenth-century Barcelona owed much to the persistent strength of its guild regime. Just as the chronology of economic change in Catalonia from the fifteenth to the eighteenth centuries differed substantially from that experienced by Castile, so too did extensive corporate organization distinguish Barcelona from the rest of Iberia. In contrast to the sporadic presence of craft confraternities in most Castilian cities, there was scarcely any economic activity in Barcelona not regulated directly by a guild. The

[33] Fontana, "Comercio Exterior"; Martínez Shaw, "Comercio Marítimo."
[34] Feliu de la Penya, *Político Discurso*, and *Fénix de Cataluña*.
[35] Vilar, *Catalogne*, II-III.

strength of local corporatism was merely one of many characteristics that linked Barcelona's history more closely to the Mediterranean than to the urban centers in the rest of the peninsula.
Most of the city's craft associations were founded in the
later Middle Ages. The resort to collective artisanal organization
represented above all a defensive reaction to the increasing economic difficulties of the fourteenth and fifteenth centuries.[36] The
expansion of the guilds in turn strengthened resistance to economic changes like the lowering of wages and the introduction
of technological innovations. Above all, the trade associations
repeatedly attempted to defend local manufacturers against competition by foreign products. In short, the corporate regime—
an involutive response to uncertain economic conditions wor-
sened by rising competition from abroad—was both a leading
cause and an effect of the "mature" economy of early modern
Barcelona.

The persistent strength of the guild regime contributed to
the essentially static occupational structure of the city during the
sixteenth and seventeenth centuries. Jordi Nadal and Emili Giralt's study of the censuses of 1516 and 1716-1717 reveals little
change in the relative weight of different professional sectors.
Their breakdown of urban trades into general categories (see Table I-1) discloses an overwhelming stability in the distribution of
work within early modern Barcelona.[37] Continuity of profession
within individual families accompanied the tendency toward occupational stasis. Further analysis of the marriage contracts cited
above reveals the extent of change in trades between the fathers
and sons surveyed. Of a total of 551 contracts studied, 233, or
42 percent, of the grooms held the same occupations as their
fathers. Sixty-five, or 12 percent, practiced a different trade
within the same general sector, such as cloth, metalwork,
leather, or agriculture. Two hundred and fifty-three, or a plu-

[36] Tintó, *Gremis*; Bonnassie, *Organización del Trabajo*; Molas, *Gremios Barceloneses*.
[37] Nadal and Giralt, "Barcelona en 1717-18."

Table I-1
Occupational Structure of Barcelona, 1516-1717:
Heads of Households

Sector	1516 (%)		1717 (%)	
Agriculture/husbandry	432	(6.7)	474	(6.1)
Fishing/maritime	284	(4.4)	297	(3.8)
Construction	329	(5.1)	542	(7.0)
Hides and leather	465	(7.2)	510	(6.6)
Cloth	979	(15.2)	949	(12.3)
Metal	229	(3.6)	361	(4.7)
Glass/ceramics	48	(0.8)	77	(1.0)
Victualing trades	230	(3.6)	427	(5.6)
Commerce and transport	530	(8.2)	602	(7.8)
Liberal professions	254	(3.9)	344	(4.5)
Public employees	117	(1.8)	173	(2.2)
Widows	1118	(17.4)	1122	(14.6)
Others	1420	(22.1)	1839	(23.8)
TOTAL	6435	(100)	7717	(100)

SOURCE: J. Nadal and E. Giralt, "Barcelona en 1717-1718: Un Modelo de Sociedad Preindustrial," *Homenaje a Ramón Carande* (Madrid, 1963), II, 277-305. (Minor inconsistencies in the calculation of several percentages have been corrected.)

rality of 46 percent, devoted themselves to entirely different occupations. In short, no fewer than one-half of the grooms surveyed continued to work in the same sector as their fathers, which demonstrated a remarkable degree of continuity.

Rigidity, stability, lack of flexibility—these were the principal characteristics of an economic order openly hostile to innovation and ruled by a fundamentally conservative spirit. In such a context, the strongest pressures for change derived from external sources, not from within. While the guilds tried to oppose legislation to the harsh realities of economic transformation, Barcelona's productive base slowly eroded under the relentless pressure of foreign competition. First the Genoese and later the French deepened their penetration into local markets while tightening their stranglehold over the domestic supply of raw materials. Giralt's study of maritime commerce during the mid-seventeenth century identifies the 1630-1640s as a significant turning point in the city's balance of trade. The latter decade in particular witnessed a reversal of the earlier prevalence of exports over imports registered in local shipping contracts. Josep Fontana's analysis of port traffic during the later years of the seventeenth century reveals a similar predominance of imports, especially from France. By the end of the seventeenth century, the most important maritime commerce passed through the hands of English, Dutch, Genoese, and French merchants, and their local factors.[38] These traders operated for the most part outside the official structures of the local economy, like the Guild Merchant and its famous "Consulate of the Sea." The preeminence of these outsiders testifies to the growing dependence on foreign economies experienced by the Principality during the early modern period. This dependence would prove one of the seventeenth century's most crucial legacies to future generations, notwithstanding Catalonia's relatively privileged status within the peninsular economy as a whole.

Barcelona's role as the leading economic power within the Principality was closely linked to its function as a political capital. Despite the comparatively reduced size of its government bureaucracy—constitutional restrictions limited the number of crown officials, in sharp contrast with the dramatic expansion of the royal bureaucracy in Castile—Barcelona was a city endowed with a strong administrative character. Not surprisingly, the concentration within its walls of the most important Catalan po-

[38] Giralt, "Comercio Marítimo," 204, and "Colonia Mercantil Francesa"; Fontana, "Comercio Exterior."

litical and legal institutions exercised a determining influence upon its fortunes during the two centuries prior to 1714.

While a large cast of characters habitually crowded the stage of local politics, three in particular stood out as protagonists. The most venerable was the municipal government of Barcelona. Its two more prominent bodies were the general assembly known as the *Consell de Cent*, or Council of the Hundred, and the five (six after 1641) Councillors who presided over it. King James I established the procedures for governance by the magistrates and plenary Council in the mid-thirteenth century. A generation later, Peter II decreed the definitive form and composition of municipal administration in the famous privilege of 1283 known as *Recognoverunt Proceres*.[39] The impressive array of powers and jurisdictions conferred upon Barcelona increased with the passage of time. Following the reforms undertaken by Ferdinand the Catholic between 1490 and 1510, its municipal government disposed of prerogatives unrivalled by any other city in the peninsula. As such, Barcelona proved a singularly formidable contender in the political struggles of the late medieval and early modern eras.

The second participant in the institutional trio was the *Generalitat* of Catalonia, also known as the *Diputació*. This organ had emerged during the fourteenth century as the permanent representative commission between sessions of the Catalan *Corts*, or parliament.[40] Its membership consisted of three *Diputats* or Deputies drawn from each of the three parliamentary Estates: Clergy, Nobility, and Commons. Three *Oïdors de Comptes*, or Overseers of Accounts, also selected by lot from the ranks of the different Estates, aided the Deputies. The principal task of the *Generalitat* was to supervise the collection of parliamentary taxes, and to ensure that the conduct of royal officials did not contravene the *constitutions*, or laws passed jointly by the Estates and

[39] Maluquer, *Derecho Civil Especial*, 236-260.
[40] Elliott, *Revolt*, 46 and 130-137.

the crown in parliament. Traditionally dominated by the rural aristocracy, the *Generalitat* saw itself as the guardian of a venerable arrangement whose substantial limitations on monarchical prerogative lent such a distinctive—and disruptive—flavor to Catalan politics.

The third member—the royal administration—proved a relative newcomer to this cast of characters. While a small staff of crown officials had long existed in Barcelona, it did not obtain definitive shape until the later decades of the fifteenth century. Royal government in Catalonia was divided into three parts. At its apex stood the leading official, the viceroy.[41] His post originally developed during the later Middle Ages as an administrative expedient for the rule of the far-flung Mediterranean dominions of the Crown of Aragon. The viceroy gradually became a familiar and influential figure in local politics, thanks to the prolonged periods of royal absenteeism that proved the norm, beginning with the succession of Charles V in 1516. He presided in turn over a small complement of officials, including the Governor General, the Treasurer, and the overseers of the accounts of the royal patrimony. Most important among these, however, were the dozen or so members of the *Audiència*, a body reorganized by Ferdinand the Catholic in the 1490s. This powerful institution combined the functions of the traditional Royal Council—charged with advising the king or viceroy in political matters—with the judicial task of serving as a high court of appeals. The *Audiència* provided an essential element of continuity in royal administration amid the frequent changes of the viceroys. Moreover, it numbered among its ranks the most prominent native members of the crown administration, as the viceroys assigned to the Principality were more often than not titled aristocrats from Castile.

The final component of central government in Catalonia resided not in the Principality, but rather (beginning in the late

---

[41] Lalinde, *Institución Virreinal*; Reglà, *Virreis de Catalunya*, II.

sixteenth century) in Madrid. This was the Council of Aragon, established in 1494 by Ferdinand the Catholic to advise the frequently absent king on the affairs of the Crown of Aragon.[42] Each of the separate members of the Aragonese confederation— Catalonia, Valencia, the Balearic Islands, southern Italy/Sicily, and Aragon itself—was represented by both a native regent and a secretary in charge of correspondence with the kingdom. Despite the physical distance separating it from the Principality, the Council intervened quite actively in local politics. Not surprisingly, its members frequently clashed with the viceroy, who resented conciliar control over the most potent instrument for commanding obedience to the king's authority—patronage of favors and posts within the royal administration.

The political history of early modern Barcelona was shaped above all by the rising influence of the monarchy, despite frequent absenteeism and its increasingly Castilian flavor.[43] That the growing pretensions of the crown would clash with the firm particularist defense of local privilege by national and municipal institutions became readily apparent in the early years of the seventeenth century. However, it was not until the administration of the royal favorite, the Count-Duke of Olivares (1621- 1643), that relations between the Principality and the central government degenerated to the point of open rupture. The crown's previous success in playing off the Barcelona municipal government against the rival *Generalitat* gradually evaporated during the 1630s, as the rising fiscal demands occasioned by Spanish participation in the Thirty Years' War alienated practically all levels of Catalan society. Violent peasant uprisings in 1639-1640 triggered a general revolt which led in 1641 to the separation of the Principality from the Spanish monarchy and its annexation by France. The reconquest of Barcelona following

---

[42] Riba, *Consejo Supremo de Aragón*.
[43] Soldevila, *Història de Catalunya*, II-III; Reglà, *Virreis*; Nadal, *Dos Segles d'Oscuritat*. By far the most important accounts are Elliott's *Revolt of the Catalans*, and Vilar's *Catalogne*, I.

the bitter siege of 1652 ushered in a new period of relative calm. This so-called "neo-foral" epoch was characterized above all by the political quiescence of the ruling classes of the Principality, chastened by the recent experience of direct French rule.[44] The second half of the seventeenth century witnessed near-constant warfare between Catalonia and its powerful northern neighbor. These hostilities encouraged the Catalans in 1705-1706 to support the Habsburg pretender to the Spanish throne, the Archduke Charles, over the French candidate, Philip of Anjou. The defeat of the Austrian coalition in the War of Spanish Succession—the final act of which was the storming of Barcelona on September 11, 1714—constituted a decisive event for the Catalan nation. Beginning in 1714, the Principality ceased to exist as a separate institutional body within the Hispanic monarchy. The social and political consequences of its forcible annexation by Castile—known as the *Nova Planta*, or "new beginning"—will be alluded to in the course of this study.

A singular contradiction marked the history of Barcelona during the sixteenth and seventeenth centuries. Seen from a strictly local perspective, Barcelona was Catalonia's *cap i casal*—literally its "head and hearth." As a local preacher noted, Barcelona was the "head of the entire Principality of Catalonia, and the mirror by which all other cities and towns measure themselves."[45] As such it led the Principality in size, wealth, prestige, and political influence. Yet the same city viewed from the outside revealed itself a provincial, second-rate power. For a center of its political im-

[44] The term "neo-foral" (etym. *for*, meaning "privilege" or "franchise") refers to the later seventeenth century, when the control exercised by the central government over the Crown of Aragon slackened considerably. One important consequence was the abrupt disappearance of the violent confrontations with local constitutional traditions that had marked the first half of the century. For a recent study, see Kamen, *Spain in the Later Seventeenth Century*.

[45] Sala, *Govern Polítich*, 10r.

portance, its demographic strength was quite deficient by European, and even Iberian, standards.[46] Moreover, economically it was on the defensive, exercising a mere shadow of its former primacy within the western Mediterranean. Guicciardini doubtless summed up the attitude of many foreign observers when he remarked in 1512 that "its commerce does not flourish as it did in the past, and it no longer disposes of its former wealth, especially now that the court has moved to Castile."[47]

The image of Barcelona as a lethargic city mired in the backwaters of the Hispanic monarchy has found widespread acceptance among historians of early modern Spain. One well-known scholar has even labelled Barcelona in this period the "Sleeping Beauty of the Mediterranean." One might hesitate to apply this label to the city in which events like the Corpus revolt of 1640 took place. Still, what strikes the observer's eye is the essential stability and strong sense of continuity underlying local society over the course of these two centuries. There was, however, at least one sphere which experienced fundamental change during the early modern era. The governing elite of the city suffered profound alterations in its social composition, professional activities, and public identity. At no point did these new developments represent a dramatic rupture with the past. They nevertheless contributed to the most significant transformation in the lengthy history of the Catalan ruling class prior to the industrial era. The following pages trace the contours of this change. They also explore the vital connection between the successful recomposition of the urban elite, and the construction of ruling-class hegemony within local society, politics, and culture.

[46] For example, neighboring Valencia contained some 12,000 hearths in the early seventeenth century: Casey, *Kingdom of Valencia*, 154.

[47] Guicciardini, *Diario*, 51.

II

THE EVOLUTION OF
OLIGARCHY

"*Knights* of the city-state"—well-chosen words, even if they served to bridge two hopeless anachronisms. For when in 1628 the Catalan jurist Andreu Bosch coined this description of the "honored citizens" of Barcelona, neither chivalry nor independent urban polities were much the fashion in a Europe given to the expanding power of centralizing states.[1] It is precisely this issue of power which engages our attention, as the history of the Barcelona oligarchy is a chronicle of power, both formal and informal.[2] Its sources, distribution, and the ways and means of its manipulation determined the fate of all local citizens, "honored" and otherwise, during the era of the rule of the few.

In a strict sense, of course, the designation "honored citizen" refers only obliquely to power itself. Since the days of classical Athens the term "citizen" had been employed to single out a recognized participant in urban politics. The word "honored," on the other hand, denoted neither power nor participation, but rather a certain social (and moral) standing. Those citizens "more

---

[1] Bosch, *Títols*, 417. I have translated the vexing term *ciutadans honrats* as "honored citizens," although less literal renderings like "honorable," "distinguished," or even "noble citizens" convey much the same meaning.

[2] Contemporary Italian writers also defined civic nobility in terms of public power. See Berengo, "Città del Antico Regime"; Borelli, "Problema dei Patriziati Urbani"; and Marrara, "Nobiltà Civica e Patriziato."

24

equal than others" distinguished themselves from the commonality of the republic by their claim to the higher rank conferred
upon them by public opinion—in short, to "honor." The label
thus blessed the coupling of power and reputation. "The honor
and esteem given to the citizens," wrote Bosch, "derive from
their political service and governance."[3] In this context, "honor"
defined class boundaries, marked recognizable lines of social separation, and ultimately divided the generality of citizens into the
opposed categories of rulers and ruled.

Shifting Definitions

The first explicit reference to "honored citizens" dates from the
early fourteenth century.[4] By that point, however, its usage
merely reflected a *fait accompli*—one which rested on the previous
differentiation of Barcelona's inhabitants into two discrete
groups. As early as the twelfth century, a handful of *prohoms*, or
"distinguished citizens," claimed special positions of leadership
for themselves within the municipality. The more generic *poble*,
or "populace," developed as a residual category for the vast majority of city-dwellers condemned to a subordinate role in local
affairs. Royal privileges of the later thirteenth century establishing the organs of independent civic government decisively wid-
ened this gap. Crown directives confirmed the honored citizens'
monopoly over Barcelona's six Councillorships, or superior magistracies.[5] These offices, vested with sole legislative initiative and

---

[3] Bosch, *Títols*, 418. Not surprisingly, terms of address also embodied such
distinctions. Medieval usage accorded honored citizens several forms of address,
including *mossen* (equivalent to "monsieur" or "messire"), and *honorable*. Later
centuries witnessed a general inflation in these terms of respect. Notarial documents of the seventeenth century designate guild masters and merchants as "honorable," while reserving the prefix *magnífic* for honored citizens and university
graduates.

[4] Palacio, "Contribución," 312.

[5] Their number was reduced to five in 1274.

authority over municipal expenditures, far outweighed in importance lesser bodies such as the plenary assembly of the *Consell de Cent*, or Council of the Hundred. Moreover, the procedure of election by cooptation—the selection without accountability of successors in office—ensured the citizens ongoing control over Barcelona's political life.

Despite the lack of a firm juridical formula defining its membership, there emerged a ruling class possessed of a strong sense of its own identity. Although later texts hint at the existence of an unofficial *matrícula*, or register of citizens, the prevailing criteria for inclusion in this group seemed studiously informal. According to Bosch, the "old way"—that is, prior to 1510—of determining membership in the elite "consisted in being considered an honored citizen in terms of treatment, respect, esteem, and distinction, or by living nobly, or through the greater honor certain persons receive in cities and towns according to public opinion."[6] Such a definition is casual only in appearance. Extension of marriage alliances, recruitment into political factions, and other strategic devices provided mechanisms for integration into an elite whose grip on government made it all too easy to recognize.

Insistence upon the role institutional power played in delineating the public identity of the oligarchy should not obscure the influence of less formal sources of cohesion and strength. In fact, the most distinctive mark of the citizenry in the eyes of contemporaries was its collective existence as a rentier class. The Abbé Xaupí, the honored citizens' most enthusiastic chronicler, underscored the explicit connection between the homogeneous economic base of the oligarchy and its control over the local polity. When posing the question of the "true estate" of an honored citizen, he singled out the qualities of "warriors living honorably from their rents, established by the feudal order within the lead-

---

[6] Bosch, *Títols*, 413.

ing cities to exercise civil and military authority."[7] Many other commentaries, however, limited characterization of the citizens to their disengagement from any but a passive economic role. "Those who live nobly off their rents, and do not work with their hands"; "distinguished city-dwellers with rents of their own, not exercising the mechanical arts"—virtually all such texts focused upon the citizens' unique economic function—or, rather, their lack of one.[8]

Contemporary emphasis on the economic dimensions of oligarchical identity was not misplaced. The shared rentier existence proved vital to fostering the social differentiation by which the citizens rose from their origins as local *prohoms* to constitute the ruling class of the later Middle Ages. The turning point was reached when they triumphantly distanced themselves from the real loser in the struggle for local hegemony, the merchant community. The citizens' assumption of military responsibilities accounts in part for this success.[9] Even more important, however, was their gradual disengagement from the very commercial ventures which had originally financed their bid for power. Withdrawal from direct involvement in trade rested upon a skillful transposition to the urban sphere of the values and modes of behavior of the feudal aristocracy. This rudimentary system of social classification permitted citizens with a rentier income to pose as those "living as nobles do." As such it drove a wedge between a ruling group not directly engaged in economic enterprise and the vast majority of city-dwellers inescapably linked to the "mechanical arts." While in fact the wealthier merchants involved in international trade commanded economic resources far superior to those of citizen or even gentry families, the association of commerce with manual labor and the pursuit of gain derogated the former to the lower sphere of the commons. A

---

[7] Xaupí, *Recherches*, 362.

[8] Tristany, *Discurs de les Contrafactions*, 6v.; Soler, *Discurs*, 23; Fossa, *Mémoire*, 44.

[9] Alós, "Disputa sobre la Noblesa."

more complex and markedly inegalitarian social structure thus arose amid the ruins of the (at least theoretical) equality of the early medieval commune. Presiding over it was an elite whose pretensions to higher rank depended on maintaining distance from the world of industry and trade.

The rise of oligarchy in Barcelona did not go unchallenged. Opposition to the exclusive practices and widespread corruption of the local ruling class erupted sporadically beginning in the thirteenth century. Apart from an isolated revolt in 1285, the first widespread movement to offer a specific alternative to citizen monopoly over local government appeared in 1386.[10] A coalition of lesser merchants and guild masters, angered by the mismanagement of public funds and alarmed by the recent increase in municipal debt, obtained royal support for an ambitious reform of local government. The key feature of its program was a proposal to expand the number of Councillors from five to six, now to be composed of two citizens, two merchants, and two guild masters. The death of Peter IV in 1387 and his successor's hasty revocation of this legislation dashed the reformers' hopes.[11] Nevertheless, opposition to the citizen oligarchy did not die out. It surfaced again during the turbulent decades of the mid-fifteenth century in the guise of a *sindicat del poble*, or "union of the people." This unique example of late medieval popular mobilization provided the nucleus of the so-called *Busca*, or reform party, that, with the support of royal officials, seized control of the city government in 1453. In that year, according to an outraged chronicler of the seventeenth century, King Alphonso the Magnanimous "made a huge effort to show support for the *pobles menuts* ['lesser people'] against the honored citizens," charging that, "the *grossos* [lit., 'big men'] had ruled the city up to now, and had completely robbed and ruined it."[12] The royal

---

[10] Batlle, *Crisis Social*, I.

[11] B.C./Ms. 1479, untitled history of Barcelona, 27r.-v.

[12] A.H.M.B./Ms. B-44, *Catálogo de Consellers de la present Ciutat de Barcelona*, 22v.

28

governor suspended the annual elections for the Councillorships, and in their place filled the vacant posts with two citizens and three merchants, all members of the *Busca*. Other crown measures included an edict expanding the Council of the Hundred and altering the balance between the social classes represented within it. The decrees of 1454 fixed the Council's membership at 32 citizens (a category to which physicians and barristers were now added); 32 merchants; 32 *artistes*, or upper guild masters; and 32 *menestrals*, or masters from the lesser guilds.[13]

The citizens and their *Biga* party launched a violent counterattack against this challenge to their privileges, thus plunging Barcelona into three decades of turbulent civil strife. The eventual triumph of the urban oligarchs and rural nobility following the bitterly destructive Catalan civil wars of the late fifteenth century did not remove the original causes of discontent. A new formula clearly had to be found to provide more stable municipal government. Despite various tentative measures, including the creation of separate registries for honored citizens and merchants in 1479, no significant steps were taken to redress the still-precarious situation until the middle years of the reign of Ferdinand the Catholic (1479-1516).[14]

The royal reforms of 1490 to 1510 attempted to pacify the city by constructing a new political balance skillfully weighted in favor of the honored citizens. It was apparent that a simple return to the *status quo ante bellum* would not achieve civic peace. Restoring power to the citizen oligarchy depended on recasting the hitherto-informal procedures for determining both membership in the citizen group and its representation within the various organs of local government. Seen as a whole, the Fernandine program embodied four profound alterations of the municipal power structure inherited from Alphonso's privilege of 1454. First, it reduced the representation of the lower classes at the

[13] Batlle, *Crisis*, II, 466-475.
[14] A.H.M.B./Consell de Cent, XV, *Diversorum*, 1, 2v.-3r.

highest level of city government from three Councillors to two. The separate guild magistrates (the fourth and fifth) were now combined in the figure of a single fifth *Conseller*, alternating each year between upper and lower guild masters. By thus lowering the status of the merchants' representative (now the fourth Councillor) and limiting artisan participation to merely one post, the effective balance of power within the magistracy reverted back to the citizens, who controlled three of the five offices. [15]

Ferdinand also encouraged the aristocratization of local government by admitting the urban gentry for the first time to the ruling institutions of the city. The fusion in 1498 of these *cavallers* with the honored citizens through the exercise of joint control over the local polity was achieved by mandating the representation of one gentleman for every two citizen Councillors. The inclusion of the gentry within these nominally citizen posts could not help but confer added lustre on the increasingly powerful oligarchy. The further aggregation of physicians and barristers to this category—a reform originally countenanced in the decree of 1454—also expanded the ranks of the composite elite.

The king sought to prevent the resurgence of the factionalism so prominent a feature of the city's recent history by instituting a system of "insaculation," or lottery, for all major public offices. Ferdinand thus hoped to neutralize the rivalries and discontent provoked by certain families' monopolizing the resources and patronage of local institutions. He initially took care to retain control over the key step in the insaculation process—the *habilitació*, or scrutiny governing admission to the lists of candidates. However, in 1516 Ferdinand permanently transferred this power to a commission of twelve chosen by lot among the members of the Council of the Hundred. While the Councillors apparently managed to exercise some favoritism within this seemingly neutral framework, the measure proved remarkably successful in discouraging the bitter factional disputes that so

---

[15] Vicens, *Ferran II*; Reglà, "Política Municipal." A sixth full-time *menestral* Councillor was created in 1641: Amelang, "Oligarquia Ciutadana," 16-19.

often had threatened the public peace during the later Middle Ages.[16]

Yet all these measures would have been ineffective without a more acceptable means of determining membership in the citizen oligarchy. The pressing need for a clear public definition of the composition and legal status of the honored citizenry gave rise to the capstone of the royal program: the edict of 1510, awarding noble privileges to the specific families named as *ciutadans honrats* of Barcelona. The decree conferred upon the citizens and their direct male descendants "all the privileges, immunities, liberties, franchises, honors, favors, and prerogatives pertaining to gentlemen and other noble persons in Catalonia."[17] Two exceptions were made to this sweeping concession of privileges. Honored citizens were not permitted to sit or vote in the Noble Estate during parliamentary sessions. Neither could they occupy the two positions reserved for nobles in the *Generalitat*, the *Diputat* and *Oïdor Militars*. In all other instances, however, citizens were to be regarded as equal to the gentry, a clause which enabled their admission to sessions of the Noble Estate when parliament was not convened. The privilege concluded with a list of the approximately 100 persons[18] specifically named citizens, along with provisions for the future admission of new members to the group.

The four-pronged reform program left the citizens in unambiguous if not exclusive control over the governance of Barcelona. While representatives of the craft guilds were not wholly removed from power, and even enjoyed parity with citizens and merchants in various committees, the balance of power within

---

[16] The scrutiny was carried out every four years until 1587, when it became annual. The crown resumed direct control over the *habilitació* following the surrender of Barcelona in 1652. See Xammar, *Civilis Doctrina*, chaps. 20-22; Mercader, *Fin de La Insaculación Fernandina*; and Torras Ribé, *Municipis Catalans*, 108-116.

[17] A.C.A./Can., reg. 3558, 314r.-318v.; Solà-Morales, *Création de Noblesse Patricienne*, 69.

[18] The exact number cannot be ascertained because of several references to unnamed relatives (e.g., "et eius fratres") within the original list.

local government had shifted back to the citizens and their new-found gentry and professional allies (see Table II-1).[19] The key to citizen predominance lay in the superior power of the Councillorships in relation to the larger bodies of civic government. The latter were: the *Trentenari*, a thirty-six member council whose principal task was to screen legislation presented by the Councillors to the Council of the Hundred; the various committees of eight, twelve, sixteen, or twenty-four members established to advise the Councillors on matters of public policy; and the Council of the Hundred itself. All legislative initiative lay with the Councillors, as did the right to name those eligible to serve on the plenary Council and in other municipal offices.[20]

Table II-1
Reforms of the Municipal Government of Barcelona: Representation by Social Rank during the Fifteenth Century

		Citizens and gentry	Merchants	Upper guild masters	Lower guild masters
Councillors	After 1454 reform[19]	2	1	1	1
	After 1493 reform	3	1	1	
Committees	Eight members	2	2	2	2
	Twelve	3	3	3	3
	Sixteen	4	4	4	4
	Twenty-four	6	6	6	6
Trentenari	Before 1498 reform	8	8	8	8
	After 1498 reform	12	8	8	8
Council of the Hundred	After 1454 reform	36	32	32	32
	After 1493 reform	48	32	32	32

SOURCES: J. Vicens Vives, *Ferran II i la Ciutat de Barcelona* (1936), II, chapter 8; J. P. Xammar, *Civilis Doctrina Civitatis Barchinonae* (1644), 191-192; C. Batlle, "Trentenari," in the *Gran Enciclopèdia Catalana* (1979).

[19] Prior to 1454 virtually all Councillors were honored citizens.
[20] A.H.M.B./Consellers, C-VIII, *Insaculacions*, I.

The power to appoint candidates for citizen rank also rested with the magistrates. Contemporaries did not fail to remark the preeminent position enjoyed by the Councillors in relation to the other organs of local government, where the citizens and gentry wielded a plurality but not the majority of votes. In the eyes of the late seventeenth-century diarist Josep Montfar i Sorts, the control the Councillors exercised over prospective legislation enabled them to pose as "the lords of all proposals," and thus to manipulate with ease the pliant *Trentenari*.[21] Apologists for the citizens, such as the barrister Francesch Soler and the Abbé Xaupí, likened their predominance within the Barcelona government to similar political institutions in the rest of Europe. Not surprisingly, a favored comparison was with the famed conciliar system of Venice.[22] But above all the citizen oligarchy loved to depict itself in the guise of the patriciate of late Republican Rome. The strong Latin resonance of the label "citizen," the constant references to the ruling elite as "senators" and "patricians," and the alleged derivation of the term *conseller* from the Roman "consul"—all helped foster a marked if spurious sense of historical continuity with the most glorious oligarchy in western history.[23] Mixing Ciceronian gravity with the self-righteousness of Cato, the honored citizens emerged rejuvenated from the Fernandine epoch. They were, moreover, prepared to resume responsibility over a temporarily weakened yet still powerful city.

The King's Two Bodies

The oligarchy's ability to perpetuate its rule during the next two centuries rested in part upon the calculated absorption of new-

---

[21] J. Montfar i Sorts, *Diario de Barcelona*, B.U.B./Ms. 398, 21 Jan. 1686. Montfar i Sorts was a barrister from a prominent citizen family.

[22] Soler, *Discurs*, 17; Xaupí, *Recherches*, 34.

[23] Numerous examples can be found in Bosch, *Títols*; Soler, *Discurs*; and Xammar, *Civilis Doctrina*.

comers into its midst. The royal privilege of 1510 spelled out the procedures for the appointment of new members. A typical assembly began with the call on May 1 for all honored citizens to gather at the city hall in the presence of the Councillors and other officials. After attendance was taken, the municipal notaries inscribed into the *matrícula* all the direct male descendants of citizens who had reached the age of twenty. If a two-thirds quorum could be established, the assembly voted by secret ballot on the candidates nominated for membership by the Councillors. The names of those lucky enough to have obtained unanimous approval were then entered in the registry, an act which brought the solemn ceremony to a close.[24]

Royal intervention soon threatened the citizens' exclusive control over the matriculation process promised in the edict of 1510. In 1519 Charles V lowered the minimum for acceptance to three-fourths of those present.[25] He also personally named at least three honored citizens between the years 1528 and 1532.[26] The threat of increased crown intervention had the desired effect. The citizens relaxed their tacit ban on admissions and, beginning in 1531, held regular meetings to approve new candidates for membership. The "extremely rigorous examination and most severe judgment" of election to citizen rank nevertheless obliged many potential or failed candidates to seek alternate means of gaining admission to this exclusive group.[27] Philip II's decision to revert to his father's tactic of creating citizens by royal fiat led to the awarding of twenty-two patents prior to his

[24] A.H.M.B./Mss. L-56 and 57, *Matrícula dels Ciutadans Honrats*. These terse minutes provide a mere summary of the proceedings. They do not specify the number or names of all candidates for new membership, nor the actual deliberations of the assembly itself. Chance references from diaries or the minutes of the city Council can supplement this bare outline. Nevertheless, evidence for internal history of this group—including the criteria for admission—is quite limited.

[25] *Matrícula*, 13r.-14r.

[26] A.C.A./Can., reg. 3915, 302r.

[27] Fontanella, *Sacri Regii Senatus*, I, 392.

death in 1598. Fearing loss of control over admission to this rank, the matriculants opposed stubborn resistance to exercise of the royal prerogative. The controversy came to a head in 1586, when the head Councillor ordered the municipal notary to matriculate four lawyers created citizens by royal privilege following the parliamentary session of the previous year. Although the *ciutadans de matrícula* responded with a lawsuit defending their exclusive right to inscribe new members, an appellate judgment of 1588 ruled against them. The matriculants retaliated in 1591 by declaring a boycott of new admissions. However, this self-defeating measure merely lent the king added justification for awarding new privileges.[28]

In 1599 the new monarch, Phillip III, and the government of Barcelona finally reached a compromise. Threats of obstructionism in the Commons forced the crown to promise that in the future no citizen created by royal privilege would be inscribed in the *matrícula*. In exchange for this substantial limitation upon the royal prerogative of ennoblement, the "old citizens" agreed to inscribe all the royal nominees appointed to that date. More importantly, the matriculants finally accepted the legitimacy of the royal creation of citizens despite the exclusive powers of nomination Ferdinand had conferred upon them in 1510.[29] The compromise of 1599 thus fostered the emergence of two different bodies of citizens. The *ciutadans de matrícula*, or "old" citizens, continued to be elected through the procedures established in 1510. The *ciutadans de nómina reial*, or "new" citizens, were appointed directly by the king. Contemporary observers unfailingly attributed higher social status to the first group. Commenting upon the legal status and privileges of Barcelona's honored citizenry, the distinguished jurisconsult Joan Pere Fontanella assigned higher social standing to the *ciutadans de matrícula*. "In all meetings and public acts," he remarked, "the citizens

[28] *Matrícula*, 68v.-69v.
[29] A.H.M.B./Ms. A-1, *Copia de Varios Diarios de Sucesos Memorables*, 159v.; *Matrícula*, ff. 72r.-76v.

made by the city, even those not yet of legal age, are to be preferred to those by royal privilege."[30] Nevertheless, the royal *potestas* of naming citizens had survived a crucial challenge, and was soon exercised on a scale hardly to be imagined by the relatively tight-fisted monarchs of the sixteenth century.

The evolution of the *ciutadans de matrícula* from the creation of this registry to 1699, the last year in which an assembly met to elect new members, is portrayed in Table II-2. The first admissions to citizen rank took place immediately after Charles V's intervention. The figures then level out for three to four decades prior to the dramatic rise of 1590 to 1600. The flood of new applicants began with the acceptance in 1590 of twelve nominees, the largest number of members absorbed through a single election to that date. After the matriculation of three other nominees in 1591, the citizens declared a boycott of new admissions. They did not reconvene as a body until 1600, following the compromise reached the previous year with Philip III. By that point a considerable backlog of applicants had developed, which that year's ballot duly reflected. The *annus mirabilis* of 1600 witnessed the creation of an extraordinary number of new citizens. These included the fifteen chosen from a total of twenty-seven candidates, a further half-dozen inscribed as a condition of the royal privilege of 1599, and some ten sons of citizens who had reached the age of twenty.[31] The first half of the seventeenth century saw the regular admission of a moderately high number of citizens, averaging some ten new members per decade. The siege of 1651-1652 and the accompanying famine and plague disrupted this steady influx; the assemblies of that decade admitted only three candidates.[32] The final years of the century experienced a gradual return to earlier levels of admission, until the annual assemblies ground to a halt in 1699.

[30] Fontanella, *Sacri Regii Senatus*, I, 392. Fontanella himself was a *ciutadà de matrícula*.

[31] *Matrícula*, 70r.-71v.

[32] *Ibid.*, 118v.-119r.

The contrast between the numbers of new admissions and the sons of citizens inscribed following their twentieth birthday shows the latter consistently outstripping the former except during the extraordinary decade of the 1590s. The self-perpetuation of the elite clearly depended more on the biological issue of existing citizens than on the election of new members. Still, the admission of the latter proved crucial to the continued existence of the group as a whole. Of the 250 families registered as *ciutadans de matrícula* during the period under study, approximately 100 contributed only one member to the group. Among the remaining 150 families, 46 were represented by just two generations.[33] Upward mobility out of citizen status joined biological extinction in accounting for the failure to contribute more members to the group. Hence the reproduction of the citizens as a distinct social class depended vitally upon the constant replacement of old members by new families.

The concession of royal privileges of honored citizenship of Barcelona and other Catalan cities and towns is detailed in Table II-3.[34] The crown awarded only three letters-patent prior to 1585, when Philip II created a dozen new citizens following the conclusion of parliament. The number of *ciutadans de nómina reial* steadily rose during the early decades of the seventeenth century, to culminate in the dispatch of some sixty privileges in the later 1630s. The revolt of 1640 and the subsequent collapse of royal government in Catalonia accounted for the sharp drop in the number of citizens named by the king.[35] Not surprisingly, a

---

[33] Cabestany, "Nómina de los Ciudadanos Honrados de Barcelona."

[34] Llaris indices to the Chancery section of the A.C.A.; index of letters-patent of nobility during the reign of Philip IV prepared by E. González Hurtebise (manuscript in A.C.A.); Morales Roca, "Privilegios Nobiliarios: Reinado de Carlos II." For further discussion of these figures, see Amelang, "Honored Citizens," 84, note 65.

[35] The French government in Catalonia (1641-1652) awarded 210 privileges of citizenship of Barcelona (Morales Roca, "Privilegios Nobiliarios: Gobierno Intruso de Luis XIII y Luis XIV"). While the Castilian government revoked these privileges following the restoration of 1652, some families nevertheless succeeded in retaining citizen status.

Table II-2

Admissions to the *Ciutadans de Matrícula*, 1510–1699

Years	No. of mtgs.	No. of mtgs. when new members admitted	Estimated no. of cits.[1]	No. of new admissions	No. of sons of cits. admitted at the age of 20	Total no. of new citizens
1510–19	1	0	61–120	2[2]	25[3]	27[3]
1520–29	0	0	—	0	0	0
1530–39	7	3	52–55	9	24	33
1540–49	8	5	36–51	14	17	31
1550–59	7	5	63–64	7	12	19
1560–69	10	9	61–66	9	18	27
1570–79	9	8	61–67	8	17	25
1580–89	5	5	27–48	11[4]	17	28
1590–99	2	2	29–53	19[4]	9	28
1600–09	9	9	43–66	30[5]	28	58
1610–19	8	8	44–67	10	24	34
1620–29	9	7	61–64	13	18	31
1630–39	8	7	34–52	8	19	27
1640–49	6	6	30–46	10	14	24
1650–59	4	2	39–45	3	7	10

1660-69	7	5	32-49	9	9	18
1670-79	4	4	28-43	10	14	24
1680-89	5	5	25-39	8	15	23
1690-99	6	6	31-48	12	18	30
TOTALS	115	96		192	305	497

SOURCE: *Matrícula dels Ciutadans Honrats*, A.H.M.B./Mss. L-56 and L-57.

[1] These figures give an estimate of the approximate number of honored citizens in Barcelona. I have used two procedures in calculating the minimum number. When the 2/3 quorum was obtained at every meeting during the decade, I give the lowest number of citizens in attendance. Otherwise, I take the highest number when quorum was not achieved, multiply it by 1.5 to make up the missing third, and then add one to reach the minimum possible number of citizens. I derive the figure for the maximum by taking the lowest number at which quorum is achieved, then multiplying it by 1.5 and adding one; or I take the largest attendance figure, if it exceeds the first calculation. Naturally, the actual ceiling for this later figure may be slightly underestimated due to later admissions.

The figure for the maximum of the 1510 meeting is the approximate number of honored citizens named in the royal edict of that year, combined with the sons and brothers added in 1511.

[2] Admitted by royal privilege of 14 Nov. 1511, adding two brothers of a citizen named in the original edict of 1510 (*Matrícula*, 12r.-v.).

[3] This number includes the many sons and brothers of the citizens specifically named in the privilege of 1510 already over the age of twenty whose names were entered into the *matrícula* in 1511. There were thus in reality no new citizens admitted during this first decade (*Matrícula*, 10v.-11v.).

[4] These totals include seven citizens by royal privilege ordered inscribed in the *matrícula*.

[5] This total comprises six citizens by royal privilege not voted for admission but accepted according to the compromise of 1599.

Table II-3
Creation of Honored Citizens by Royal Privilege, 1560-1699

Years	Barcelona	Perpignan	Girona	Lleida	Tortosa	Others[1]	Totals
1560-69	0	8	0	0	0	3	11
1570-79	0	8	0	0	0	3	11
1580-89	12	7	0	0	0	5	24
1590-99	10	6	4	4	3	6	33
1600-09	17	16	0	2	6	9	50
1610-19	13	9	1	1	1	6	31
1620-29	22	5	1	3	2	4	37
1630-39	80	31	4	1	0	2	118
1640-49	25	2	0	0	1	0	28
1650-59	57	15	0	0	0	0	72
1600-69	98	0	0	0	0	0	98
1670-79	101	0	0	0	0	0	101
1680-89	43	0	0	0	0	0	43
1690-99	15	0	14	0	0	0	29
TOTALS	493	107	24	11	13	38	686

Sources: see footnote 34.

[1] The other towns include: Berga, Manresa, Vic, Camprodon, Vilafranca del Penedès, Ribes, Vilafranca del Conflent, Tarragona, Puigcerdà, Cervera, Mataró, St. Joan de les Abadesses, Besalú, Sabadell, Olot, and Ripoll.

dramatic increase in privileges followed the reimposition of Castilian authority in 1652.[36] The later 1670s witnessed the creation of a record-breaking number of citizens. The annual averages then began slowly to taper off, and the century closed with the granting of only one privilege during the last five years of the reign of Charles II. Philip V created seven new citizens of Barcelona from 1702 to 1704, while the Pretender Archduke Charles of Austria issued some 82 patents during his brief rule (1705-1714). The Bourbons awarded a modest 206 *ciutadanias* prior to the abolition of this rank in the Liberal reform of 1838.[37]

The rates of expansion of the two groups of citizens are contrasted in Table II-4 and Graph 1. There is little difference between the level of admissions to either category at the beginning and end of the period under review. However, the dramatic expansion in royal privileges during the mid- and late-seventeenth century far outdistanced the remarkably stable number of citizens elected to the registry. Any explanation of the variation in the rate of new creations must take into account two key factors pressuring the royal government to issue these patents: the "excessive severity" of the *matrícula* test and the crown's own fiscal and political necessities.

Contemporary observers like Fontanella were quick to point to the highly restrictive character of the matriculation process. The rhythm of admission to the *matrícula* obviously failed to accommodate local demand for citizen status. The bizarre case of Joan Francesch Rossell, one of the most prominent Catalan physicians of the seventeenth century, vividly illustrates the frustration produced by failure to gain entry into the elite. In the wake of repeated rejections by the *ciutadans de matrícula*, Rossell finally resorted to the desperate expedient of forging a royal

[36] This growth proved all the more significant considering the pronounced demographic contraction of Barcelona following the siege and plague of 1651-1652.

[37] Morales Roca, "Privilegios Nobiliarios: Gobierno Intruso del Archiduque D. Carlos," and his "Privilegios Nobiliarios: Dinastía de Borbón, 1700-1838."

Table II-4
Creation of Honored Citizens of Barcelona, 1516-1700

Reign	New admissions to the Ciutadans de Matrícula	Average number per year	Citizens by royal privilege	Average number per year	Totals
Charles V 1516-1558 (42 yrs.)	20	0.46	3	0.07	23
Philip II 1558-1598 (40 yrs.)	44	1.10	22	0.55	66
Philip III 1598-1621 (23 yrs.)	40	1.70	30	1.30	70
Philip IV 1621-1665 (44 yrs.)					
1621-40	21	1.10	102	5.36	123
1641-52	11	1.00	25	2.27	36
1653-65	11	0.92	113	9.41	124
Total	43	0.97	240	5.45	283
Charles II 1665-1700 (35 yrs.)	30	0.85	201	5.74	231
TOTALS	177[1]	0.96	496	2.70	673

SOURCES: same as Tables II-2 and II-3.

[1] This total does not exactly coincide with the number of matriculants in Table II-2 due to the deliberate omission in the former list of: two citizens admitted in 1511 (i.e., prior to the reign of Charles V); seven citizens the *Audiència* ordered entered in the *matrícula* during the 1580s and 1590s (Table II-2, note 4); and six citizens by royal privilege inscribed in 1600 (Table II-2, note 5).

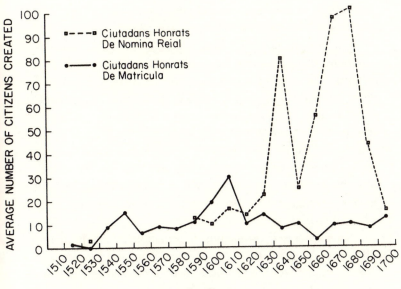

Graph 1

Creation of Honored Citizens of Barcelona, 1510-1700

patent in order to be inscribed along with the crown nominees included in the compromise of 1599. A group of citizens—most likely personal enemies of this apparently distasteful character—searched the chancery registers and discovered the forgery. Rossell immediately took refuge in a local monastery, and later fled to Madrid. He finally escaped punishment for his crime through an ingenious scheme countenanced by his protector D. Joan Terés, Archbishop of Tarragona and acting Viceroy of Catalonia. Rossell arranged for a peasant who had killed a bandit to deliver the corpse to him. The doctor then promptly turned it over to the government, which, in accordance with its long-standing policy of offering pardons in exchange for outlaws brought in dead or alive, dropped the charges against Rossell and restituted him *ad honorem*—much to the disgust of the citizens.[38]

[38] A.H.M.B./Ms. A-1, 16or.

43

Failure to obtain election to citizen rank did not lead everyone to seek (or forge!) a royal privilege. Analysis of the fate of the dozen candidates who failed to win admission in 1600 shows that none of these went on to obtain a crown patent. Damià Prexana, a lawyer who had narrowly escaped being elected in 1600, gained admittance at the 1602 meeting. Joan Baptista Gorí, a judge of the *Audiència*, was also later matriculated the year prior to his death at the hands of a lynch mob in 1640. Moreover, two of those rejected in 1600 had already obtained letters-patent of citizenship in 1599, and had merely sought to join the *matrícula* group as well—a telling indication of the greater prestige of the latter. Of the rest, apparently none achieved citizen status.[39]

An even more compelling explanation of the pronounced differences between the rates of creation of the two groups of citizens emphasizes the supply instead of the demand side of the equation. The crown's own motives for issuing these privileges reflected both a growing need for funds and the desire to obtain political support through a calculated strategy of individual ennoblement. Pressure upon the royal government to offer these privileges as a source of badly needed revenue increased dramatically with the onset of the Thirty Years' War. As a result, the crown sold a number of patents, especially during the early 1630s.[40] Still, the outright sale of citizenship for fiscal reasons apparently did not match in overall importance the government's attempts to use these creations as *mercedes*, or grants, designed to drum up political support among the local elite. The coincidence between the issuing of patents and meetings of the Catalan parliament (1585, 1599, 1626) highlights a deliberate if sporadic policy of granting citizenship as a reward for political favors. The

---

[39] A.H.M.B./Ms. A-25, P. Serra Postius, *Senat Barcelonés*, 395-397. Unfortunately, this is the only document which lists the names of unsuccessful aspirants to matriculation as honored citizens.

[40] Thompson, "Purchase of Nobility." The sale of nobility in Catalonia is discussed in Chapter III, below.

flood of privileges conferred following the recapture of Barcelona in 1652 also originated in the crown's need to compensate its loyal supporters. This development confirms recent interpretations of the "neo-foral" period as one which linked the new-found political quiescence of the Catalan ruling class to substantial honorific concessions by the crown.[41]

A singular feature of the postwar era was a pronounced attrition in the awarding of citizenship of towns outside Barcelona. Grants of honored citizen or burgess status for towns like Perpignan and Girona had longed played an integral role in the crown's policies of ennoblement. However, by the final decades of the seventeenth century, the only such privileges awarded were fourteen citizenships of Girona in 1693, a concession motivated by extraordinary local contributions to the war effort against the French. A growing geographical dispersion of those receiving patents of *ciutadania* of Barcelona compensated for the drop in the number of creations of citizens and burgesses of towns outside the leading city (see Table II-5). By the later seventeenth century, an impressive majority of new citizens did not originate from Barcelona. Moreover, many of the new appointees continued to live outside the capital. While all twenty-two recipients of privileges awarded by Philip II were either natives or residents of Barcelona, fewer than one-fifth of the citizens named by Charles II can be identified as such.

The crucial factor underlying the sharp rise in demand for patents of citizenship among rural elites was the rank's exemption from royal taxation. This immunity took on added importance during the second half of the century, when the crown frequently resorted to the billeting of troops as a means of offsetting diminishing income from traditional parliamentary taxation. Such generosity soon proved counterproductive, as the awarding of citizenship substantially reduced the number of eligible taxpayers in the countryside. The Council of Aragon rec-

[41] Reglà, *Historia de Cataluña*, 100; Kamen, "Forgotten Insurrection."

Table II-5
Geographical Origins of Honored Citizens of Barcelona by Royal Privilege, 1558-1700

Reigns	Barcelona			Girona	Tarragona	Lleida	Tortosa	Towns with fewer than 4,000 inhabitants	Totals
	Native	Resident							
Philip II (1558-1598)	14	8	} 22	0	0	0	0	0	22
Philip III (1598-1621)	14	8	} 22	1	1	0	1	2	27
Philip IV (1621-1665)	25	7	} 32	0	6	2	16	100	156
Charles II (1665-1700)	21	11	} 32	11	5	1	3	121	173
	—	—	32	—	—	—	—	—	—
TOTALS	74	34	108	12	12	3	20	223	378

SOURCES: same as Table II-3.

ognized the increasing difficulties these grants posed for the collection of revenue. Internal government memoranda also underscored the close connection between the excessive number of citizens created "in towns and villages" and the growing peasant unrest of the 1680s.[42] As a result, beginning in that decade the Council began to discourage the issue of patents, and continued to implement this policy until the end of Charles II's reign.

It is hard to determine the precise effects of the royal creations upon the honored citizenry of Barcelona. The lively internal debates and sharp public exchanges of the prewar period vanished from local politics in the aftermath of the restoration of 1652. The change in tone toward a studied quiescence following the turbulent decades of mid-century led to a perceptible decline in the quality of contemporary political observation. The contrast between the waspish remarks of the barrister Jeroni Pujades, writing in the opening years of the century, and the pious commonplaces of his fellow jurist Josep Montfar i Sorts during the 1680s reflects more than differences in individual temperament.[43] Their works symbolize two distinct political climates, two eras separated by the experience of revolution and civil war. Unfortunately for our purposes, the transformed mood of the second half of the century yields little in the way of perceptive social and political commentary.

The trends of the seventeenth century nevertheless point to an important shift within the civic oligarchy. Since 1510 three separate groups had competed for "citizen" posts: *ciutadans de matrícula*; citizens by royal creation; and *gaudints*, or those doctors in law and medicine who, beginning in the mid-fifteenth century, also won inclusion among the candidates for the higher magistracies. The background of the 353 citizens, professionals, and aristocrats who filled the first three Councillorships from 1600 to the final lottery of November 1713 is specified in Table

---

[42] A.C.A./C.A., llig. 242 (47). Jaume Dantí's "Revolta dels Gorretes" provides a useful introduction to this unrest.

[43] Pujades, *Dietari*, (1600-30); Montfar i Sorts, *Diario* (1685-1687).

47

II-6. Of the 171 Councillors from 1600 to 1654, 51 were *ciutadans de matrícula*, 23 citizens by royal privilege, and 97 *gaudints*. The 182 magistrates serving from 1655 to 1714 included 28 matriculants, now overshadowed by 39 crown nominees and 115 professionals. The dramatic erosion in the relative strength of the matriculants becomes even more clear when one recalls their unchallenged domination of the Councillorships throughout the sixteenth century. From the creation of the registry in 1510 to the compromise of 1599, only 43 *gaudints* and no royal citizens were admitted to over 180 magisterial posts.

Xaupí's claim that the crown nominees "did not in truth partake in the great power that the matriculants exercised" proved demonstrably false.[44] Still, one should avoid attributing the royal generosity of the "neo-foral" period to a deliberate attempt by the crown to dilute the political influence of the Barcelona oligarchy by staffing it with its own creatures. The flood of royal privileges was in fact a consequence of the government's decision not to indulge in any major institutional reform of the city administration. One might expect the crown to compensate for this unique exercise in self-restraint by promoting more dependable personnel through the manipulation of patents of citizenship. Still, there are several grounds for questioning the existence of a royal policy of using these privileges as a means of weakening Barcelona's ruling class. First, among all the major contenders in Catalan politics during the seventeenth century, the members of the citizen oligarchy had proved the most consistent backers of royal policy. The crown would thus derive little benefit from hindering or replacing its most reliable local supporters.[45] Moreover, the rise in the number of *ciutadans de nómina reial* holding Councillorships during this period should not obscure the fact that the great majority of these privileges were awarded to *coqs de village* in outlying rural areas who played

[44] Xaupí, *Recherches*, 192.
[45] Elliott, *Revolt*, Chapter 5.

48

Table II-6
Social Background of First, Second, and Third Councillors, 1600-1714

Years	Total number of offices	Honored citizens		Gaudints		Unknown	Aristocrats	
		Matriculants	Royal nominees	Barristers	Physicians		Gentry	Nobles
1600-09	31	11	1	6	1	1	11	0
1610-19	33	13	3	2	3	1	11	0
1620-29	31	11	3	2	4	1	10	0
1630-39	30	6	6	4	3	1	9	1
1640-49	30	7	5	2	4	2	7	3
1650-59	32	5	8	4	4	1	2	8
1660-69	30	4	6	3	5	2	6	4
1670-79	31	5	8	3	3	2	6	4
1680-89	30	5	8	4	2	2	8	1
1690-99	31	7	5	4	3	1	7	4
1700-09	32	5	5	5	5	0	4	8
1710-14	12	0	4	2	1	4	1	0
TOTALS	353	79	62	41	37	21	80	32

SOURCES: Bruniquer, *Rúbriques*, I; Capmany, *Memorias Históricas*, II, 1,025-1,045; Serra Postius, *Senat Barcelonés*; *Catálogo de Consellers de Barcelona*. See also Amelang, "Honored Citizens," 128, note 5.

no role in the government of the city. Finally, the figures in the table clearly indicate that the foremost threat to the matriculants' preeminence came, not from the citizens by royal creation, but rather from the growing number of *gaudints*. The rapid increase during the late sixteenth century in the number of university graduates eligible for scrutiny had already provoked a sharp response from the *ciutadans de matrícula*, who filed suit to limit *gaudint* representation to only one physician and one barrister. However, in 1602 a royal inspection commission ruled in favor of the graduates, thus provoking (according to a delighted Pujades) an explosion of rage on the part of the citizens.[46]

The dramatic rise in the number of royal creations during the "neo-foral" period had less direct impact than might be expected upon the internal cohesion and political predominance of the *ciutadans de matrícula*. The more pressing threat to their grip on the machinery of local government came, not from this direction, but from another source. By the middle of the seventeenth century, the gains made by the growing number of university graduates had substantially diminished the matriculants' control over the Councillorships. The decline in their relative share of political power thus combined with the less exalted occupational and geographic extraction of the rapidly expanding group of royal nominees to lower the status of citizen rank. Beginning in the 1630s, the increased availability of privileges of ennoblement encouraged greater numbers of aspirants to upward mobility to forego the slower if more secure method of obtaining noble rank through citizenship in favor of a dramatic leap from plebeian to gentry status. By the end of the century, the matriculants' control over the offices they had formerly dominated with ease had dwindled to a mere shadow of its former self. The revolutionary transformations of the succeeding generation severed the citizens' last formal link to municipal government, thus forcing a new accommodation with the changing realities of power.

---

[46] Pujades, *Dietari*, I, 218; Fontanella, *Tractatus De Pactis Nuptialibus*, I, 14; *Matrícula*, 106v.-108v.

The structure of local government nevertheless remained in place without substantial alteration until its reorganization by Philip V following the siege of 1714. During the previous two centuries, and despite occasional outbursts of lower-class discontent, Barcelona's political destiny lay firmly in the hands of the citizens and their professional and aristocratic allies. Effective control over municipal government endowed this composite group with a public prominence far outstripping that of civic elites in the rest of Spain. The analogy that foreign visitors frequently drew between Barcelona's distinctive polity and northern Italian and Imperial cities bore witness to the unique power and prestige wielded by its oligarchy. In like manner, the elaborate customs and rituals of local municipal ceremonial fostered the citizens' self-image as protagonists amid the pomp and display of urban politics. Proud of their heritage, though somewhat less optimistic about their ability to influence the future, the oligarchs of Barcelona soon found themselves in charge of the last remaining Iberian city to challenge the expanding powers of the modern state. Their defeat in 1714 spelled the end of the honored citizens as leading members of the urban patriciate, and opened the path of social and political hegemony to another, more exclusive, ruling class.[47]

The concentration of power and prestige in the hands of Barcelona's honored citizens was far from unique. A glance at the evolution of urban society throughout the rest of Europe reveals similar patriciates consolidating their hold upon local government during the closing years of the Middle Ages. All the leading municipalities of the Crown of Aragon—Valencia, Saragossa, and Palma de Mallorca—were dominated by a

[47] The best study of the socio-political consequences of the *Nova Planta* is Torras Ribé, *Municipis Catalans*.

distinguished "citizen" class.[48] Numerous Castilian cities also boasted the presence of an urban petty nobility, especially among their *regidores* or town Councillors. Moreover, several fifteenth-century Castilian writers referred to a *ciudadano*, or middling stratum, between nobles and commoners living, as in Catalonia, "not from labor, but from rents."[49] Beyond the Pyrenees, rentier oligarchies in Italy and France provided close parallels with the experience of Barcelona. The *bourgeoisie* of many French cities in particular similarly linked dominance in local politics to an "honorable"—that is, rentier—existence.[50]

The shared economic base and political preeminence informing ruling-class experience throughout much of the continent should nevertheless not obscure one vital characteristic distinguishing the Barcelona elite from, say, the civic oligarchies of early modern France. The crucial difference lay in the collective ennoblement in 1510 of the honored citizens. This guaranteed the Barcelona patrician a much higher (and more secure) social status than the *bourgeois*, whose strident claims to noble rank were often spurned by local aristocrats.[51] The citizens' winning of inheritable nobility proved a decisive step on the high road of acceptance by the Catalan aristocracy. Without it, the unified civic elite of early modern Barcelona would not have emerged.

[48] Madramany y Calatayud, *Tratado de la Nobleza*, 237-501; Domínguez Ortiz, *Clases Privilegiadas*, 177-184.

[49] Villena, *Doze Trabajos de Hércules*, 12; Domínguez Ortiz, *Clases Privilegiadas*, 52-54; Ruiz, "Transformation of Castilian Municipalities."

[50] Galasso, *Economia e Società*, 312-324; Vovelle and Roche, "Bourgeois, Rentiers, and Property Owners"; di Corcia, "*Bourg, Bourgeois, Bourgeoisie de Paris.*" Interestingly, Bosch discarded traditional arguments attributing the historical origins of Barcelona's honored citizens to the Roman Senate in favor of a connection with the *burgesos* of northern Europe (*Títols*, 411).

[51] Goubert, *Ancien Régime*, Chapter 10.

III

TOWARD AN URBAN
NOBILITY

The nobility of Catalonia was divided into three separate ranks, each with its own privileges, customs, and legal status. A handful of *magnates*, roughly equivalent to the grandees of Castile, presided over this social pyramid. Following the promotions of the parliamentary session of 1599, the titled nobility included one duke, one marquis, eight counts, and one viscount. These peers, led by the powerful Cardona and Queralt families, traced their ancestry back to the *rics homens*, or direct feudatories of the king who rose to prominence in the later Carolingian period. Slightly lower on the scale came the *nobles*, or aristocrats proper. This exclusive group shared with the peerage the distinctive formal address of "Don." Finally, the gentry stood at the base of the noble hierarchy. These *cavallers* or *militars* formed the single largest group within the aristocratic estate.[1]

The lack of reliable tax lists or censuses from the sixteenth and seventeenth centuries makes it difficult to fix the precise

---

[1] Fluvià, "Categorías Nobiliarias," and "Títulos Nobiliarios." It should be noted that in Catalonia the honorific title "don," which distinguished aristocrats proper from the gentry, was inherited by younger as well as eldest sons. The Castilian practice of addressing all members of the elite as "don" replaced this usage, beginning in the eighteenth century.

In this study, therefore, *noble* (when italicized) designates a member of the specific social rank between the peerage and the gentry, whereas the unitalicized term refers more generally to all persons and things aristocratic.

number of aristocrats. Elliott used convocations of the *Bras Militar*, or Noble Estate in parliament, to arrive at the following estimates:[2]

Date	Nobles	Gentry	Total
1518	37	451	488
1626	254	526	780

These figures highlight the persistent numerical predominance of the *cavallers* within the upper class throughout the sixteenth and seventeenth centuries. They also underscore an important shift within the aristocracy: the dramatic expansion of the upper ranks of *nobles*. Significant alterations in Catalan society, politics, and the economy underlay the transformation of the structure and composition of the noble estate. Migration from the country to the city, changing rhythms of social mobility, the improved fortunes of liberal professionals, and a growing resort to rentier income contributed to the emergence of a new and powerful aristocracy within Barcelona's walls.

From Country to City

"Who could describe the host of illustrious nobles and citizens of this noble city of Barcelona?" Jorba, the wrangling pedant encountered above, wasted no time in answering his own question, as he reeled off a five-page list of the distinguished families whose past feats of arms and letters had conferred glory and honor upon his home town.[3] Nor was he the only contemporary to remark about the aristocratic tone lent the city by the Catalan nobility's penchant for urban living. In 1599, the Swiss medical student Thomas Platter credited the wealth and beauty of Barcelona to the fact that "many of [its] houses look like palaces, the

[2] Elliott, "Provincial Aristocracy," 129.
[3] Jorba, *Descripción*, 26r.-28r.

gentlemen of the district having neither the custom nor desire to live in the country."[4] It is of course possible to exaggerate the extent to which Catalan aristocrats had strayed from their rural origins. After all, magnates like the Duke of Cardona exercised great power in the outlying counties, while the lesser gentry continued to plague the countryside with its turbulent feuds. All the same, by the seventeenth century the center of gravity within the Catalan nobility was clearly shifting from the country to the city.

Other contemporary accounts echoed the observations of Jorba and Platter regarding the urban proclivities of the aristocracy. An anonymous manuscript from the early seventeenth century joined them in claiming that "Barcelona has a very great number of gentlemen, because the majority of Catalan nobles has established residence there." And in the mid-eighteenth century, the *Audiència* encountered increasing difficulties in its search for resident nobles to serve in town governments outside the larger cities.[5] However, the absence of fiscal and demographic records such as hearth-lists and parish registers prevents our reconstructing the precise chronology or quantitative dimensions of this all-important event in the history of the Catalan ruling class. A list drawn up in 1639 in preparation for a military levy furnishes the best estimate of the minimum number of aristocrats residing in Barcelona. The 225 men named in the document included 103 *nobles* and 71 gentlemen—roughly a quarter of the entire Catalan aristocracy.[6] If one adds to this figure the number of nobles living in smaller cities like Girona and Tarragona, it is evident that in the mid-seventeenth century the ruling class of the Principality was predominantly urban in character.[7]

---

[4] Platter, *Journal*, 199.

[5] "Península a Principios del S. XVII," 475-476; Torras Ribé, *Municipis Catalans*, 253-262.

[6] A.C.A./Gen., caixa 26 (cited in Elliott, *Revolt*, 68). The remaining 51 names belonged to honored citizens.

[7] A.C.A./Gen., caixa 26, for lists of nobles in Agramunt, Girona, Montblanch, and Perpignan; Junyent, "Noblesa Vigatana en 1666."

The greater baronial lords now visited rather than resided on their estates. In turn, the violent highlands squires who strutted about in Castilian *comedias* faced the choice of adapting to more sedentary lives in the cities and larger towns, or of fading into relative obscurity.

Underlying this shift was the growing insecurity of the Catalan countryside. The threat was not largely physical in character, although the rising incidence of banditry during the later sixteenth and seventeenth centuries did little to make rural life more appealing. Rather, increased economic hardship drove the rustic gentry to try to better its fortunes in the cities and towns. Regrettably, little is known of the rural history of early modern Catalonia. What evidence there is suggests that, despite the apparent juridical strength of the local seigneurial regime, by the 1620s and 1630s a host of economic difficulties—especially dwindling real income due to fixed rents and rising indebtedness—prevented many noble families from making ends meet. The most important work to date on the early modern Catalan nobility—Eva Serra's study of the titled Sentmenat house—highlights the serious shortfall besetting this distinguished family's patrimony during the troubled decades of the early seventeenth century.[8] Meanwhile, misfortune was hardly limited to the more illustrious noble households. The crisis of the seigneurial regime appeared even more threatening at the lower reaches of the rural nobility, which included those without access to the power and influence enjoyed by relatively wealthy families like the Sentmenats.

The rampant inflation of the "long sixteenth century" contributed to the economic crisis of the aristocracy. Yet equally influential were the constraints that peasant initiative placed on seigneurial power in the aftermath of the Sentence of Guadalupe (1485). This royal edict attempted to pacify the Catalan countryside following the bitterly destructive civil wars of the fifteenth

[8] Serra, "Societat Rural Catalana."

century. In exchange for the confirmation of existing allodial dues and the disbanding of the leagues created to defend peasant rights, the king abolished the more abusive practices of the seigneurial regime. Even more significant were the provisions securing effective land tenure (*dominium utile*) for tenants holding long-term contracts. The extension of emphyteutic leaseholds beginning in the early seventeenth century further expanded the power of this class of middle-sized producers. Their role as bailiffs and middlemen for the lords not only provided increased control over sublessors and dependent farm workers, but also enabled them to challenge the seigneurial monopoly over local agricultural surplus. The consolidation during the early modern era of a class of substantial middling peasants did much to distinguish Catalonia from other areas within the peninsula. It also contributed decisively to the drift toward absentee lordship on the part of its nobility.[9]

Small wonder then that, as many rural nobles forsook direct management of their estates, the chance to obtain urban offices and sinecures proved all the more attractive. Cities like Barcelona boasted a wide range of alternative sources of income for hard-pressed aristocrats. For example, the benefices and chaplaincies of its cathedral chapter afforded secure and dignified livings to some one hundred members of the local nobility.[10] Equally alluring were the lucrative offices of the *Generalitat* and the municipal administration. The public returns from these posts were in themselves quite impressive—the city Councillors, for instance, earned a respectable £600 plus expenses every year.[11] Less visible forms of remuneration, such as the chance to profit from inside bidding for the city's grain contracts, often proved even more appealing. One aristocrat was so eager to obtain a

9 Vicens, *Gran Sindicato Remensa*; Serra, "Règim Feudal Català"; Serra and Garrabou, "Agricoltura Catalana."

10 A.S.V./Sac. Cong. Concilio, *Relat. Dioc. ad Liminam*, III A (Barcinon.), 11r. (1594).

11 Bruniquer, *Rúbriques*, I, 77-130.

57

Councillorship that in 1635 he renounced his privileges of nobility in order to be included in a less restrictive scrutiny for office.[12] Granted, his was an extreme case. It nevertheless underscores the fact that the nobility's shift from rural to urban living was not solely the result of worsening conditions in the countryside. The cities exercised a powerful appeal of their own. Barcelona and other urban areas functioned as centers for borrowing and lending, markets for lucrative marriages, and venues for upper-class sociability. It was there that energetic aristocrats could put their status and privileges to best use in the pursuit of wealth, influence, and social advancement.

Ennoblement and Social Mobility

The number of Catalan nobles grew dramatically during the sixteenth and seventeenth centuries. The contours of this "inflation in honors" take on greater relief when set against the background of local patterns of social mobility. The marriage contracts from the seventeenth century studied above highlight prevailing tendencies in inter-generational mobility. To be sure, the limited information provided by these documents makes it difficult to trace precise changes of occupation and status.[13] The contracts do not specify levels of individual wealth beyond dowry awards, nor do they always distinguish among apprentices, journeymen, and masters within the guild regime. Nevertheless, one can accurately chart changes in occupation between grooms and their fathers at the time of marriage (Table III-1). Shifts in status can

[12] A.H.M.B./C-VIII, *Insaculacions*, I, 11r. Nobles were not the only ones eager for these offices. For *menestral* resentment of exclusion from the honor and rewards accruing to permanent Councillorships, see *Corts Generals de Pau Claris*, 227. Interestingly, in 1626 the Inquisition complained bitterly that constitutional restrictions disqualifying familiars from municipal posts discouraged even "lowly persons" from serving the Holy Office (A.H.N./Inquisición, lib. 1267, 6v.).

[13] For remarks on the problems posed by similar documentary sources, see Sharlin, "Study of Social Mobility."

Table III-1
Grooms and Their Fathers: Occupational Mobility

FATHERS	SONS							
	Peasant	Menestral	Artista	Merchant	Professional	Honored citizen or Burgess	Gentleman or noble	Total
Peasant	91	96	17	—	5	1	—	210
Menestral	11	190	26	—	4	—	—	231
Artista	1	2	27	2	6	—	—	38
Merchant	—	—	1	7	1	1	1	11
Professional	—	—	—	—	9	—	1	10
Honored citizen or Burgess	—	—	—	—	1	3	—	4
Gentleman or noble	—	—	1	—	1	—	19	21
TOTAL	103	288	72	9	27	5	21	525

SOURCES: same as Chapter One, note 14.

Table III-2
Grooms and Their Fathers: Social Mobility

Status of fathers	Sons of lower status	Sons of same status	Sons of higher status	Total
Peasants and *menestrals*	—	388	53	441
Artistes (upper guilds)	3	27	8	38
Merchants	1	7	3	11
Honored citizens and professionals[1]	—	13	1	14
Gentlemen and *nobles*	1	20	—	21
TOTALS	5	455	65	525

SOURCES: same as Chapter One, note 14.
[1] For the equation of physicians and barristers with honored citizens, see pages 69-71 below.

also be documented by ranking individual trades according to the categories of social standing used to determine corporate representation in the municipal Council (Table III-2).

Comparison of these tables reveals a firm continuity in social status between the two generations. Of the seven categories analyzed, only one—the peasantry—witnessed a clear majority of sons (57 percent) exercising different trades from those of their fathers. Yet of these 119 grooms, 96, or 70 percent of the cohort, had merely exchanged agricultural work for the *menestralia*, or lower sector of the guild regime. The remaining members of this group included 17 *artistes* or upper guild masters, 5 liberal professionals, and 1 honored citizen. Hence, even within the category exhibiting the greatest degree of "horizontal" movement, the degree of "vertical" mobility was limited, given the equality of status between peasants and *menestrals*.[14] Moreover, the same tendency toward continuity in status is found elsewhere on the social scale. Of a total of 231 *menestrals* 210, or 87 percent, held the same rank as their fathers. Only 30 (13 percent) achieved a higher status. The stability in social level characterizing the lower ranks also prevailed among the higher categories. From the evidence of the contracts, these latter groups experienced relatively little change in standing from one generation to another, relieved only by a slightly greater degree of upward mobility among merchants and *artistes*.

These figures must be treated with caution. Sources like marriage contracts minimize the extent of vertical mobility by overlooking the tendency among families unable to maintain the minimum economic level of their social rank to disappear either by emigrating or by not marrying. Furthermore, by dealing with such broad categories as "peasant" or *menestral*, we are unable to specify less pronounced but significant movements along the social scale. That there was often a broader gulf separating a rich peasant from a poor agricultural laborer than that between upper and lower guild masters is obscured by the use of institutional categories which mask the crucial difference that wealth could make in determining social standing. All the same, these documents suggest several conclusions. They not only confirm the overwhelming predominance of horizontal over vertical movement within early modern Catalan society, but they also reveal some interesting linkages between the two. The figures from the rural sector in particular point to a dual pattern of migration through which better-off farmers either married their younger sons to peasant heiresses, or else dispatched them to the city to apprentice in *artista* guilds or study for the liberal professions. Less wealthy homesteads, on the other hand, provided a steady stream of recruits to the *menestralia*, or contributed to the large

[14] Contemporary rankings like the diocesan nuptials-tax schedule accorded the same (low) standing to *menestrals* and peasants. For a typical tariff, see A.C.B./ Esposalles, 48, 1r. (1575-1577).

number of urban casual laborers and transients living outside the confines of the guild system.[15]

A wide gap also separated occupational from status change. While there was a fair, even impressive, amount of occupational mobility—as we have seen, fewer than half of the grooms practiced the same trade as their fathers—the overwhelming majority of fathers and sons (87 percent) held the same social rank. Of the grooms experiencing status mobility, only 5 (1 percent) suffered a decline in standing, while 65 (12 percent) obtained a higher rank. Yet, despite the significant difference between "horizontal" and "vertical" mobility, these latter instances of upward advancement did not violate contemporary expectations regarding changes in social status. While the thirteenth-century mystic Raymond Lull castigated guild masters who forsook their trades for the rentier existence of the honored citizenry, many later writers took a less severe view of this aspiration.[16] In fact, they regarded *gradual* movement upward along the social scale as part of the natural order of urban society. In 1628 the jurist Andreu Bosch argued that cities proved especially receptive to "obtaining higher titles by many routes, for there one can rise degree by degree from the very lowest condition to the highest honor available, the rank of honored citizen or burgess."[17] In a similar vein his fellow barrister Aleix Tristany noted that "before obtaining their rank, many merchants had their origins in other trades in this city . . . some were *menestrals*, and other *artistes*."[18] Yet, while gradual upward mobility appears to have been an accepted feature of early modern society, the same cannot be said of those individuals who pressed their suit in the *cursus honorum* too eagerly. Hence the frequent scornful attacks in Pujades' diary on

[15] Arranz and Grau, "Problemas de Inmigración." See also: Clark, "Migration in England," 70-71; and Thirsk, "Younger Sons."

[16] Llull, *Doctrina Pueril*, 187.

[17] Bosch, *Títols*, 370.

[18] Tristany, *Discurs*, 9v.-10r.

those who climbed the social ladder without due regard for the general norm of one rank per generation.[19]

A few writers upheld the caste-like character of the "three estates." Tristany, who apparently saw nothing wrong in guildsmen becoming merchants, firmly opposed the acquisition of citizen rank by the merchants themselves. He argued that such improprieties fostered "intolerable confusion . . . everyone should be content to occupy the place he now has, without aspiring to something higher."[20] Yet, on the whole, both horizontal and vertical movement formed an integral part of contemporary attitudes toward society and the proper place of individuals within it. Not surprisingly, vertical mobility in a strongly corporate society like Barcelona possessed a well-defined and carefully graded character, with the ascent from guild to merchant to citizen *matrícules* bearing a closer resemblance to an escalator than to Lawrence Stone's elevators.[21] Enhancement of social status met with little opposition if it were discreet, as befitted a society that accorded much importance to maintaining visible, public distinctions between different occupational and social categories.

Mobility upward and downward apparently proved more intense among the higher reaches of the social scale. Both the upper guilds and the urban elite experienced constant turnover within their memberships. Only 2 of the 25 merchant families occupying municipal office during the 1480s were listed in the merchant registry a century and a half later.[22] A similar lack of biological continuity characterized the honored citizen stratum. Of the 67 families listed in the original privilege of 1510, 39—a striking 58 percent—failed to contribute any new members to

---

[19] Pujades, *Dietari*, III, 148 and IV, 128; A.H.M.B./Ms. A-1, 158v.-159r.

[20] Tristany, *Discurs*, 10r. For recent studies of the social "image" of the "three orders," see Niccoli, *Sacerdoti*, and Duby, *Three Orders*.

[21] Stone, "Social Mobility in England."

[22] Giralt, "Comercio Marítimo," 80. I am indebted to Professor Giralt for permission to consult and reproduce portions of his study.

the group. Nine families registered their last sons in the *matrícula* from 1530 to 1560; the final members from 11 other families were inducted from 1560 to 1590. Of the remaining 8 families, 6 matriculated their last sons from 1590 to 1602; the final 2 registered in 1622 and 1631.[23] While it is difficult to ascertain the precise fortunes of individual citizens in the absence of detailed genealogies, comparison with later patents of nobility issued by the crown reveals the fate of three-fourths of these households. Sixteen of the original 67 families achieved gentry rank—8 during the reign of Charles V (1516-58), 3 under Philip II (1558-98), two in the reign of Philip III (1598-1621), and the remaining 3 at unknown dates. Thirteen other families went on to obtain *noble* status—1 under Charles V, 3 during the reign of Philip II, 7 under Philip III, 1 during the French interregnum (1641-52), and 1 at an unknown date. Attendance records from the annual assemblies show that 2 of the original families retained citizen rank until the final two decades of the matriculation, which ended in 1699. Thus of a total of 31 traceable families, 29 of them moved upward from citizenship to the gentry and aristocracy proper, while only 2 continued as citizens. The rest apparently emigrated or suffered biological extinction in the years immediately following the generation of 1510.[24]

The general patterns of mobility underlying the constant renovation of the upper classes serve as background for the figures on ennoblement listed in Table III-3. This chart presents minimum estimates of letters-patent issued by the Catalan chancery from the beginning of the reign of Philip II to the abolition of aristocratic privileges in the Liberal reform of 1838.[25] A clear

[23] *Matrícula dels Ciutadans Honrats.*

[24] The sixteen families I was unable to trace probably either emigrated from the Principality or died out during the sixteenth century. Studies of the biological "scissors" discouraging elite family reproduction include: Zanetti, *Demografía del Patriziato Milanese*; Litchfield, "Demographic Characteristics of Florentine Patrician Families"; and Pedlow, "Marriage, Family Size, and Inheritance."

[25] For discussion of the methods used to derive these figures, see Amelang, "Honored Citizens," 262-263.

chronology of ennoblement emerges from these statistics. The first notable expansion in the number of patents took place immediately following the conclusion of the parliamentary session of 1599—a pattern remarkably similar to the "inflation of honors" in early modern England.[26] The upward trend continued unabated throughout the seventeenth century, reaching a climax during the final years of the reign of Philip IV (1621-1665). Even if one subtracts the number of patents issued during the French and later Habsburg interregna, it is evident that the high point of the royal creation of nobles during the Old Regime occurred in the mid-seventeenth century. The rhythm of ennoblement slacked off under the new Bourbon dynasty, at no point recovering the intensity that marked the early years of the neo-foral period.[27]

The reign of Philip IV and the first two decades under Charles II provided ample opportunities for rapid ennoblement to those willing to place their economic and political resources at the disposal of the crown. During the middle years of the seventeenth century, the monarchy translated its pressing financial needs into the issue of an unprecedented number of awards of nobility. The government first sold patents in order to raise funds in the early 1630s. As in Castile, this desperate fiscal expedient met with little success.[28] Although these privileges were generally regarded as negotiable and thus often substituted for cash payments, few showed interest in their outright purchase. They were most often issued in the Crown of Aragon as rewards for political loyalty, such as the approval of royal legislation in parliament. As noted above, the flood of awards beginning in the 1640s represented an impoverished crown's means of compensating its followers for privations suffered during the recent

---

[26] Elliott, *Revolt*, 49; Stone, *Crisis of the Aristocracy*, 65-128.
[27] Morales Roca, "Privilegios Nobiliarios. Dinastía de Borbón."
[28] A.C.A./C.A., leg. 242 (7), 13 June 1633; Thompson, "Purchase of Nobility." During the 1630s, the government attempted to sell *cavaller* patents for £800, and honored citizenship for £400.

Table III-3
Ennoblement in Catalonia 1558-1838

Reign	Honored citizens Barcelona	Honored burgesses Perpignan	Honored citizens other towns	Gentlemen	Nobles	Total No.	Avg. no. patents per annum
Philip II 1558-98	22	28	23	74	35	182	4.6
Philip III 1598-1621	30	24	34	82	88	258	11.3
Philip IV 1621-65	240	52	14	208	96	610	13.8
Interregnum Louis XIII-XIV 1641-52	194	31	17	65	15	322	29.0
Charles II 1665-1700	201	—	14	150	101	466	13.4

Archduke Charles 1705-14	82	—	—	51	49	182	20.0
Bourbons 1700-1838	213	3	—	181	126	523	3.8
TOTAL	982	138	102	811	510	2,543	9.1

SOURCE: J. S. Amelang, "The Purchase of Nobility in Castile 1552-1700: A Comment," *Journal of European Economic History*, 11, 1982, 220-221.

civil war. However, fear of the fiscal and political consequences of swelling the ranks of the tax-exempt eventually obliged the government to halt their issue.[29]

A recent characterization of mid-seventeenth century Bordeaux as a society where "mobility had virtually ceased" would have found scant echo in early modern Catalonia.[30] Despite the lack of a well-defined institutional structure of ennoblement through the purchase of venal office as under the *paulette* system in France, during the mid-seventeenth century more Catalans obtained privileges of nobility in a shorter length of time than in any other period since the later Middle Ages. Contemporaries were well aware of the extraordinary number of privileges being awarded, and some did not hesitate to protest what they considered excessive generosity on the part of the crown.[31] All the same, royal liberality probably contributed substantially to easing tensions between the king and at least certain of his subjects in the years following the revolt of 1640. The ample opportunities for both horizontal and vertical mobility at all levels of Catalan society may well have proved one of its leading sources of stability throughout the early modern era.

Rise of the Lawyers

The renovation of the Catalan aristocracy was scarcely limited to a mere increase in numbers. Crucial transformations in its social composition and public functions accompanied this expansion. One of the most significant of these alterations was the increased representation within all sectors of the ruling class of university-educated professionals, especially barristers.[32]

The number of jurists elected to honored citizenship during

[29] A.C.A./C.A., leg. 240 (16), 2 May 1692.
[30] Westrich, *Ormée of Bordeaux*, 2-3.
[31] Tristany, *Discurs*, 11v.
[32] For a more detailed discussion, see Amelang, "Barristers and Judges."

the sixteenth and seventeenth centuries provides one clear index of the growing importance of lawyers within the urban oligarchy. Slightly over one-half of all new matriculants from 1510 to 1714 held advanced degrees in law. This was a remarkably high proportion, considering the diverse social and occupational origins of the citizen oligarchy, which found recruits among merchants, physicians, notaries, and upper guild masters. The incidence of lawyers among both old and new honored citizens gives an even clearer picture of the rise of jurists within the oligarchy. Graph 2 depicts the percentage of lawyers among those attending citizen assemblies at twenty- to thirty-year intervals from 1510 to 1691. The royal privilege of 1510 included some fifteen barristers (14 percent) among the approximately 110 individuals specifically named honored citizens. This proportion tripled, beginning in the mid-sixteenth century, and reached a climax during the final decades of elections when lawyers made up almost one-half of all *ciutadans de matrícula*. In short, jurists played an increasingly important role among the honored citizens, constituting at all times the single largest occupational group within the body of matriculants.

The participation of liberal professionals in the organs of municipal government also reflected their growing influence in urban society. As we have seen, royal policies formally permitting doctors in law and medicine to share the powers and privileges of honored citizens dated to the mid-fifteenth century. In 1447, for example, the royal council guaranteed physicians the same rights as citizens.[33] Beginning in 1455, *gaudints* (literally, "those who enjoy" doctorates in law or medicine) won inclusion in the roster of candidates from whom were chosen the first three magistrates and the first forty-eight members of the Council of the Hundred. These were all positions formerly reserved exclusively to the honored citizenry. Members of the liberal professions thus obtained the right to compete for these posts, regard-

[33] Bruniquer, *Rúbriques*, V, 153.

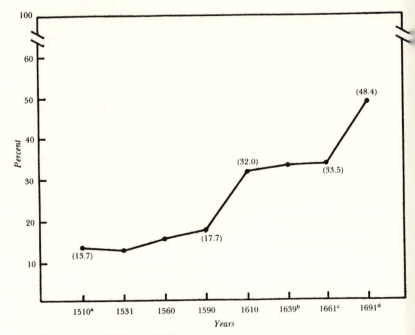

ᵃ An approximation of the number of honored citizens in 1510, compiled from the individuals listed in the origin. privilege, was used to calculate this percentage.
ᵇ There was no meeting held in 1640. The next assembly was on May 1, 1642.
ᶜ There is no record of attendance for the meeting of 1660.
ᵈ There was no meeting in 1690.
SOURCE: *Matrícula dels ciutadans de Barcelona*, Arxiu Històric Municipal de Barcelona, MSS. L-56, L-57.

Graph 2
Percentage of Jurists in Attendance at Assemblies of
Honored Citizens, 1510-1691

less of whether they formed part of the citizen oligarchy.[34] While only a handful of lawyers and physicians held Councillorships from their establishment in the mid-thirteenth century to the late fifteenth century, this began to change during the sixteenth century (see Graph 3).[35] Beginning in the 1550s, the number of lawyers and physicians serving as Councillors increased steadily

[34] Batlle, *Crisis*, II, 466–475.
[35] Amelang, "Honored Citizens," 128.

70

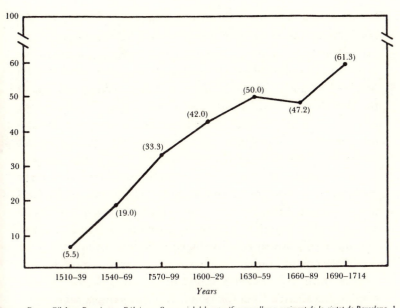

ɔURCE: Esteve Gilabert Bruniquer, *Rúbriques: Ceremonial dels magnífics consellers y regiment de la ciutat de Barcelona*, 1 *Barcelona*, 1912); and James S. Amelang, "Honored Citizens and Shameful Poor: Social and Cultural Change in arcelona, 1518–1714" (Ph.D. dissertation, Princeton University, 1981), 128.

Graph 3
Percentage of Barristers and Physicians among Councillors,
1510-1714

until levelling off at a plateau of 35-45 percent from 1610 to
1680. Further growth in the representation of liberal professionals marked the final years of this regime, reaching record pro-
portions during the 1690s and the first decade and a half of the
eighteenth century. As one anonymous chronicler of the late seventeenth century complained, liberal professionals "have multi-
plied so much that today they fill almost half these posts."[36]

A significant, if somewhat less striking, reorientation of existing noble families toward the practice of law accompanied the
intensified upward mobility of the city's jurists. This point deserves emphasis. The growing resort to university education

[36] A.H.M.B./Ms. B-44, 34v.

within the upper ranks of Catalan society was not merely the result of the absorption of lawyers and physicians within the urban oligarchy. Rather, these newcomers were joined by an expanding number of gentry and even aristocrats proper who obtained advanced university degrees. The surviving *matrícula* of the Barcelona criminal court reveals that during the years 1551 to 1703, some 85 of a total of 563 practicing lawyers were gentlemen and *nobles*. The nobility thus accounted for a full 15 percent of this wide sampling of the local bar.[37] Other, more fragmentary evidence highlights the aristocracy's increasing involvement in the legal profession. Prominent *noble* houses such as the Cardona, Queralt, Erill, Fivaller, Paguera, and Xammar families all contributed sons to the bar.[38] Symbolizing the growing predilection for legal study among the highest reaches of the aristocracy was the signature on the title-page of one of the most famous local political tracts of the seventeenth-century, D. Ramon Dalmau de Rocabertí's *Fatal Omens of French Rule in Catalonia* (1646). This Viscount, one of the Principality's leading peers, ended the long list of his baronies and jurisdictions by referring to himself as a "graduate in canon and civil law"—a distinction virtually impossible to find among titled nobles a mere century before.[39]

The causes of the growing incidence of liberal professionals within the urban nobility are varied and complex. Not least among them was the considerable intellectual prestige of the Catalan legal tradition, which provided the theoretical underpin-

---

[37] A.H.M.B./Vegueria XV, *Matrícula dels Jurisperits*, IX-XIV. The relatively small numbers involved do not permit a more precise chronology of nobles registering in the Barcelona court, especially since documentation is lacking for the years 1574-1605, 1640-1642, and 1654-1658. The 1660s and 1670s apparently saw a record number of both noble and commoner matriculants to the local bar (Amelang, "Barristers and Judges," 1,272 and 1,279).

[38] Other such noble families include the Agullana, Cancer, Cassador, Copons, Despalau, Marimon, Meca, Vilaplana, and Vilossa.

[39] Rocabertí, *Presagios Fatales*, title-page. A noble law student from Barcelona was the hero of Lope de Vega's play *Los Ponces de Barcelona: Obras*, VIII, 569-601.

nings for one of the most active constitutional regimes of the sixteenth and seventeenth centuries. Nor can one overlook the political influence accruing to jurists in early modern Catalonia. Lawyers played a crucial role not only in the municipal government of Barcelona but also in the royal administration, especially through service on the *Audiència* or appellate court. Yet perhaps the most important factor influencing the nobility's resort to university study was economic. Maintenance of the family patrimony occupied a central place in elite career strategies throughout this period. It is to the intersection of economic choice and familial advancement that we must now turn our attention.

Economic Foundations

The urban economy of early modern Catalonia can be divided into two discrete spheres. The first centered around direct productive activity per se. This everyday world of industry and exchange absorbed the efforts of merchants, guildsmen and their dependents, and casual or non-artisanal laborers. The other sector embraced what historians have labelled the "proprietary system," whose mainstay was the passive administration of fixed returns from investments.[40] A rentier class of honored citizens and urban nobles loomed most prominently within this sphere. To be sure, numerous points of contact linked the two sectors. However, our focus will be on the latter economy, and the changing economic base of the urban ruling class—what Pierre Vilar has labelled the "transformation of a society of entrepreneurs into a society of rentiers."[41] Until recently, most studies in early modern economic history have placed overriding emphasis on the role of the entrepreneur. This brief sketch seeks to redress this imbalance by examining the only apparently less

---

[40] Taylor, "Non-Capitalist Wealth." See also Giesey, "Rules of Inheritance," and Schnapper, *Rentes au 16ᵉ Siècle.*
[41] Vilar, *Catalogne,* I, 569.

"dynamic" system of rents, credit, and professional services underlying the "mature economy" of early modern Barcelona.[42] Identification with a rentier existence was a longstanding attribute of the Catalan nobility. Aristocratic "honor" centered around the ability to live off one's rents, in contrast with commoners, who engaged directly in agriculture, trade, or the "mechanical" arts. It would of course be a mistake to take these claims to economic passivity too literally. The customary social codes buttressing the nobility's rentier style of life made a fundamental distinction between direct and indirect participation in economic enterprise. Insistence by contemporaries that the public functions of aristocrats not include physical exertion or "work with their hands" should be read at face value.[43] The system of classification informing this imagery left ample room for the upper class to engage in a variety of disguised or secondhand commercial and investment ventures. There were in fact exceptions even to this relaxed set of norms. Several honored citizens actively participated in crafts and trade, especially during the neoforal period. As previously noted, during the later seventeenth century the royal government bestowed many privileges of citizenship upon wealthy peasants or artisans in provincial towns. While some of these fortunate individuals abandoned their plows and shops upon ennoblement, others continued to ply their trades,[44] hence the references to citizens serving as merchants (1640s), silversmiths (1683), or even as *bacaladeros* or codfish importers (1706).[45] Small wonder then that by 1681 the Noble Es-

[42] C.M. Cipolla coined this term in his "The Decline of Italy."

[43] Molas, *Comerç*, 6-19.

[44] In 1706 Antoni Rovira, an esparto-weaver from St. Boi, complained that the local peasant Joan Martí had hidden behind a privilege of honored citizenship to avoid returning a borrowed mule. The indignant Rovira marked that "Martí was to him a peasant and not a knight, for nobles did not plow the ground the way Martí did": A.H.M.B./Vegueria, leg. 362, 81 (2). (I am grateful to Kazuko Mitsuhata for this reference.)

[45] Catalogue of Civil Suits, Audiència de Catalunya (A.C.A.); Molas, *Economia i Societat*, 132; A.C.A./Gen., G-68, I, 307r.

tate felt compelled to protest the crown's "dispatch of patents of nobility and citizenship to persons exercising mechanical arts."[46] Yet, these examples of direct participation by honored citizens in industry and trade were apparently exceptions proving the general rule forbidding such activities. By the early sixteenth century, the citizen oligarchy had abandoned its medieval heritage of large-scale mercantile enterprise for the rentier style of life so firmly identified with the traditional nobility. The patricians of Barcelona proved no more immune to the "contagion of rent" than did urban notables throughout the rest of Europe.[47] The dictates of aristocratic comportment and the related fear of status loss through derogation left them little room for maneuver.[48]

The later Middle Ages set the stage for the consolidation of the "proprietary system" that served as the economic foundation of Barcelona's expanding ruling class. The depression of the fourteenth and fifteenth centuries merely encouraged the elite's drift toward non-commercial investment. As the upper class increasingly resorted to fixed rents, it placed growing emphasis on monetary stability. Exporters and artisans, on the other hand, hoped to check the decline in exports through protectionism. They sought more power for the guilds, and called for the revitalization of production and trade through the twin instruments of import tariffs and monetary devaluation. Direct confrontation between these conflicting sets of interests underlay the bitter class struggle of the mid-fifteenth century.[49] The eventual

---

[46] A.C.A./Gen., G-68, *Dietari del Bras Militar*, III, 542r.

[47] Bennassar, *Valladolid au Siècle d'Or*, Chapter 8; Domínguez Ortiz, *Clases Privilegiadas*, Chapter 3; Phillips, *Ciudad Real*, Chapter 7. Studies of European cities where merchants continued to dominate local government include: Strauss, *Nuremberg in the 16th Century*; Friedrichs, *Urban Society*; and Benedict, *Rouen during the Wars of Religion*.

[48] Interestingly, the 1620s witnessed an unsuccessful movement to make wholesale trade compatible with nobility: Wright, "Military Orders," 63.

[49] Vilar, *Catalogne*, I, 461-520; Batlle, *Crisis*, I, Chapters 4-6; Bonnassie, *Organización del Trabajo*, especially Chapter 5.

triumph of the nobles and citizen oligarchy ensured that henceforth there would be no political tampering with the instruments and institutions of the rentier system.

The gradual contraction of Barcelona's trading area and the generally risky conditions prevailing throughout much of the Mediterranean "long century" sustained the elite's resort to the proprietary system.[50] A sluggish economic climate joined rising social pretensions in encouraging the upper class to eschew direct involvement in trade in favor of less lucrative but more secure sources of income. The consolidation of the citizen oligarchy favored the transformation of wealth originally amassed through commerce into a structure of diverse investments yielding stable if lower fixed returns.[51] Full assumption of the rentier habits of the nobility thus represented the end-point of a fairly uniform pattern of economic activity. Individual patterns of capital accumulation recapitulated the experience of the class as a whole. The first stage of the cycle was based upon a high level of business activity, whose purpose was to generate sufficient funds to establish the income necessary to aspire to citizen status. In the succeeding phase, these activities were either abandoned or disguised through the adoption of more indirect pursuits of wealth. The fundamental aim at this juncture was not so much to expand the family patrimony as to preserve it—a difficult task even in the best of times.

What were the sources of rentier income? How did the elite secure the fixed returns that formed the backbone of this system? Early modern marriage contracts contained detailed provisions regarding the transfer of patrimonial wealth both within and between families. These notarial records constituted a binding agreement fixing the distribution of family resources among at

[50] Giralt, "Comercio Marítimo." See also Braudel, *Mediterranean*, 865-891; Tenenti, *Piracy and the Decline of Venice*; and Rapp, "Unmaking of the Mediterranean Trade Hegemony."

[51] See also Friedrichs, *Urban Society*, 142, and Burke, *Venice and Amsterdam*, 101-114.

least two sets of participants. These included the houses allied by the marriage, along with the different generations within each family whose present or future transfers of property made up either the bride's dowry (*dot*) or the groom's dower (*escreix*).[52] The act of marriage thus not only involved the transmission of economic resources from one family to another. It also required the settlement of future testatory succession with the families involved, as the dowry and *escreix* were almost always secured against the offspring's legacies. The patrimony was in turn distributed between a single principal heir (*hereu/hereva*) and the other children, who were each awarded *llegítimes*, or equal portions of the remainder of the estate. Given the overriding need to secure future returns, upper-class marriage contracts usually contained elaborate lists of properties producing fixed rents. As such they are useful guides to the composition of elite family patrimonies.

A representative list can be found in the marriage contract drawn up in 1635 by the *Audiència* judge and honored citizen Miquel Joan Magarola.[53] Therein the magistrate settled upon his eldest son and heir Magí de Magarola approximately £1,370 in annual rents. The purpose of this *donatio inter vivos* was to secure the dowry of £4,000 brought by the bride, *Doña* Francesca de Perellòs i de Aragó, the daughter of a provincial gentleman from the nearby town of Tàrrega. Following customary practice, Miquel Joan reserved usufruct over the gift for the remainder of his life. He in turn promised the newlyweds both room and board in his house, and a yearly cash allowance of £300. Magí's settlement—which involved the transfer of most of the economic resources of his branch of the family—comprised forty-four sepa-

[52] Catalan civil law regarding marriage settlements followed the Roman custom of *dos* and *antefactum*. See Fontanella, *De Pactis Nuptialibus*; Maspons, *Nostre Dret Familiar*; and Maluquer, *Derecho Civil*, chap. 4.

[53] A.H.P.B./Antic Servat major, *Capitula Matrimonialia et Concordia 1635-37*, 74r.-77v. (21 Nov. 1635).

rate items, distributed among the ten categories outlined in Table III-4.

Two features of this patrimony merit comment. First, by far the greatest portion of the family's fixed income derived from rural sources. Most important were the fourteen pieces of land

Table III-4
The Magarola Patrimony of 1635

Source	No. of items	Total annual rent
Seigneurial dues and tithes	2	215 £
Censos (leases)		
RURAL REAL ESTATE		
outside district of Barcelona	1	25 £
within district of Barcelona	14	495 £
subtotal	15	520 £
URBAN REAL ESTATE (Barcelona)		
cases (houses)	3	100 £
botigues (shops)	2	39 £
horts (gardens)	7	137 £ 10 s
subtotal	12	276 £ 10 s
Censals (personal loans and annuities)		
to the *Generalitat*	2	80 £ 14 s
to rural property-holders	6	200 £ 16 s
to urban property-holders	6	64 £ 6 s
undetermined	1	14 £ 12 s
subtotal	15	360 £ 8 s
TOTAL	44	1,371 £ 18 s

SOURCE: A.H.P.B./Antic Servat major, *Capitula Matrimonialia et Concordie* 1635-37, 74r.-77r. (21 Nov. 1635).

in the immediate vicinity of Barcelona. These produced revenue (£495 p.a.) over twice the value of the seigneurial rights, dues, and tithes from the family's recently purchased barony (£215 p.a.). If we add to these holdings income from *censals* or mortgaged loans to rural property-owners, we find that a full two-thirds of Magarola's revenues derived from the nearby countryside. Thus, while land was hardly the most lucrative investment, its combination of ease of transfer, security of return, and high prestige value clearly rendered it attractive to wealthy city-dwellers.

The size of this patrimony also deserves emphasis. The effort required to amass this inheritance was obviously a considerable one. With only two exceptions, the loans, mortgages, and other investments listed in the document yielded a steady 5 percent return. The capital originally required to form this patrimony thus totalled some £30,000—an extremely large sum, even given the father's respectable professional income (£1,000-2,000 p.a.).[54] The sheer size of the principal helps explain the incremental and piecemeal acquisition of the holdings, their wide geographical distribution, and Magarola's resort to a broad range of repayment mechanisms—all characteristic features of such patrimonies during this era.

Dowries played a central role within the economic life of the upper class, as bridal portions provided an important source of fixed revenue. As a consequence, many aristocratic houses sought to improve their finances by taking wives from wealthy families, often of lower social status. Moreover, dowry levels rose dramatically in the early modern period. Even taking contemporary inflation into account, during the sixteenth and early seventeenth centuries the average dowry of an honored citizen's daughter apparently doubled from £2,000 to £4,000. This meant that a greater proportion of the elite's economic resources had to be devoted to investments producing the secured returns re-

[54] Amelang, "Barristers and Judges."

quired by pre-nuptial contracts.[55] The principal consequence of dowry inflation was to reinforce the existing tendency to divert capital toward investments yielding stable returns. In other words, as dowries grew, so did the need for annuities and long-term contracts securing the fixed revenues needed for their payment.

While changing economic circumstances fostered the upper class's growing resort to the proprietary system, the strengthening of the rentier sector in turn placed new pressures on the urban economy. Especially important was its impact on the local capital structure. The emphasis rentiers placed on security of returns encouraged reliance upon a wide range of sources of income. This led in turn to a notable dispersion of investments.[56] The lack of concentration of capital—more symptom than cause of the economic difficulties of the sixteenth and seventeenth centuries—was reflected in Feliu de la Penya's 1683 project for the establishment of a trading company in Barcelona. His proposal to draw together a large number of small investments from the upper class as well as from merchants and guild masters obviously suited a capital structure whose aversion to risk fostered a marked dispersion of resources.[57]

Equally grave in its consequences for the urban economy was the neutralization of wealth in the complicated tangle of long-term instruments such as government bonds and annuities. The ultimate effect of the elite's predilection for rentier income was to reduce the role of capital as a dynamic force within the

[55] These figures derive from the study of 33 dowries given by honored citizen fathers from 1576 to 1689 (documents in A.H.P.B.). The nominal sums were specified in fixed proportion to gold, whose price was relatively stable during these years (Elliott, *Revolt*, 553-554). For interesting perspectives on early modern dowries, see: Nader, "Noble Income In 16th-Century Castile"; Chojnacki, "Dowries and Kinsmen"; and Stone, *Crisis of the Aristocracy*, 632-649.

[56] Vilar, *Catalogne*, I, 661; Ruiz Martín, "Joan y Pau Saurí"; Nadal and Giralt, "Barcelona en 1717-18," 299-302.

[57] Feliu de la Penya, *Fénix de Cataluña*, 80-81.

economic life of the city.[58] The need to yield secure returns literally immobilized economic resources. The upper class neutralized its economic strength in the form of low-risk investments
which, while transferred with ease from one family to another,
nevertheless did little to stimulate either trade or production.[59]

Symbolizing this "sterilization" of capital was the very
prominence of Barcelona's famed *Taula de Canvis*, or public de-
posits bank.[60] The annual interest of 3 percent on *taula* accounts
represented the minimum yield on the sort of high-security returns sought by local investors. A considerable gap separated
interest rates for these low-risk investments—ranging from the 3
percent bank dividend to the 5 percent standard *censal* rate—and
the interest charged for less secure commercial undertakings.
Thus in March 1606 the directors of the Merchant Consulate
protested the exorbitant rates (30-40 percent) charged for mercantile ventures, and urged a maximum of 10 percent.[61] This
episode indicates that by the early seventeenth century at least
two separate channels of capitalization existed in Barcelona. The
supply of capital available for secure investments had overtaken
the market for high-risk commercial ventures. Worsening economic conditions thus joined aristocratic decorum to discourage
entrepreneurial initiative on the part of the social class with the
greatest economic resources at its disposal—the urban ruling
class.

How, then, was wealth generated within the confines of the
proprietary system? The few detailed account books that survive
from this period reveal that the close management of investments

[58] Of course, the passive administration encouraged by the rentier system may
well have aided the more prosperous peasants who could benefit from long-term
contracts during years of rising agricultural prices. My discussion here is limited
to the effects of this system on the urban economy.

[59] Vilar, *Catalogne*, I, 565. For the dependence of the Valencian patriciate on
censals, see Casey, *Valencia*, chaps. 5-6.

[60] Usher, *Early History of Deposit Banking*, II; Riu, "Banking and Society in
Late Medieval and Early Modern Aragon."

[61] *Dietari*, VIII, 263; Smith, *Spanish Guild Merchant*, 58.

81

by aristocrats was not uncommon. They also suggest that certain nobles showed an active interest in agriculture and mining on their estates.[62] The elite gained revenue from rural properties by encouraging agricultural improvement in lands not subject to the expanding regime of tenant farming. Citizens and nobles also assumed active roles as intermediaries in the sale of produce in urban areas.[63] Yet, as noted above, aristocrats did not involve themselves in trading ventures of the sort envisioned by Feliu de la Penya. Neither did they evince much interest in direct participation in manufacture.

Indirect involvement in local enterprise, however, was a different matter. Early modern notarial documents reveal urban nobles investing capital as silent partners in both wholesale and retail trade.[64] Aristocrats seeking profits greater than the 5 percent return on annuities and other fixed investments could also turn their money to account by farming out public taxes and supply contracts. Manuel Arranz's study of bids for municipal excises on goods entering Barcelona highlights substantial participation by honored citizens and gentry, who acted as guarantors of consortia competing for this monopoly.[65] The 272 investors in these contracts from 1665 to 1712 included 23 honored citizens, 7 gentlemen, and 9 *nobles*. Together they pledged approximately £1,043,000—over 15 percent of the total guaranteed capital. Urban notables also bid for contracts for municipal supplies of grain and other staples. In 1667, for example, an honored citizen joined with a *noble* to provide the city with wheat and

[62] Vilar, "Explotació Agrícola d'una Proprietat a la Horta de Tàrrega," in his *Assaigs*, 11-42; Serra, "Consideracions entorn de la Producció"; Canales, "Producció a la Comarca de La Selva"; and Vázquez, "Aportación al Estudio de la Siderurgía Catalana."

[63] Hence the entry in the account books of the Montalegre monastery noting £201 paid out for "olive oil delivered by Francesch Marí, honored citizen of Barcelona": A.H.M.B./Patrimonial X-17 (G), 5 March 1642.

[64] Giralt, "Comercio Marítimo," II, 15-16, 48, 78, and 80; Molas, *Comerç*, 122-164; Martínez Shaw, "Construcción Naval," 234-236.

[65] A.H.M.B./Consell de Cent, XIII, *Manuals*, 1655 et seq. I am grateful to Professor Arranz for sharing this and other references with me.

rye.[66] Finally, Barcelona's aristocrats invested heavily in local real estate. The *catastro* or tax-registry of 1716-1717 documents extensive participation by nobles in the city's active housing market.[67]

Yet, of all these means of earning income, only a handful did not require a considerable initial investment. Opportunities for less wealthy members of the elite to improve their families' position were in fact quite limited. There was only one sphere of lucrative endeavor in which nobles could engage without incurring the risk of status derogation—the liberal professions. The exercise of law in particular played a crucial role in sustaining the local ruling class during its transition from merchant oligarchy and feudal aristocracy to a unified civic elite. The substantial earnings accruing from legal practice and judicial service did much to compensate for the shortfall in income that aristocrats experienced during the later sixteenth and seventeenth centuries. The negative economic climate of the latter century in particular not only improved the chances of successful lawyers being absorbed into the elite. It also encouraged established nobles to try their luck at the bar. It was thus hardly a coincidence that the years of most severe economic depression—the 1630s to the 1670s—witnessed a record number of both aristocratic and commoner law graduates registering for local practice.[68]

The sixteenth and seventeenth centuries represented a crucial turning point in the history of the Catalan aristocracy. Increasingly unfavorable social and economic conditions encour-

---

[66] Giralt, "Comercio Marítimo," II, 61.

[67] A.H.M.B./Cadastre, vols. 11-15. Fewer than half of Barcelona's heads of households in 1716 actually owned the houses in which they lived: Nadal and Giralt, "Barcelona en 1717-18," 297-299.

[68] *Matrícula dels Jurisperits.* That a record number of lawyers registered at mid-century is even more striking, given the severe demographic losses from the siege and plague of 1651-1652. For a more detailed exposition of this argument, see Amelang, "Barristers and Judges."

aged the traditional nobility to forsake its rural origins for residence in nearby cities. Just as the town walls had provided military protection to newcomers during the Middle Ages, they now afforded economic shelter to an aristocracy pressed by inflation and falling seigneurial income. In Barcelona, in particular, nobles eagerly joined in pursuit of the "treasures of knowledge," hoping to garner through the practice of law the earnings needed to maintain the style of life judged proper for members of the civic elite. The main consequences of the demographic reverses and economic depression of the mid-seventeenth century were a further decline in Barcelona's commerce and industry and a corresponding strengthening of its rentier and professional sectors. Thus in many respects aristocratic investment patterns and economic behavior constituted a rational response to prevailing conditions. Finally, the decisive shift toward sources of income that were both more secure and fully compatible with aristocratic "honor" not only represented the final stage in the upper class's retreat from direct farming and commercial investment. The proprietary system also provided a meeting-ground for the gradual merger of the urban oligarchy with the traditional aristocracy—a merger born of common economic values and interests, and bound by ties of shared power and authority.

IV

THE MAKING OF
A RULING CLASS

Barcelona's honored citizens occupied an ambiguous position within local society prior to the sixteenth century. This ambiguity was rooted in a fundamental contradiction—that between their firm control over substantial political and economic resources, and the uncertain social status born of their lack of a clear juridical standing. The Fernandine reforms—especially the decree of 1510 endowing this group with gentry privileges—not only lent the crucial impetus to the emergence of a single class of notables. A considerably simplified social structure also resulted from these measures. In characteristic fashion, Xaupí spelled out the long-term consequences of the citizens' elevation from an intermediate position between nobles and commoners to full integration into a unitary civic elite. "Is this not the same," he asked, "as saying that all men are either nobles or commoners, and that our honored citizens and burgesses should be counted among the ranks of the nobles?"[1]

Several special characteristics of the Catalan aristocracy contributed to the success of this amalgam. First, the local nobility comprised a well-defined social group whose membership was ascertained by a variety of legal prescriptions. Summons to the aristocratic house in parliament; inclusion in lists of candidates

[1] Xaupí, *Recherches*, 98.

for specifically noble offices such as the *Diputat Militar*; inscription (beginning in 1604) in the registry of the Noble Estate—all these provided clear, public tests of membership in the aristocracy. The hard-fought struggles for informal social recognition and the endless stream of appeals to the heraldic chamber of the royal chancery in Castile found little counterpart in Catalonia. In the Principality more precise juridical mechanisms replaced the vagaries of public repute as the leading determinants of *nobilitas*. In the absence of bitter disputes over the specific status of individual families, the boundaries separating the different ranks within the upper class could be more easily relaxed. As a result, the Catalan nobility developed as a more homogeneous social class than in many other realms.

The relatively undifferentiated character of the local aristocracy also fostered an integrated civic elite. The absence of a strong magnate group—small in number to begin with, and largely absentee by the seventeenth century—narrowed the distance between ranks within the estate. The cohesion born of a shared style of life differed sharply from the wide gap found among the privileged classes of neighboring lands. The Catalan nobility certainly did not lack its own indigent members. These poorer country squires, however, did not offer as stark a contrast with the higher ranks of the aristocracy as that between Castile's powerful grandees and often-impoverished *hidalgos*, or French peers and their *hobereaux* cousins. Once again, contemporaries did not fail to remark the difference. Xaupí noted that, unlike Catalonia, the fundamental division within the aristocracy of Castile was that "between the titled and untitled nobility." The *cavaller* barrister Josep de Amigant argued the same point in 1670. Citing the works of eminent local jurists like Fontanella, Bosch, and Acaci Ripoll, he proclaimed that "in Catalonia there are few distinctions separating *nobles* from gentlemen."[2]

The principal cause, however, of this successful integration

[2] *Ibid.*, 60; Amigant, *Discurso*, 3 and 7.

was the equally strong bargaining positions of the two contending sides. The unified ruling class of early modern Barcelona issued from a pact between the citizen oligarchy and the established aristocracy, each covetous of the resources monopolized by the other. Aristocrats increasingly hard-pressed by inflation and stagnant seigneurial income envied the honored citizens' control over local politics and government office. Conversely, urban oligarchs eager to obtain recognition of their claims to gentle rank realized that only the nobles could guarantee their acceptance as aristocrats. Admission of first gentlemen and later *nobles* to the municipal government of Barcelona and other Catalan cities found reciprocation in the acceptance of citizens as integral members of the second estate. The equal exchange between power and status found strikingly overt expression in the case of Barcelona and the neighboring town of Perpignan.

The Art of Compromise

Ferdinand's restructuring of the Barcelona civic regime cleared the way for the social pact uniting the new ruling class. As we have seen, in 1498 he ordered the urban gentry admitted to citizen offices in the municipal government. He subsequently elevated honored citizens to noble status in 1510, thus "cementing," in the words of Xaupí, "the union of two rival groups of nobles."[3] Citizens and *cavallers* soon formed a compact bloc of privilege against outside pressure. In 1547, for example, they stood firmly united in opposition to a proposal by the merchant and guild magistrates to add a sixth, permanent *menestral* Councillor.[4] Yet this condominium of power did not of itself achieve the full integration of citizens and nobles. The upper ranks of the aristocracy continued to be barred from posts in local administra-

[3] Xaupí, *Recherches*, 119.
[4] *Cartas del Emperador Carlos V*, 182.

tion: hence the second estate's protest during the parliamentary session of 1599 against the ongoing exclusion of *nobles* from the governments of Barcelona and other cities—an exclusion Catalan aristocrats found especially irritating, given their liability to municipal taxation. The Noble Estate thus accompanied its petition with a veiled threat to refuse to pay civic assessments if its members were not admitted to local office.[5]

The aristocrats did not fulfill their ambitions until 1621. Following a brief flurry of opposition, they were accorded four places on the Council of the Hundred and inclusion in scrutinies for the leading Councillorships. The debate surrounding this reform affords an interesting glimpse into the relations between different strata of the urban elite. The episode began on January 25 with a joint proposal by the royal governor, D. Bernardino de Marimon, and the Noble Estate in parliament to allow aristocrats proper entry into the city government. Their petition argued that "in Catalonia *militars* and *nobles* are members of the same estate"—an eloquent testimony to the cohesion binding the different ranks of the upper class.[6] However, "unrest and dissension" on the part of unidentified members spurred the Council to appoint a committee of sixteen to discuss the proposal. Shortly thereafter several gentlemen serving on the Council presented a brief opposing the *nobles'* pretensions. The document expressed fear that the *nobles*, because of their overweening "arrogance, wealth, and ambition," would be unable to function effectively in a government which included commoners and even guildsmen.[7] On March 16 an indignant aristocratic Estate replied to this paper. It accused the latter's authors of inventing spurious objections in order to mask the fact that their opposition was motivated solely by the fear of losing their own places on the

---

[5] *Constitutions*, 63. In 1626 the Noble Estate once again referred to its members' tax burdens while seeking the admission of *nobles* to town governments throughout the rest of Catalonia; A.H.M.B./Consell de Cent, XVI, *Corts*, vol. 82, no. 73.

[6] A.H.M.B./Consell de Cent, II, *Deliberacions*, vol. 130.

[7] One of the members of this group—the barrister Francesch Soler—published a separate pamphlet opposing the *nobles'* project; see Soler, *Discurs*.

Council to the newly admitted *nobles*. Thereafter, a small group of honored citizens submitted another brief. Defending their opposition to the aristocrats' entry, they argued that the new competition would cause many *gaudint* professionals to lose their positions. Nevertheless, on June 6 the *ad hoc* committee joined the city's legal staff in recommending the aristocrats' admission, provided that gentry representation within the noble category could be protected.

Three features in particular emerge from the discussions surrounding the reform. Foremost was the striking absence of opposition to the *nobles'* project on ideological grounds. The content of both the gentry and citizen briefs, as well as the accompanying pamphlet by the *militar* barrister Francesch Soler, bore out the Estate's contention that the protest was not grounded in ideological incompatibility with the upper ranks of the aristocracy. Rather, it drew upon the dominant group's fear of increased competition for the limited number of posts within the civic administration. That the underlying conflict was basically one of "ins" versus "outs" is suggested by another characteristic of the dispute—leadership of the reform party by new *nobles* seeking to recover posts recently lost through their passing from gentry to full aristocratic rank. Pujades identified the prime movers of the measure as "some youthful spirits and new *nobles*, such as D. Bernardino de Marimon, who until recently were content to be honored citizens."[8] His account depicted the two parties in the dispute as "factions" (*bàndols*), and attributed the enmity between them to personal rivalries and questions of punctilio. Finally, the Noble Estate's firm support of the reform clearly contributed to the ultimate success of the measure. The stance of this aristocratic institution—which, as we shall see, numbered honored citizens among its members—provides additional evidence for the absence of principled opposition to the new legislation on the part of the urban elite.

The reform of the municipal government of Perpignan from

---

[8] Pujades, *Dietari*, III, 25-26. The first Council to seat *nobles* included Marimon among the handful of aristocratic representatives; *Dietari*, X, 7 Dec. 1621.

1599 to 1602 offers an even more explicit instance of the direct exchange of political power for social acceptance.[9] The fusion of the town's honored burgess oligarchy and aristocratic residents had in fact commenced some twenty-five years earlier. The urban gentry won access to municipal posts in 1572, thus reshaping the *mà major*—literally the "upper hand" in charge of the leading offices in local administration. In the following year, the noble confraternity of St. George, founded in 1562 in imitation of a similar brotherhood in Barcelona, obligingly began to admit honored burgesses as members. However, Philip II nullified these acts in 1580, and the town government reverted to the *status quo ante*. The next change came after the parliamentary session of 1599, when the new king, Philip III, conferred upon the burgesses all the privileges of nobility enjoyed by honored citizens of Barcelona. While this measure entitled burgesses to automatic membership in the confraternity of St. George, it did not resolve the problem of gentry participation in local government. The crown therefore issued a supplementary edict stipulating that the *cavaller* privileges of the burgesses did not prevent their occupying posts in the Perpignan administration. This measure cleared the way for the reinstatement of the original compromise of 1572-1573. The final decree of 1601 permitted the insaculation of both gentry and *nobles* in the *mà major*, in exchange for the permanent admission of burgesses to the noble confraternity.

Elite Sociability

The examples of Barcelona and Perpignan illustrate the extent to which, in the historian Antoni Capmany's words, the "privileges and supreme power of municipal government" equipped

[9] Elliott, *Revolt*, 125-126; Torras Ribé, *Municipis Catalans*, 84-86; Palacio, "Contribución," 667-671; Bosch, *Títols*, 383-408; Xaupí, *Recherches*, 122-260. The royal writ of 1599 is in A.C.A./Can., reg. 4885, 248r.-273r.

the citizen oligarchy with a strong counter in negotiating its status with the traditional aristocracy.[10] In both cases the linkage between shared political power and the acceptance of citizens as nobles was evident to all concerned. Thus by the late 1620s one finds Bosch warmly commending the "perfect brotherhood" uniting civic "patricians" and the "equestrian order."[11] Yet the fusion of the two strata into a single "class of power" dominating urban government did not by any means represent the sole embodiment of their new-found solidarity. Various formal and informal reminders pointed to growing cohesion within the second estate. Foremost among the institutional expressions of this new class identity was the *Bras Militar*, or Noble Estate of the Catalan parliament.

The *Bras Militar* first emerged as the permanent commission of lesser nobles in parliament.[12] In 1389 King John I empowered the Estate to draw up statutes to govern its meetings when parliament was not in session. Although its initial organization deliberately excluded barons, peers, and aristocrats proper, in 1481 Ferdinand joined the upper nobility to the body. There is little evidence of activity on the part of the Estate until the campaign for its reorganization launched at the beginning of the seventeenth century by a handful of Barcelona nobles under the leadership of D. Aleix de Alentorn. At its first meeting in 1602, the group appointed a committee of twelve to draft new statutes for its internal governance. The nobles' purpose in reviving the long-dormant institution was to assure the "preservation of the prerogatives, immunities, and privileges" specified in the original decree of 1389.[13]

At least two developments contributed to the reemergence of the *Bras* as a separate political organization at this moment. First,

[10] Capmany, *Memorias Históricas*, I, 447.

[11] Bosch, *Títols*, 418-419.

[12] *Constitutions*, 53-55; Salvador, "Real Cuerpo"; Vilaplana, *Tractatus de Brachio Militari*.

[13] *Ordinacions y Statuts del Bras Militar*.

one should note the influence of the aristocracy's prolonged dispute with the vice-regal government concerning a 1599 law forbidding nobles to bear firearms. This conflict encouraged the upper class to close ranks in a single, permanent "guild" whose principal task was to guard against similar encroachments upon aristocratic privilege.[14] The other issue concerned the shift within the aristocracy from the country to the city. The clear predominance of the urban nobility within the *Bras* reflected the desire of Barcelona's aristocrats to see their greater political activism rewarded by a like predominance within the two leading Catalan political institutions: parliament and the *Generalitat*. The reactivation of the *Bras* in the opening years of the seventeenth century not only represented a victory for those urging a permanent, more effective defense of noble privilege. It also confirmed the dominant voice of Barcelonans within the Catalan aristocracy as a whole.

One of the first acts of the newly founded corporation was to institute a *matrícula*, or formal membership list, along the lines of those already established for merchants, jurists, and honored citizens.[15] No one was to be inscribed in the register without the prior approval of at least three of the Estate's five elected officers. Membership in the *Bras* was construed as an official recognition of nobility; similarly, failure to obtain admission signified lack of aristocratic status. The initial functions of the body were thus twofold: to defend class privileges increasingly threatened by the central government, and to establish objective means of defining and thus controlling admission to the nobility. Active recourse to these instruments assured Barcelona's nobles an overwhelming predominance within the estate as a whole.

[14] Elliott, *Revolt*, 103-110.

[15] The statutes and subsequent minutes of the Estate repeatedly employed the corporate idiom so characteristic a feature of early modern civic discourse. Hence the constant references to the *Bras* as a guild (*gremi*) or corporation (*col.legi*). The *matrícula* of the Estate—the famous *Llibre Verd*, or "Green Book"—is located in A.C.A./Gen., G-225. The Estate's *Dietari* can be found in A.C.A./Gen., G-68 and G-69 (seven volumes).

The subsequent history of the *Bras* and of its considerable involvement in local politics during the 1620s and 1630s need not concern us here. More relevant to the coalescence of ruling-class identity was the extent to which honored citizens won acceptance within this body. Citizen integration into the most prominent institution of the Catalan aristocracy can be examined from two perspectives. The first concerns their direct participation in the ongoing activities of the Estate, while the second involves the *Bras*'s defense of citizens against challenges to their noble status.

A sample of attendance at assemblies of the Estate reveals substantial citizen participation throughout the seventeenth century (Table IV-1). Records of eleven meetings from 1624 to 1704 show that roughly one-fourth (23 percent) of those present were honored citizens. This proportion compares with a slightly higher average number of gentlemen (27 percent), and the strik-

Table IV-1
Attendance at Meetings of the Noble Estate: A Sample

Date	Honored citizens %		Matriculants	Royal privilege	Gentry %		Nobles %		Total
1624	2	(7)	2	0	15	(50)	13	(43)	30
1629	2	(7)	2	0	7	(26)	18	(67)	27
1631	13	(16)	9	4	28	(35)	39	(49)	80
1637	9	(23)	8	1	12	(31)	18	(46)	39
1639	13	(23)	10	3	15	(27)	28	(50)	56
1660	23	(28)	10	13	30	(36)	30	(36)	83
1672	11	(35)	4	7	4	(13)	16	(52)	31
1686	15	(15)	7	8	20	(20)	65	(65)	100
1693	13	(36)	8	5	8	(22)	15	(42)	36
1699	20	(32)	7	13	9	(15)	33	(53)	62
1704	20	(33)	6	14	13	(21)	28	(46)	61
TOTALS	141	(23)	73	68	161	(27)	303	(50)	605

SOURCE: A.C.A./Gen., G-68 and G-69, *Dietari del Bras Militar*.

ing predominance of the aristocracy proper with its 50 percent.[16] The table also reveals a shift in the balance between *ciutadans de matrícula* and those by royal creation. The gradual rise in importance of the latter closely resembles the changing representation of the two groups in municipal Councillorships during the same years. Yet the integration of the civic oligarchy into the *Bras* was not limited to the numerous citizens in attendance. While the aristocracy proper at no point ceased to dominate the Estate, it is also true that citizens exercised the same voting rights as gentlemen and *nobles*. The persistence of a clear internal hierarchy within the Estate did not detract from the equality of rights enjoyed by citizen members. To the contrary, the placing of citizens on a par with the highest levels of the aristocracy bears eloquent testimony to their public recognition as members of the nobility.

The Estate's unhesitating defense of the citizens' noble privileges completed their absorption into the urban elite. The campaign undertaken by the *Bras* during the late 1670s and 1680s to protect its members against attacks on their rights (especially exemption from taxation) by municipal and royal officials provided ample opportunities to come to the citizens' aid. Thus in 1677 the *Bras* agreed to subsidize the legal expenses of two honored citizens of Barcelona by royal creation who sought protection against town governments attempting to billet troops on their property in violation of Catalan constitutional practice. Equally illustrative of this solidarity was the Estate's decision in 1685 to support the cause of another citizen by royal privilege, whom a royal official had arrested without due regard for his immunity as a noble. These and other examples document the

[16] There were approximately four hundred meetings of the plenary assembly of the Estate during these years. The original commission set up in 1602 to draft the *Bras* statutes included five *ciutadans de matrícula*, along with three gentlemen and four *nobles: Ordinacions*, introduction.

extent to which citizens had won acceptance by local aristocrats as full members of the Catalan nobility.[17]

Another mechanism for the integration of honored citizens into the elite was the confraternity of St. George. Unlike the *Bras Militar*, this association was strictly ceremonial in character. As such it proved an equally if not more visible feature of urban life. King Peter IV founded the brotherhood in 1371 and charged it with regulating jousts and other aristocratic ceremonies. From its inception the association numbered among its members such leading noble families as the Sentmenat, Montcada, Rocabertí, and Erill. While the *Diputat Militar* served as the Prior of the confraternity, and its membership soon overlapped with that of the *Bras*, the two groups retained their individual autonomy throughout the sixteenth century. However, in 1610 the confraternity issued an ordinance forbidding election to its offices of any member not previously registered in the *matrícula* of the Estate.[18] While there is ample evidence of jousting in the *Born*, or market square near the Carrer de Montcada, during the fifteenth and early sixteenth centuries, the confraternity itself appears to have been inactive during this period. In the 1550s a campaign began to restore the association, on the grounds that the "decline" in the martial spirit of the Catalan aristocracy could be arrested only by renewed devotion to the display of arms in jousts and tourneys. Local nobles drew up new ordinances in 1565 and 1573. They once again commended the brotherhood to the protection of St. George, patron both of Aragon-Catalonia and of the most fervent sponsor of the association, the *Generalitat*.[19]

[17] A.C.A./Gen., G-69, III, 5 April 1677 and 12 Nov. 1685.

[18] Salvador, "Real Cuerpo"; Xaupí, *Recherches*, 489.

[19] Duran, "L'Estament Militar: Els Cavallers i la Cavalleria," in his *Barcelona i la Seva Història*, III, 171-259. For aristocratic confraternities elsewhere in Spain, see: Domínguez Ortiz, *Clases Privilegiadas*, 46-48; Ocerín, "Cofradías Nobles"; and Liehr, *Sozialgeschichte Spanischer Adelskorpörationen*, I.

Honored citizens actively participated in the confraternity from the beginning of its revival in the mid-sixteenth century. The membership register created in 1565 included a number of citizens—a point of no small import, as this list served as the roll-book of the Catalan nobility prior to the inauguration of the *matrícula* of the Noble Estate in 1604.[20] While the upper ranks of the aristocracy—particularly the titled noble families—dominated its proceedings, the list of prizes awarded at the annual jousts bears witness to the citizens' enthusiasm for chivalric sports. Honored citizens garnered 41 of a total of 429 prizes conferred from 1556 to 1640, including 11 awards for the "most gallant" horsemen and 7 for the most interesting emblem (*millor invenció*).[21] Citizen participation in this body's activities not only lent visible expression to their acceptance by the traditional aristocracy. It also schooled them in the values of the higher nobility, and encouraged assimilation of distinctively aristocratic modes of comportment.

The admission of citizens to other institutions reserved to members of the nobility provides additional evidence for the public recognition of their aristocratic status. That citizenship was deemed sufficient proof for entry into the military orders of Santiago, Montesa, and St. John of Jerusalem lent weight to arguments for their *nobilitas*. Similarly, acceptance of sons and daughters of citizens by exclusively aristocratic monasteries and convents such as the local houses of the Benedictine order reinforced their claim to full noble standing.[22] However, proof of the citizens' nobility was not confined to strictly institutional settings. Numerous informal indicators underscored the new-found cohesion of the city's burgeoning upper class. Contem-

---

[20] A.H.M.B./Ms. B-64 covers the years 1565-1586; registers for 1596-1701 are found in A.C.A./Gen., G-75. The *matrícules* of local confraternities of St. George also served as roll books of nobles in Girona, Perpignan, and Tortosa. See, for example, Montoto, "Cofradía de San Jorge."

[21] Duran, "Estament Militar," 223-235.

[22] Xaupí, *Recherches*, 299-332; Pujades, *Dietari*, I, 366; Domínguez Ortiz, *Clases Privilegiadas*, 322.

porary census records, for example, confirmed the privileged standing of honored citizens. The royal officials who drew up the list of nobles residing in Barcelona in 1639 did not fail to include members of the oligarchy. Citizens also figured prominently in a 1649 registry of nobles living in the quarter of Santa Maria del Pi.[23]

Ample evidence documents the citizens' absorption of various features of aristocratic comportment. These ranged from forms of honorific address and the bearing of arms, to more general patterns of conspicuous consumption and display, public dress, and precedence in municipal ceremonies. A revealing embodiment of these shared norms of behavior is found in a published description of an aristocratic *fête* of 1637.[24] The pamphlet's author was one Miquel Cervera i de Armengol, the son of an upwardly mobile citizen and a *noble* mother.[25] The poem's central *leitmotiv* is the constant intertwining of the two ranks. D. Ramon de Salba i de Cardona, a descendant of two of the leading Catalan aristocratic houses, penned a laudatory preface to the work. The text itself heaped fulsome praise upon citizens riding at the side of *nobles* in the colorful jousts. Hosting the spectacle was D. Pere Reguer, a shining exemplar of the country gentleman who had abandoned his rural estate for life in the city. Interestingly, Reguer's palace in the Plaça de Sta. Ana stood next door to that of D. Lluís de Paguera, one of the most famous Catalan jurisconsults and the first of many *nobles* to serve in the *Audiència*.

One could pursue these inner connections endlessly. The

---

[23] A.C.A./Gen., caixa 26, varis; A.H.M.B./Fogatges XIX-20. Nobles and citizens also served together as captains in the Barcelona civic militia (see for example the list of *cavallers y Ciutedans* heading the levy of 1542 in the *Dietari*, IV, 110-116). This and other aspects of local military organization in early modern Catalonia merit further study.

[24] Cervera i de Armengol, *A la Grave Ostentación, Al Admirable Recreo, que a lo Festivo del Tiempo Dedicó la Grandeza* . . . (1637), in B.N./V.E. Cᵃ-538-14.

[25] His father was Rafel Cervera, author of a 1616 Castilian translation of the famed medieval chronicle of Bernat Desclot.

sociability born of a shared style of life, both everyday and festive, was a significant informal source of ruling-class cohesion. Yet it was not the only one. The marriage strategies of citizen families also served as mechanisms of entry into the local aristocracy.[26] Of the 27 citizens appearing as grooms in the marriage contracts studied above, 7 married daughters of *nobles* (3) or gentlemen (4). Fourteen, or slightly more than one-half, married into the families of other citizens (5), or of *gaudints* (9). In contrast, only 6 married beneath their rank, to daughters of merchants (3), wealthy *artistes* (2), and a *menestral*. Of the 34 daughters of citizens included in this sample, over one-third married gentlemen (9) or aristocrats proper (4). A plurality of 16 wed honored citizens (8) or *gaudints* (8). Only 5 married commoners, including 4 merchants and a *menestral*.

Certain restrictions did of course limit the full integration of citizens into the established nobility. Most irksome was their exclusion from the Noble Estate when parliament was in session, and from the posts reserved to aristocrats in the *Generalitat*. Although the privilege of 1510 specified that these exclusions did not prejudice the citizens' juridical status as nobles, the two reservations nevertheless proved a source of embarrassment. Similarly, other, less institutional means also limited their absorption into the aristocracy. In 1604, the Duke of Sessa was quite content to watch the annual ceramics fair in the *Born* from the balcony of the honored citizen Rafel Cervera, father of the author of the 1637 *fête* pamphlet. However, some twenty years later his close relative the Duke of Cardona did not know the first name of 14 of the 25 citizens invited to his daughter's wedding. Furthermore, while members of the citizen oligarchy were allowed

---

[26] For a discussion of the marriage patterns of the early modern Parisian elite, see Diefendorf, *Paris City Councillors*, III-IV.

to take part in the lavish masquerades organized by the Duke to entertain the visiting monarchs in 1632, only 3 of the 44 upper-class participants in the masques and mock battles were honored citizens.[27]

The consolidation of a unified ruling class in early modern Barcelona did not take place entirely without friction. The rising tensions during the late seventeenth century between public students and private pupils of the local Jesuit school may well have originated in the traditional rivalry between the Society and the Dominicans in charge of the University. Demographic factors may also have entered into play, as both institutions eagerly competed for students in the years following the plague of 1651-1652. Yet the diverse class origins of the two student bodies doubtless contributed to the quarrel. The University served as the leading vehicle for the upwardly mobile *gaudints*, whose presence in the municipal government was on the rise. The Jesuit *collegium*, to be sure, also numbered students of *gaudint* background among its pupils. Yet it functioned primarily as an instrument for the socialization of those already fully integrated into the elite. Achieved status thus confronted aspiration in the guise of student riots. On the surface, this hardly appeared a serious problem. Underneath, it suggests the presence of deep tensions in local society.

The limits to the full absorption of the civic oligarchy into the aristocracy confirm the persistence of a well-defined hierarchy within the noble estate. Conferral upon honored citizens of aristocratic privileges; enjoyment of personal nobility by doctors in law and medicine; equal representation of all ranks within the Estate's public institutions; association of citizens and aristocrats in less formal venues—all were accepted characteristics of Barcelonan society. That the willingness of the traditional nobility to share its prerogatives and privileges with the civic elite

---

[27] Pujades, *Dietari*, I, 336; B.C./Ms. 979, 208r.-217r., *Memoria de Todas las Casas de Caballeros que ay en Barcelona hecha con Ocasión de Dar Parte del Casamiento de la Hija del Duque de Cardona*, undated; Parets, "Sucesos," vol. 20, 84-85.

did not erase certain other social distinctions should come as no surprise.[28] Our overriding emphasis, however, has been on those elements of authority—power, wealth, and prestige—which all members of the ruling class shared in common.

Traditional interpretations of early modern society have insisted upon the crucial importance of conflict between "new" and "old" elites.[29] Other studies have challenged this view by focusing instead upon the successful recomposition of governing classes throughout Europe during the sixteenth and seventeenth centuries. In the case of early modern France, many scholars now question the true extent of friction between "robe" and "sword" nobilities, and place renewed emphasis on the interests and identity binding the two strata together.[30] As should be apparent, changes in the economic, social, and political structures of early modern Barcelona bear closer resemblance to the latter interpretation. I have tried to isolate the specific causes underlaying this crucial development in the history of the Catalan ruling class. Still, one more point remains to be made. The successful admixture of upwardly mobile citizens and *gaudints* with the traditional aristocracy was fundamentally a product of an urban setting. It was surely no accident that new and old experienced fullest integration in the two institutions most closely identified with the city, the *Bras Militar* and the confraternity of St. George. Conversely, the institutions dominated by the rural aristocracy—parliament and its inter-term representative, the *Generalitat*—were the only ones to challenge the citizens' full exercise of noble privilege. The new, cohesive upper class born of

---

[28] The concept of mesalliance also defined the accepted relations between different ranks within the noble estate. As usual, Pujades' diary is an excellent source for this sort of scandal.

[29] Mousnier, *Institutions of France*, 202-210; Hamscher, *Parlement of Paris*, Chapters 1-2; Coveney, *France in Crisis*, 16-20; Morrill, "French Absolutism," 969-971; Salmon, "Storm over the Noblesse."

[30] Alatri, "Formazione della Élite"; Dewald, *Formation of a Provincial Nobility*; Diefendorf, *Paris City Councillors*, xxv. See also Berengo, *Nobili e Mercanti*, Chapter 4; and Vasoli, *Cultura delle Corti*, 75.

the fusion of the citizen oligarchy and feudal aristocracy thrived best amid the more expansive atmosphere of the city.[31] The multiple forms of power and, above all, the shared identity of the ruling class were overwhelmingly urban in character. Outside the city walls lay a far less secure world—one that challenged its proud certainties, and called into question its authority.

[31] Villari, "Città e la Cultura," 754.

V

IDEOLOGIES OF
NOBILITY

"*Camillo*, as you are certainly a gentleman, thereto clerk-like experienced, which no less adorns our gentry than our parents' noble names, in whose success we are gentle. . . ." Polixenes' remark in the second scene of *The Winter's Tale* aptly summarizes the most significant change experienced by early modern nobles: their transformation from a wide-ranging assortment of rural magnates and squires into an educated, more urban ruling class. The phrase "a gentleman, thereto clerk-like experienced" presumes an identification between noble birth and formal education scarcely conceivable during the Middle Ages. Prior to the "educational revolution" of the early modern era, clerks and knights hailed from distinct social backgrounds. With few exceptions, relations between the two orders were rarely characterized by admixture, much less equality. When such integration did occur, it was limited to the higher reaches of the church hierarchy, and to exceptional religious orders like the Benedictines. And while in clerical depictions of the "three orders" the sacred enjoyed precedence, in the more profane sphere of reality learning consistently deferred to chivalry.[1]

[1] Stone, "Educational Revolution"; Clanchy, *From Memory to Written Record*, 173-201. Russo, "Cavalliers e Clercs," deals with the contrast between clerks and knights, so prominent a theme in medieval literature (but cf. Turner, "*Miles Literatus*").

The transformation was neither abrupt nor uniform. After all, few subsequent aristocracies could boast the artistic refinement and opulent display of the late medieval Burgundian court. Meanwhile, on the other side of the "revolutionary" divide, affable boors like Squire Western chased foxes and damned the court well into the modern era. Yet these apparent exceptions merely confirmed the rule of the profound change experienced by this "nobility in search of a definition."[2] Significantly, the case of the Burgundian court differed sharply from that of future generations of aristocrats. Its extensive patronage of art and highly stylized existence issued, not from the formal education characteristic of later centuries; rather, they were the product of a singular aesthetic ethos whose roots lay well outside the academy. Similarly, the vitality of Fielding's congenial rustic squire was made possible by a political structure in which substantial power and prestige accrued to the country as well as to the cities and the court in London. By and large, this configuration proved unique to England and certain areas of eastern Europe.[3] In the rest of the continent, centralization of government and domestication of the rural nobility proceeded apace. The persistent strength of the seigneurial regime throughout the later years of the old regime scarcely concealed the forging of new power relations among aristocracy, cities, and the central government. The nobility's successful adaptation to changing political and economic circumstances found sustenance in a broadened conception of elite identity—one that rested upon novel justifications of aristocratic privilege.

[2] Goubert, *Ancien Régime*, Chapter 7. See also: Hexter, "Education of the Aristocracy"; Stone, *Crisis of the Aristocracy*, 672-724; Labatut, *Noblesses Européenes*, 85-101; Bitton, *French Nobility*, Chapter 2; Sales, "Desaparición"; Wood, *Nobility*, Chapter 3; and Vale, *War and Chivalry*.

[3] For a revealing sketch of the unlettered rural nobility of 17th-century Poland, see Sienkiewicz' *The Deluge*. This novel—originally published in 1886—drew heavily upon the fascinating memoirs of a noble military commander during the Commonwealth Wars (Leach, *Memoirs of the Polish Baroque*).

Virtuous Letters

That the essence of nobility was a loosely defined ideal of "virtue" was a concept with deep roots in classical and Scholastic thought. Both Stoic and later neo-Aristotelian writings singled out *virtus* as the leading characteristic of the aristocracy—a choice that accorded well with depictions of chivalry in medieval imaginative literature.[4] However, during the later Middle Ages and Renaissance this formulation changed significantly, as humanists and lawyers argued for the acquisition of virtue through study of the liberal arts. The case for the "nobility of letters" had not lacked intellectual precursors among classical authors or medieval jurists. Nevertheless, writers, academics, and liberal professionals pressed it with unprecedented vigor beginning in the early fifteenth century. From their efforts a novel definition of nobility emerged—one that placed less emphasis upon lineage and racial descent in favor of a broader vision of "virtue" as a product of education, not of birth.[5]

The new definition of *virtus* first appeared in the city-states of the early Italian Renaissance. Florentine humanists in particular discussed the essence of nobility in numerous writings. Texts like the *Disputation of Nobility*, written around 1420 by Buonaccorso da Montemagno the Younger, and the 1440 dialogue of the same title by Poggio Bracciolini directly addressed the problem of aristocratic identity.[6] The work by Buonaccorso—a professor of jurisprudence at the University of Florence and a member of the circle of Leonardo Bruni—explicitly de-

---

[4] E.g., the *Decameron*, fourth day, first story. See also Huizinga, *Waning of the Middle Ages*, chapters 3-4; and Duby, *Chivalrous Society*, 86.

[5] Skinner, *Foundations of Modern Political Thought*, I, Chapters 2, 4, 8, and 9.

[6] Garin, *Prosatori Latini*, 141-168; Baron, *Crisis*, 420-423; Poggio, *Opera*, 64-83; Holmes, *Florentine Enlightenment*, 148, and his "Emergence of Urban Ideology," 126-128.

fined nobility as virtue acquired through learning. It also sought to demonstrate the superior merit of the "self-made" commoner who had risen in society through his own efforts and innate capabilities. This intensely personal vision of nobility, which shone forth in adages like "whosoever has not attained distinction should blame himself," was also propounded by Poggio a generation later. His dialogue opened with a survey of views from both ancient and contemporary writers. Poggio concluded that, given the absence of uniform criteria within descriptions of nobles in Antiquity and his own era, personal virtue should be regarded the exclusive hallmark of the aristocratic spirit. The most famous passage of the treatise argued that "true nobility" was the "splendor proceeding from virtue, which illumines those possessing it regardless of their social extraction."[7]

A similar view of *nobilitas* informed the protracted discussions among Florentine intellectuals concerning the relative nobility of law versus medicine—the famed *disputa delle arti*. The most representative contribution to this debate was Coluccio Salutati's *On the Nobility of Law and Medicine*, written around 1399 and published by Girolamo Giganti in 1542. In the opening chapter Coluccio affirmed that "true nobility is not a matter of ancestors or of lineage, but rather resides solely in virtue." The author went on to note that the first nobles among the Israelites were those chosen upon Moses' advice among "learned and wise men . . . excelling through their knowledge and virtue."[8] This brief but significant passage sums up prevailing attitudes toward the aristocracy among many early Florentine humanists. Their dialogues and treatises not only defined nobility as *virtus*. The humanists' true innovation was to argue that virtue could best be acquired through "learning," that is, education in humane letters and the liberal arts.

---

[7] Poggio, *Opera*, 79 and 85.

[8] Salutati, *De Nobilitate Legum et Medicinae*, 8. See also: Garin, *Disputa delle Arti*, and his *L'Educazione in Europa*, 145-148; Thorndike, "Medicine vs. Law"; and Ullman, *Humanism of Coluccio Salutati*, 31-32.

The most influential discussion of *nobilitas* to issue from the Italian Renaissance was Baldesar Castiglione's *The Book of the Courtier*, finished around 1516 and published by Manutius in 1528. Set against the background of the decline of the civic nobility's power following the French invasion of 1494, this treatise sought to resolve the aristocracy's crisis of confidence by proposing a new social role of public spectacle and display. While earlier briefs for the nobility of letters read as apologia for the aristocratic pretensions of liberally educated civic elites, Castiglione urged the humanistic education of the established court aristocracy. He also argued for a remarkably self-conscious manipulation of letters and comportment by the ruling class as a whole. In his view, education, manners, and demeanor not only distinguished nobles from commoners, but also lent renewed justification to the social hierarchy inherited from the past. Every detail of aristocratic life was thus to be governed as if nobles were actors in a spectacle whose audience was society at large. Learning, grace, refinement—these were the badges of distinction to be worn by the aristocracy. While older arguments for the nobility of letters provided the necessary foundations for this imposing edifice of studied display, his new definition of nobility superseded the original humanist program by strengthening the role of formal knowledge and manners as conscious instruments of social separation. As the pursuit of "humane letters" gradually emerged as a central element in the aristocracy's own self-consciousness, theatrical presentation of the new learning began to dominate the face shown by the nobility to the rest of society.

The remarkable popularity of Castiglione's book throughout early modern Europe ensured that there would be no retreat from the path explored in his novel formulation of aristocratic intent. The flood of treatises written in imitation of *The Book of the Courtier* partook of a common attempt to adapt arguments for the nobility of letters to the needs of established aristocracies as well as urban oligarchies. Sixteenth-century Italy in particular saw a host of elaborations on the themes propounded by the

Florentine humanists and Castiglione. These usually took the form of courtesy books, the best-known of which was Giovanni Della Casa's *Galateo*, first published in Venice in 1558. The shift in the meaning of *virtus* away from ideals of medieval chivalry toward new standards of learning and behavior was nowhere made more apparent than in the preamble to this widely read text:

> We wish to be courteous, agreeable, and good-man-nered in our conversation and dealings with others. If this is not virtue, it is not far removed from it. For though generosity, loyalty, and moral courage are without doubt nobler and more praiseworthy qualities than charm and courtesy, nevertheless polite habits and a correct manner of speech and behavior may benefit those who possess them no less than a noble spirit and a stout heart benefit others. . . .[9]

Della Casa devoted the rest of his treatise to prescribing the knowledge and manners needed to distinguish the "noble" from the "obscure," placing special emphasis on bodily comportment, dress, and language.

The new vision of gentility which took as its point of departure the nobility of learning also found expression in the hackneyed debate over arms versus letters. Perhaps the most influential treatise on this subject was Girolamo Muzio's *The Gentleman* (1571).[10] After subjecting the reader to the habitual review of classical and contemporary definitions of nobility, Muzio opted in the end for the ultimate superiority of letters. In the words of Marino Berengo,

[9] Della Casa, *Galateo*, 21 (R. S. Pine-Coffin's translation). Pages 101-131 of this edition discuss courtesy books in England, as does Woodward, *Studies in Education*, 268-382. For this text's diffusion in the rest of Europe, see: Retali, *Galateo*, and Richter, *Giovanni Della Casa in Francia*. A Castilian translation by Domingo de Becerra was published in Venice in 1585.

[10] Muzio, *Gentilhuomo*. Also see Clements, *Picta Poesis*, Chapter 7.

The figure of the noble versed in letters and law, whose birth served above all to guarantee a virtuous education, came to dominate the public vision of this author who for many years served in the ranks of the Spanish administration, a body singularly mindful of class distinctions and so little disposed to forget the noble or common status determined by birth. . . .[11]

Other early modern Italian writers like Giovanni Botero and Daniello Bartoli defended the nobility of letters in similar terms.[12] By the late sixteenth century, the power of liberal education to confer the lustre of gentle rank had in fact become a stock theme of most contemporary discussions of *nobilitas*.

The nobility of letters also found defenders outside the realm of humanist discourse and social commentary. Not surprisingly, jurists numbered themselves among the best-known proponents of this theme. Particularly influential were the *Commentaries on Nobility* published in 1543 by André Tiraqueau, a renowned legal scholar and magistrate of the *Parlement* of Paris.[13] An even more famous defense of the acquisition of noble virtue through the study of letters was Charles Loyseau's *Treatise on the Orders* (1610). This distinguished barrister's advocacy of the *noblesse de robe*'s claim to gentle rank placed overriding emphasis on the power of education to confer virtue. "If at times children's characters happen to conform to those of their parents," he argued, "this is not the result of descent, which plays no part in character, but rather of education and upbringing."[14]

[11] Berengo, *Nobili e Mercanti*, 254.

[12] Botero, "Treatise of the Greatness of Cities," in his *The Reason of State*, 251; Bartoli, *L'Uomo di Lettere*. Both works were translated into Castilian and published in Barcelona, respectively in 1603 and 1744. Bartoli's work in particular was popular with local readers, as evidenced by its frequent appearance in notarial inventories.

[13] Tiraqueau, *Commentarii de Nobilitate*. See also Brejon, *André Tiraqueau*.

[14] Loyseau, *Traité des Ordres et Simples Dignitez*, IV, 1. My citation is from Peter Evans' translation of Mousnier, *Social Hierarchies*, 84, which reproduces Loyseau's arguments in detail.

Castile also made important contributions to this genre of apologetic literature. The influential thirteenth-century law code known as the *Siete Partidas* enshrined the juridical tradition assigning the origins of nobility to "lineage" and "knowledge." The power of learning to bestow nobility found ample resonance in later writings as well. One representative text was the oft-cited legal treatise by the Salamancan jurist Andrés Mendo, *On Academic Law* (1665), which contained an exhaustive discussion of the noble rights and privileges enjoyed by holders of university degrees throughout Europe.[15] Other authors, like Alonso Núñez de Castro, Diego de Saavedra Fajardo, Juan de Zabaleta, and Cristóbal Suárez de Figueroa, elaborated at length on the theme of the *nobleza de letras*.[16] One of the most famous of these treatises was the *Discourses on the Nobility of Spain*, published in 1622 by D. Bernabé Moreno de Vargas, an urban *hidalgo* from Extremadura. Moreno's pithy phrase "letters and arms confer nobility, valor and wealth conserve it" underscores the extent to which this doctrine had become part of the common currency of political and legal thought in early modern Spain.[17]

By the late sixteenth and seventeenth centuries, arguments for the nobility of letters contributed vitally to a basic consensus on the sources of *nobilitas*. Of course, many writers continued to champion the hereditary quality of virtue, and thus the superiority of established aristocrats over educated newcomers—a precedence rarely called into question.[18] Nevertheless, the successful linkage of noble "virtue" with learning and mannered comportment represented a significant ideological gain by up-

[15] Fayard, *Membres du Conseil de Castile*, 181; Mendo, *De Iure Academico*. Chapter 6 of Fayard's study, entitled "Nobles et *Letrados*," provides a succinct review of the literature in Castilian.

[16] Maravall, *Poder, Honor y Elites*, 41-61; Arriaza, "Nobility in Renaissance Castile."

[17] Cited in Palacio, "Contribución," 307. See also Fayard, *Membres du Conseil de Castile*, 181-185.

[18] Stone, *Crisis of the Aristocracy*, 21; Diefendorf, *Paris City Councillors*, 168; Jouanna, *Ordre Social*, I-II.

wardly mobile urban elites. It also lent fresh impetus to the older aristocracy's effort to adapt itself to political and social change at the threshold of the modern era.

Local Arguments

Early modern Catalan arguments for the redefinition of nobility generally followed patterns laid out in the rest of Europe. In fact, the writer Joan Boscà (Juan Boscán), the most famous honored citizen of Barcelona, translated Castiglione's *The Book of the Courtier* into Spanish, publishing the first edition in his native city in 1534.[19] Nevertheless, one is struck by the singular predominance of legal exposition within Catalan commentaries on *nobilitas*. The most ardent local supporters of the nobility of letters were jurisconsults like Fontanella, Bosch, and Antoni de Vilaplana.[20] Their works drew upon the glosses of medieval canonists, Tiraqueau's treatise on the nobility, and Catalan constitutional traditions. Later generations of jurists even turned to extra-legal texts to uphold belief in the ennobling quality of learning. Representative of this latter tendency were the inaugural addresses delivered by the presidents of the Academy of Jurisprudence, founded in 1777. In these declamations prominent Catalan barristers ransacked a wide variety of lay sources

[19] Boscán, *Cuatro Libros del Cortesano*. See also Morreale, *Castiglione y Boscán*. While Boscà and other early modern Catalan writers followed Castiglione in according considerable importance to inherited *nobilitas*, they rarely seem to have associated *nobility* with race. This not only contrasts with Arlette Jouanna's findings for sixteenth-century France, but also raises questions about the stereotype of early modern Iberian obsession with *limpieza*, or "racial purity." I have been struck by the virtual absence of references to *conversos* (converted Jews) in local documents from this period. For further discussion of this anomaly, see Amelang, "Honored Citizens," 271-273.

[20] Fontanella, *Sacri Regii Senatus*, section 29; Bosch, *Títols*, 29-32, 65-68, and 348-365; Vilaplana, *Tractatus*, 221-225 and 256-268.

to bolster their contention that letters endowed their possessors with true "nobility of character."[21]

These legal expositions ostensibly defended the thesis that all forms of learning—most commonly interpreted to mean a university degree—conferred noble privilege. Nevertheless, the lawyers transformed the case for the nobility of letters into a brief for the privileged status of jurisprudence in particular. This narrow outlook was hardly surprising, given the overwhelming predominance in numbers, social prominence, and political and intellectual activism of lawyers in relation to other educated members of the urban elite. Their strongly corporate vision found eloquent depiction in the role jurists played in the canonization in 1601 of Saint Raymond Penyafort. The renowned Dominican numbered among his many qualities the happy coincidence of being a native of Barcelona, the scion of a local noble family, and a noted canon lawyer. Not surprisingly, the city's barristers became fervent devotees of the cult of this model saint, who, in the words of one contemporary, combined the exercise of law with "virtue, letters, and nobility."[22]

There existed, however, a parallel line of reasoning whose advocacy of the nobility of letters found expression in treatises on moral theology. Much of this discourse centered around the question of leisure, long a concern of political commentary on the aristocracy. Classical writers, for instance, had contrasted the *otium* of the Roman governing class to the *negotium* (literally "business") burdening the plebs.[23] Later writers justified both leisure and the rentier existence that supported it as a necessary means to two ends: responsibility for public affairs and, in the

[21] Magarola's *El Abogado Perfecto* of 1789, for example, borrowed arguments from Xenophon, Plutarch, Cicero, and Seneca to support his characterization of jurisprudence as a liberal, and thus "noble art."
[22] Pujades, *Dietari*, II, 219; Amargós, *Relació*.
[23] Godelier, "Work and Its Representations," 172. Especially influential in this regard was Aristotle's *Politics*, VII-VIII.

private sphere, commitment to humane and divine studies. Conversely, nobles who did not take proper advantage of their leisure to pursue *virtus* and wisdom were chastised as idle wastrels.[24] This sort of criticism—a predictable wedding of intense moralism to studious apoliticism—loomed prominently in the erudite discussions of Barcelona's noble academy. Its members devoted at least two sessions to weighing the merits of acquired versus hereditary nobility. On July 22, 1700, D. Josep de Rius drew heavily on conventional moralistic emblem literature to support his contention that "virtue," "good works," and "merit" were the true sources of nobility.[25] Some thirty years later, his fellow academician, the Baron of Rocafort, also defended the superiority of acquired over inherited *nobilitas*. Citing the works of Poggio, Tiraqueau, and numerous theologians and moralists, he argued that "true nobility comes not from lineage, but solely from virtue." Rocafort was no up-and-coming *gaudint* lawyer; rather, he was a prominent member of the established aristocracy.[26] His arguing such a position demonstrates the inroads moralistic assessments of personal merits had made within the burgeoning genre of upper-class apologetics.

Another representative text was the local theologian Francesch Garau's *The Wise Man Instructed in Grace* (1688). "Everyone is what he is, not what his parents were"; "it is better to make oneself [noble] than to be born noble"; "no lively spirit is content

[24] One of the most interesting texts to sound this theme was the *Vicios de las Tertulias* (1785), a free translation by the cleric Gabriel Quijano of the abbé Zucchino Stafni's *Lo Specchio del Disinganno* (Rome, 1751). See also Martín Gaite, *Usos Amorosos*, and Deacon, "Cortejo."

[25] A.H.M.B./Ms. B-98, June 10 and July 22, 1700. Rius specifically cited Saavedra Fajardo's *Emblemas Políticas*, no. 8. The most famous early modern emblem book, Alciati's *Emblemata*, also defended the superiority of letters over arms; see nos. 132 and 180 of the Spanish translation (Lyon, 1549). For a brief study of this literary genre in Spain, see Sánchez Pérez, *Literatura Emblemática*.

[26] A. de Armengol i de Aymerich, *Libro de los Assumptos que . . . ha Trabajado para la Academia de Buenas Letras*, B.C./Ms. 1874, 1 Jan. 1731, 25r. In 1607 the Saragossa academy also railed against noble idleness: B.N./Ms. 9396, *Pitima Contra la Ociosidad*. See also Chisick, *Limits of Reform*, 99 and 153.

with what is inherited"; "the greatest heroes founded their own lineage"; "let no one be discouraged, as each can 'make' his own nobility"—these were but a few of the maxims illustrated in what was perhaps the most widely read (and optimistic) of early modern Catalan emblem books.[27] Naturally, we should not exaggerate the significance of these passages. Their importance lay, not in their strident if quite routine claims for the superiority of acquired over inherited nobility; rather, such texts provide a useful index of the extent to which many influential contemporaries regarded the acquisition of nobility through the study of liberal arts a legitimate source of aristocratic rank. After all, ideological justification of the union of the traditional nobility and the civic oligarchy rested ultimately upon establishing liberal education as an essential characteristic of *all* members of the upper class. Distinctions between acquired or inherited virtue played a far lesser role in defining the new, united ruling class of the early modern period than did the binding tie of shared knowledge.

Gilabert and the Letrados

The attitude of the traditional nobility toward formal education greatly preoccupied D. Francesch de Gilabert. His reflections on the problem took the form of *The Discourse on the Source of True Nobility* (1616), the single most important treatise on the Catalan aristocracy.[28] Unfortunately, little is known about the author, save that his father won *noble* rank during the reign of Philip II, and that the son had previously served in the Spanish army overseas and as a courtier in Madrid. He was also deeply involved in Catalan urban affairs, having occupied at least once the office of head Councillor of the city of Lleida. His other works included a reply to Antonio de Herrera's commentary on the Ar-

---

[27] Garau, *Sabio Instruido*, "Sumario del Libro."
[28] Gilabert, *Discurso*.

agonese crisis of 1591; a short treatise on agriculture edited in 1626; and four other texts on Catalan society and politics published along with the *Discourse* in 1616. The literary citations in these treatises reveal a man well-versed in the Latin classics and later Patristic works. They also betray a certain familiarity with the Legists, possibly the product of a legal education.[29]

The declared purpose of the *Discourse*—formally addressed to the *Bras Militar* and its leading member, the Duke of Cardona—was to warn the Catalan aristocracy of the harmful consequences of its lack of letters. The text opened with the predictable erudite catalogue of answers to the age-old question "what is nobility?" Significantly, the author favored the definition penned by the fifteenth-century jurist Felino Sandeo as the best amid a barrage of responses. "Nobility," according to Felino, "proceeds from three sources: first, lineage and blood; second, virtue and letters; third, a mixture of these two."[30] Gilabert then traced the history of knowledge from its origins in Greek and Persian Antiquity through the Roman and later Scholastic periods. He emphasized the concurrence of all authorities in the belief that knowledge not only ennobles but also confers the power (*virtud de mandar*) that most distinguishes nobles from commoners. After reviewing various practical applications of knowledge—which included praise for the utility of mechanical arts[31]—he then discussed individual theoretical disciplines like theology, law, and medicine. He attached special importance to the impact on the aristocracy of the changing character of warfare, and underscored the need to absorb the new forms of knowledge underlying the revolution in military technology.

[29] Elliott, *Revolt*, 69. A Hierònim Gilabert, *utriusque iuris doctor*, registered in the Barcelona criminal court in 1551; however, I have not been able to determine his relation to the author. Gilabert was apparently the central figure within a small group of humanist intellectuals in Lleida. This circle also included the Aragonese physician Jerónimo de Mondragón, who in 1598 dedicated his eccentric *Censura de la Locura Humana* to Gilabert.

[30] Gilabert, *Discurso*, 3v.

[31] His passage strongly echoes part 19 of the Barcelona theologian Narcís Antoni Camós' *Microcosmia* of 1592.

These specifically included geometry—"necessary to build fortresses, dig mines, and lay trenches"—and other "mechanical arts, in order to create deadly weapons, both offensive and defensive."[32] The treatise closed with a blanket condemnation of the Catalan nobility's insufficient application to liberal and technical studies. According to Gilabert, while aristocrats wasted their energies in internal rivalries and feuds, upstart commoners supplanted their rightful place at the helm of local society and government.

Several interesting themes emerge from this essay in political and social commentary by a Catalan provincial aristocrat. First, one should remark the uniqueness of this document within the Spanish context.[33] The typology of the *Discourse*—a discussion of the nature and functions of the nobility by a nobleman himself—had little counterpart in the rest of the peninsula. Rather, it more closely resembled contemporary French treatises like François de la Noue's *Political and Military Discourses*.[34] This new generation of aristocratic self-assessment demonstrated a realism far removed from the chivalric and courtly literature of the later Middle Ages.[35] The work of Gilabert and others like him also represented a clear break with the abstract, legalistic approach of jurisprudence and moral theology. Finally, its focus on the problems of adjustment faced by the older established nobility brought it much closer to the writings of Castiglione than to those of the early Italian humanists.

[32] Gilabert, *Discurso*, 16v.-17r.

[33] In the eighteenth century the Catalan aristocrat D. Joan de Sagarriga penned a work entitled *Como deve Pintarse o Describirse el Noble*, which has unfortunately been lost; see Cosme Parpal's introduction to Sagarriga's *Dietario de Barcelona*, xvii-xx.

[34] Huseman, "François de la Noue"; Schalk, "Appearance and Reality of Nobility." There are also some intriguing parallels between Gilabert and the Austrian provincial nobleman Wolf Helmhard von Hohberg. For a suggestive study of the latter's writings, see Brunner, *Adeliges Landleben*.

[35] The best-known Catalan chivalric tracts were Lull's *Orde de Cavalleria* (late thirteenth century) and Ponç de Menaguerra's fifteenth-century *Lo Cavaller*, both edited by Pere Bohigas in the anthology *Tractats de Cavalleria*.

The clear note of self-doubt and loss of direction pervading the work conveys the impression of a traditional nobility in crisis. The text's opening pages breathe an atmosphere of instability, with Gilabert railing against the "inconstancy of the world, which treats each of us like a ball—playing with it, now hitting it forward, then back, sending it up or casting it down, propelling it against the wall of care, or puffing it up with the air of prosperity."[36] To be sure, such passages draw to some extent upon traditional topoi bemoaning the vagaries of worldly fortune. Still, they betray a sense of urgency and resolution that leaves little room to doubt the author's belief that his were special times calling for special measures. As a consequence, Gilabert's depiction of the contemporary ruling class was far from encouraging. He portrayed a rural gentry fragmented into warring factions and plagued by internecine disputes, thus paving the way for anarchy and social unrest. Moreover, a challenge from below threatened this traditional squirearchy—that of the *letrados*, or educated bureaucrats, to whom noble gentlemen must now submit as "subjects." While Gilabert never ceased to affirm the superiority of arms over letters, he nevertheless admitted that unless the older aristocracy successfully reformed itself, nobles ran the risk of losing their power and preeminence. "Learned men and knowledgeable persons exercise dominion and power over those who are not," he lamented. "It is a thing worthy of tears, and hard to believe, how nobles reject such dominion through their ignorance."[37] The only means by which the Catalan nobility might escape the consequences of the rise to power of "the favorite, the *letrado*, and the Viceroy's scribe" was thus the "study of letters and virtue."[38]

[36] Gilabert, *Discurso*, 1r.-v.

[37] *Ibid.*, 8v. and 21r. The first part of this section consciously draws upon Aristotle's *Politics*, I.

[38] Gilabert, *Discurso*, 22r. Francisco Núñez de Velasco's *Diálogos De Contención entre la Milicia y la Ciencia*, while not cited by Gilabert, was probably a source for this portion of his treatise.

The experience of Gilabert symbolized that of the traditional Catalan aristocracy as a whole. In his view, *virtus* still defined nobility: "antiquity of lineage and knowledge of letters do not in themselves constitute nobility, if they are not joined by virtue."[39] But this elusive quality had to change in order to meet the challenge of modern times—a challenge born of profound transformations in the nature of warfare and the instruments of government. Both military and political leadership constituted traditional reserves of power and patronage slipping rapidly from the hands of a nobility forced to "modernize" in order to survive. While his work referred to tensions between new and old nobility—especially those between robe and sword—we should avoid being sidetracked by the familiar opposition to upstart *letrados*. Much more significant was Gilabert's pointing directly to the solution at hand—change on the part of the traditional aristocracy which would permit reconquest of its former "power of rulership" through the absorption of *scientia*. Both nobles and their "virtue" were to be recast to embrace letters as well as arms and lineage. The final product of the transformation would be a unified upper class, freed of internal tensions and strengthened in its efforts to resist monarchical encroachment on its prerogatives.[40]

Ironically, Gilabert's prescription for the aristocracy's vigorous response to the *letrado* challenge—a challenge forcefully stated in the juridical and moralistic texts studied earlier in this chapter—paved the way for the emergence of a spirit of commonality between older and newer members of the nobility. According to his and other contemporary texts, the proper relation between "arms and letters" was complementarity, not opposition. "He united Mars and Minerva in himself"—thus read a

---

[39] Gilabert, *Discurso*, 12v.

[40] Significantly, Gilabert played a key role in combatting royal policy during the parliamentary session of 1626. See Pujades, *Dietari*, IV, 33, and B.U.B./Ms. 1009, 61r.-63v., *Discurs sobre lo Servey que lo Rey, N^re Senyor, Demana en Catalunya, per D. Francesch Gilabert.*

description of Joan Tomàs de Rocabertí, Archbishop of Valencia and younger brother of the learned Viscount cited above.[41] And D. Josep de Avilés, author of a widely read heraldic treatise published in 1725, was also extolled as a noble "known not less for his valor and military prowess on the field of Mars than for his pen's successes in the school of Minerva."[42] The wedding of Mars and Minerva provided a literary analogue to the merger of the civic oligarchy with the traditional nobility. I have already commented upon the institutional expressions of this amalgam. What remains to be examined are the ideological characterizations of their solidarity. The most significant development in the latter sphere was the gradual emergence of a binding ideal of a distinctive high "culture"—a concept that soon moved to the fore of the self-definition and comportment of urban notables.

Exemplars for Aristocrats

A remarkable literary genre flourished in late seventeenth- and eighteenth-century Catalonia: the funeral oration for prominent members of the aristocracy.[43] While the same years witnessed the apogee of this type of sermon literature throughout Spain,[44] the appearance of the *elogios* at this juncture owed much to the peculiar biological fortunes of the Catalan titled nobility. During the later decades of the seventeenth century, direct male succession failed in all four of the leading families of the Catalan peer-

---

[41] Cited in Torras Bages, *En Rocabertí*, 17.

[42] Avilés, *Ciencia Heroyca*, I, "Aprobación" of D. José Ventura Güell i Trelles. For the topos of "arms and letters" in early modern Spanish literature, see: Curtius, *European Literature*, 178-179; Russell, "Arms vs. Letters"; and Gutiérrez, "Armas, Letras, y Estoicismo." The most famous version of this *disputa* is found in *Don Quijote*, I, Chapters 37-38.

[43] Representative examples other than the ones cited below include: Potau, *Oración Fúnebre*; Miracle, *Llanto de los Hombres*; and Rocabertí, *Sermón Fúnebre*.

[44] Herrero Salgado, *Aportación Bibliográfica*, 739-741. For sermon literature in early seventeenth-century Spain, see Smith, *Preaching*.

age: the Cardona, Queralt, Montcada, and Rocabertí. These lineages followed the path traced earlier by the noted Requesens house: that is, the absorption of their titles and estates by collateral branches of Castilian origin.

The orations themselves—habitually declaimed and then published by the leading preachers of the city[45]—followed a set pattern organized around a single theme, usually a verse from the Psalms or the New Testament. Their highly formalized and stereotyped exposition oscillated between systematic theological exegesis and increasingly strained linguistic *invenciones*, which often included puns and other word-play. A stock repertory of attributes deemed typical of the exemplary aristocrat informed these frequently bizarre exercises in verbal artistry. The evolution of the concept of *nobilitas*, and the growing success of the formulaic wedding of noble virtue to the twin qualities of education and service to the state, can best be studied in the context of a single lineage. Descriptions of members of the Rocabertí family—heirs to the title of Viscount of Rocabertí, and (after 1599) Counts of Peralada—illustrate the changing public image of the traditional aristocrat.

One of the earliest and most interesting panegyrics of the family was pronounced, not on the occasion of a funeral; rather, it was included in the preface to the *Fatal Omens* tract published in 1646 by D. Ramon Dalmau de Rocabertí. In his flattering introduction to the treatise, Friar Gabriel Agustí Rius praised the "full and overwhelmingly qualified nobility" of its author, eulogizing him as an exemplar of Ovid's four "notable proofs" of *nobilitas*: "estates or wealth; antiquity of lineage; personal virtue; and *ingenio* (genius)."[46] Rius went on to note the tested fidelity

---

[45] One Pere Dimas Potau apparently led the pack of local orators, rushing into print over a dozen such sermons from the 1680s to 1710. Noble funeral laments drew heavily from imagery used in other threnodies, especially those of monarchs like the unfortunate Charles II, whose eulogies started well before his death in 1700.

[46] Rocabertí, *Presagios Fatales*, A3.

of the Viscount to the Spanish monarchy, and concluded with fulsome praise of his "virtuous employment" in letters. In this eulogy, one already notes the convergence of common themes of later funeral panegyrics: stock references to aristocratic *virtus*; emphasis placed on loyalty to the crown; and, most significantly, the close identification between intellectual attainment and membership in the ruling class embodied in the concept of noble *ingenio*.

Two texts from 1676 drew upon more conventional depictions of the exemplary aristocrat. The funeral oration preached by Francisco Sobrecasas for Ramon Dalmau's brother-in-law, D. Joan de Boixadors i de Rocabertí, scarcely departed from the traditional themes of noble description, military prowess, and other chivalric virtues. A similar emphasis pervaded Josep Dromendari's lengthy genealogy, commissioned by the family and published in a lavish folio edition in Genoa.[47] Both texts elaborated liberally upon the older conception of nobility which prized martial valor and personal fidelity to the monarch. That such themes should have been emphasized at this moment hardly seems surprising, given the widespread "disloyalty" to the Castilian monarch among the lower ranks of the Catalan nobility during the revolt of 1640-1652 and the corresponding exile imposed upon the peerage for its adherence to the Castilian cause.[48]

Later funeral orations stressed a different conception of nobility, one closer to the terms depicting Ramon Dalmau in 1646. This *exemplum* received its most refined formulation in the exequies for his grand-nephew and successor, D. Bernat Antoni de Boixadors, fifth Count of Peralada. Friar Josep Mercader preached the sermon in 1755 at the Dominican monastery of St. Catherine's. He divided the text into three parts, corresponding to the deceased's leading realms of accomplishment: "letters,

[47] Sobrecasas, *Oración Fúnebre*; Dromendari, *Arbol Genealógico*.
[48] Vidal Pla, *Guerra dels Segadors*.

arms, and statecraft." Significantly, Mercader interpreted the Count's precocious enthusiasm for humanistic studies as an obligation imposed by rank. "He knew that the glory of Julius Caesar derived as much from letters as from military triumphs, and that Alexander the Great had become even greater through his studies with Aristotle."[49] Boixadors' early predilection for literary study found later expression in a multitude of works. The most important of these were his numerous presentations to the local Academy, which ultimately named him its president.[50]

The "greatness of soul" revealed by youthful absorption in study could not but foster a "noble inclination to serve Prince and homeland"—hence the beginnings of Peralada's lengthy career in military campaigns throughout Europe. However, Mercader took pains to stress that the Count's many services to the crown were not exclusively indebted to mere martial prowess. To the contrary, both his readings in the classics and the "geographical and historical studies he had made of Italy constantly brought to mind famous deeds both ancient and modern."[51] Classical erudition thus joined physical strength and skill to serve the monarch on the field of battle. Furthermore, this scholarly soldier employed his learning to further the interests of the crown in yet another field, that of statecraft. Like that other warrior-poet David, Boixadors also felt the attraction of political service in the court. Frequent assignments as ambassador to the leading capitals of Europe tested time and again his diplomatic skills and cosmopolitan education. Thus Mercader recounts that Philip V's respect for the "erudition and *cultura*" of the Count was such that after receiving a cipher from the Republic of Hol-

---

[49] Mercader, *Oración Fúnebre*, 10-11.

[50] Miret Sans, "Dos Siglos de Vida Académica," 31; Carreras Bulbena, "Estudis Biogràfichs," 187-191; *Memorias . . . R. Academia de Buenas Letras de Barcelona*, I, 1756, "Resumen Histórico." At one point Boixadors' literary curiosity got him into trouble with the Inquisition, which suspected him of owning forbidden books: A.H.N./ Inquisición, leg. 3724 (30), undated.

[51] Mercader, *Oración Fúnebre*, 11 and 15.

land, the King remarked that only Peralada could interpret it correctly.[52]

Rulers habitually say this sort of thing to keep their followers happy. And one can guess that the troops serving under the learned Count held a rather different opinion of his penchant for quoting Tacitus on the battlefield. Still, we are dealing here not with the *reality* of court and country. Rather, our concern is with the face aristocrats chose to show to the rest of society, and the willingness of scribes to reproduce this image. In this regard it can hardly be doubted that such a paragon of erudition—to whom (it was said) the great Muratori planned to dedicate his *De Moderatione Ingeniorum*—proved a shining exemplar of the noble "great in letters, great in arms, and great in *política*."[53] The lavish funeral monument by the sculptor Manuel Tramulles (Illustration 2) also emphasized this "image" of the learned aristocrat. The catafalque itself was divided into four stories. The statues on the bottom tier of the "symbolic cenotaph" represented the four principal objects of study in Barcelona's Academy: History, Moral Philosophy, Eloquence, and Poetry. The figures on the second level symbolized the four countries where Peralada had carried out military and diplomatic missions: Spain, Portugal, France, and Italy. The third stage comprised a temple erected by the twin deities of Honor and Virtue, while the skeletal figure of Death bearing the legend *Hinc Raptus ad Astra* crowned the top of the bier.[54]

The inscriptions on the plaques surrounding the base of the tomb also drew heavily upon the vocabulary and imagery of contemporary academic discourse—hence the familiar mixture of crushing erudition with puns and other rhetorical devices; the

[52] *Ibid.*, 13 and 20.

[53] *Ibid.*, 20-21. There is no mention of Boixadors in the edition I have consulted (Muratori, *Opere*, I, 294-325).

[54] The iconographic program of this engraving was published along with the inscriptions as a preface to Mercader's sermon. For aristocratic funeral monuments in the rest of Spain, see Lleó, *Nueva Roma*, 95-149; and Gallego, *Visión*, 139-150.

2

Funeral Monument for the Count of Peralada (1756).
Designed by Manuel Tramulles; engraving by Ignasi Valls.
From Josep Mercader, *Oración Fúnebre . . . Conde de Peralada*
(1755), s.n.

presence of standard figures like Hercules, Orpheus, Phoebus, and Minerva; and the constant association of "virtue, wealth, merit, and studies." While the relatively uncomplicated prose of Mercader's sermon may have been linked to the extraordinary circumstances of the Count's demise—his death in the Lisbon earthquake of 1755 must have rendered him the envy of Enlightened intellectuals throughout Europe—its continuity with past academic style is nevertheless quite striking. The eulogy and monument constituted the most explicit local statement of the concept of the nobility of letters argued during the early modern era. By the mid-eighteenth century, the association of nobility with *cultura* provided an exemplar for aristocrats both old and new. For, as Mercader piously noted, even as a child Boixadors had learned the elementary lesson that "a noble without letters was like a ship without oars, or a bird without feathers."[55]

"Even today there are scholars who feel that working in laboratory experiments hardly suits the decorum of the nobility—as if it were more honorable to study the purely abstract ideas of men than the works of God . . . in . . . nature."[56] Local Jesuits penned this complaint in 1762, hoping to justify adding experiments in physics to their traditional scholastic curriculum. On the one hand, the statement illustrates the efforts made to absorb newer, more empirical forms of knowledge and techniques into the corpus of elite learning. It also bears witness to continued resistance to such innovations—a resistance whose intellectual foundations rested upon a firm distinction between the theoret-

[55] Mercader, *Oración Fúnebre*, 10. Apparently the Count's moral virtues were not inherited by his son, described by a hardened reprobate like Casanova as "a great debauchee and lover of bad company, an enemy of religion, morality, and law"; Casanova, *Memoirs*, VI, 209. Another noble writer, the Baron of Maldà, also referred in disgusted tones to the young Count's *vida putesca*, which led eventually to the latter's imprisonment (Galí, *Maldà*, 256).

[56] Galí, *Maldà*, 153.

ical *sapientia* identified with aristocrats, and the more practical and "impure" lore of the artisan.[57]

The time-worn dichotomy between empirical and theoretical knowledge—the object of growing intellectual debate throughout eighteenth-century Spain[58]—underlay and was in turn reinforced by existing patterns of social hierarchy. As we have seen, one of the more striking features of this configuration was the way in which humanist and juridical arguments for the "nobility of letters" lent impetus to a novel characterization of the aristocracy. This ideology did much to dignify the status of upwardly mobile urban elites determined to redefine the boundaries of the ruling class. Yet by erecting new foundations for upper-class identity, it also cleared the way for a "reconversion" of the existing aristocracy. Noble urbanity and *cultura* formed a crucible for the merger of the two strata. The amalgam's final issue was a unified civic ruling class, tightly bonded by a common public *persona*.

There was of course nothing new in the association of social and political elites with the instruments of learning. Skillful manipulation of literacy and other forms of knowledge had lent powerful support to class dominance in many previous societies.[59] Nor was elite monopolization of specific cultural activities limited to the explicitly theocratic states of the Middle Ages. The possession of learning provided an "argument for the superiority of the upper class" as far back as Antiquity. Both Aris-

[57] Rossi, *Philosophy*, Chapter 1. The principal aim of this stimulating work is to study those early modern writers whose positive reassessment of manual labor contributed to the rise of experimental science and applied technology. My interest is in the other side of the coin—the older world-view, quite healthy in this period, perhaps even strengthened by the partial incorporation within elite *scientia* of experimental methods. For a revised chronology of the latter, see Kuhn, "Mathematical Vs. Experimental Traditions."

[58] See for example Feijoo's famous essay "Causas del Atraso que se Padece en España en Orden a la Ciencias Naturales" and other texts in García Camarero, *Polémica de la Ciencia Española*.

[59] J. Goody and I. Watt, "The Consequences of Literacy," in Goody, *Literacy in Traditional Societies*, 27-68.

totelian and Platonic traditions emphasized the close ties linking empirical knowledge, manual labor, and the lower classes. They similarly associated the nobility with more abstract, speculative thought, and conceived knowledge to be a "disinterested contemplation of conceptual truths" exclusively limited to the upper class. In the eyes of most classical writers and their successors, the hierarchy of labor was in fact a hierarchy of intelligence. Individual forms of economic endeavor arrayed themselves along a spectrum bounded by the twin poles of manual labor/social inferiority, and intellectual contemplation/social superiority.[60]

The longstanding association of the "upper" class with superior intellect and education nevertheless experienced a significant transformation during the early modern period. For the first time, the identification of *nobilitas* with distinct patterns of knowledge and behavior became automatic, even necessary. Simply put, at the end of the Middle Ages it was still possible—albeit increasingly less common—to be both noble and illiterate. By the end of the period under study, an illiterate aristocrat was regarded as an intolerable contradiction. Gone were the days of the medieval knight Perceval, whose noble blood had triumphed over a lack of education.[61] The possession of some measure of "culture" had in the meantime become an essential hallmark of nobility. In the words of the most popular courtesy manual of eighteenth-century Barcelona, "be he a prince, be he the wisest man, be he powerful or rich, if he lacks education, or is uncivil, he will surely be despised. . . . Incivility is low and plebeian, courtesy is always noble."[62]

---

[60] Bauman, "Marxism and the Contemporary Theory of Culture"; Mondolfo, "Greek Attitude To Manual Labour," and "Trabajo Manual y Trabajo Intelectual Desde la Antigüedad Hasta El Renacimiento," in his *Orígenes*, 121-144; Rossi, *Philosophy*, 55.

[61] Duby, *Chivalrous Society*, 107.

[62] *Reglas de Buena Crianza Civil y Christiana*, 5. I owe this reference to Gary McDonogh, whose translation I have used.

VI

STUDIES IN SOCIAL
VOCABULARY

A notion of difference resides at the core of all complex social structures. Coherent patterns of distinction are held to delimit and render intelligible virtually every sphere of collective belief and activity. Systems of social classification range from the simple to the highly elaborate—from elementary binary oppositions like male/female or left/right, to infinitely articulated hierarchies and gradations. Whether couched in the static language of stratification or in the kinesis of changing relations, the principle of distinction is seen to influence both social organization and its symbolic representations.

Early modern men and women employed a host of criteria in forging their own categories of social analysis. There was no single, overriding mode of determining "place" in society. Rather, numerous systems of classification complemented (and contradicted) each other, as a broad range of discriminatory schemae—some strictly functional, others more broadly "ideological"—vied for the allegiance of contemporaries.[1] To be sure, certain factors of selection were acknowledged explicitly as such; others won more muted recognition. A brief remark from one of the more shrewd observers of the seventeenth century reveals

[1] Duby, "The Origins of a System of Social Classification," in *Chivalrous Society*, 88-93.

the possibilities of implicit overlap between rival categories. Sancho Panza's weary dictum that "there are only two families in the world . . . the haves and the have-nots," is a time-honored description of contemporary society.[2] As a characterization of early modern realities, it is at the same time compelling and over-simplified. One could hardly quibble with its allusion to the inescapable connection between wealth and power. Yet it also appears simplistic, in that during the *ancien régime* social distinctions were never so starkly (nor effortlessly) delineated. At no point did wealth automatically translate itself into prestige and political power. Yet high social status and political influence were difficult to maintain, much less achieve, without substantial economic resources. In short, there is more to Sancho's observation than meets the eye. This caution applies to virtually all contemporary social classifications. The juridical separation of nobles and commoners; the moralistic distinction between "shameful" and "dishonest" poor; the hierarchy of corporations defining representation in city government—the full meaning of any of these ideal systems cannot be perceived without reference to a host of implicit assumptions regarding, say, the association of different social groups with specific productive functions.

The very multiplicity of definitions of public identity obliges the historian to pay close attention to the precise terms that contemporaries used to describe their world. Study of early modern "social vocabulary" helps us unravel the mystery of how (and why) the social, economic, and political transformations described above found representation in the cultural sphere.[3] This bygone lexicon constitutes a decipherable code through which historical actors articulated their values and beliefs. At the same time, the continual reproduction of language patterns—the con-

---

[2] *Don Quijote*, II, 20.

[3] W. H. Sewell, Jr. advocates studying the "linguistic postulates" of the Old Regime in his *"État, Corps,* and *Ordre."* See also: Sewell, *Work and Revolution*; Chisick, *Limits to Reform*, 48; Agulhon, *Vie Sociale*, 247-256; and Tournier, "Vocabulaire de la Révolution."

struction of imagination within the "prison-house of language"—decisively influenced the identity and comportment of all social classes.

Examination of linguistic usage is an especially valuable approach to the study of periods of intense social transformation. Shifts in language reflected and in turn helped shape patterns of change. As we have seen, the early modern era witnessed a crucial alteration in the patrician image of self and society. Elite visions of hierarchy formerly centering around racial and biological determinants of character and social standing now took on a new dimension. Perceived *cultural* differences irrevocably joined or replaced these criteria in depicting—and justifying—the existence of a separate ruling class.[4] To a large degree the elite manipulated knowledge as a public test—one that presupposed a schema of cultural differentiation closely modelled after existing patterns of power and subordination. A shared vocabulary distinguishing "high" from "low" in explicitly cultural terms bound together diverse expressions of patrician self-consciousness. This lexicon rested upon a series of stark dichotomies opposing elite "knowledge" to popular "ignorance," high "enlightenment" to base "obscurity." The promotion of a reified notion of *cultura* itself placed the finishing touches on the quest for legitimacy by the recomposed upper class of early modern Barcelona. It is to "culture" and other such terms that we must now turn in order to trace their role in marking class boundaries.

Most previous surveys of "keywords" like *cultura* have approached them from the perspective of the "history of ideas." This method focuses on the evolving use of terms within imaginative literature and philosophy. Shifts in linguistic usage are held to represent larger transformations in the realm of normative thought. The task of the historian of ideas is "to observe the ways in which the multivocality of the word sometimes facili-

[4] Ginzburg, "High and Low"; Payne, "Elite vs. Popular Mentality"; Wrightson, "Two Concepts of Order," 46.

tates or promotes (though it doubtless seldom or never solely causes) changes—some of them revolutionary changes—in the reigning fashions in ideas."[5] Individual words and their multiple meanings thus serve as keys to the philosophical beliefs underlying them. As a result, they are habitually sought within the formal discourse of the elite.[6]

Another dominant tendency within the historiography of the term "culture" has been to emphasize its role as an antecedent to present-day anthropological usage. "Culture" in the sense of the discrete body of "manners" and "customs" of diverse social and ethnic groups first emerged during the eighteenth century. However, this meaning had deep roots in much older cognates.[7] The word "civility," in particular, with its strong classical resonance, enjoyed a major revival during the Renaissance and early modern period. Writers initially employed it to denote the mental categories and comportment of educated Europeans coming into increasingly close contact with peoples outside their continent. Soon this normative concept of a single, unitary *civilitas* gave way to a more relativistic notion of diverse "civilizations," each with its own language, ecology, and mores.[8] The eventual supplanting of "civilization" in the latter sense by "culture" owed much to the German Enlightenment, which consciously extended the term *Kultur* to the customs and "folkways" of native Europeans as well.[9]

Neither approach to the linguistic history of "culture" has examined the full historical record. Rather, they have limited

[5] Lovejoy, *Essays in the History of Ideas*, xiii.

[6] For good general discussions of the *idea* of "culture," see the separate entries by Thomas Cole and Frederick M. Barnard in the *Dictionary of the History of Ideas*, I, 607-621.

[7] Hogden, *Early Anthropology*, Chapters 6 and 7; Moravia, *Scienza dell'Uomo*, II; Davis, *Society and Culture*, 254-257.

[8] Febvre, "Civilization"; Benveniste, "Civilisation"; Vivanti, "Origini dell'Idea di Civiltà"; Weintraub, *Visions of Culture*, Chapter 1; Huppert, "Idea of Civilization"; Ryan, "Assimilating New Worlds."

[9] A. L. Kroeber and C. Kluckhohn focus exclusively on the Germanic tradition and omit the earlier Latin background of the term in their *Culture: A Critical Review*.

study of its usage exclusively to the expository writings—usually philosophical—of the intellectual elite. Little attempt has been made to bring to bear documents emanating from other levels of discourse.[10] In the following pages we shall see how "culture" and other keywords were used not only in formal argumentation, but also in school ceremonies, pamphlet literature, carnival poems, diaries, civic *fêtes*, and even in the manifesto of a peasant revolt. Expanding the scope of study from the relatively narrow confines of philosophical commentary to a more broadly based social etymology brings us much closer to the meaning of *cultura* most familiar to early modern men and women. Resort to a wider range of sources also affords insights into the distant origins of the term's present usage.

From Genius to Culture

Learned and distinguished Ripoll, to whom Heaven gave
A Genius so divine, and so much knowledge
That the world is amazed, while subtle flight
Lifts your work so high . . .
May time learn wisdom from you,
For I see you are another Athena;
And although the sun be called by others the light of day,
May it shine only for you;
For upon returning from study in your Temple,
Time will become wiser, and Apollo more discreet.[11]

This anonymous sonnet was published along with a dozen similar panegyrics in—of all things—a 1648 guide to Catalan criminal court procedure. It invites examination less for its literary

---

[10] This is true even of such revolutionary texts in intellectual history like Raymond Williams's *Culture and Society 1780-1950*. The same author's *Keywords* is an indispensable reference for the sort of linguistic history undertaken in this chapter.

[11] Ripoll, *Additiones*, introduction.

merits (although it is by no means the most unreadable sample of this tortured genre) than for the way in which it conveniently brings together virtually all the terms contemporaries used to highlight social distinction. Learned, *claro*, genius, *sciència*, high, subtle, sun, light, discreet—time and again these words set apart those whose intelligence, learning, and wisdom distinguished them from the rest of men. Differential intellectual endowment functioned as a potent myth explaining contemporary patterns of social hierarchy. Although such terms were rarely employed in isolation, for the sake of clarity they will be considered separately here. Our starting-point will be the early modern noun closest to the modern concept of intellect: *ingenio*, or genius.

The word "genius" possessed a variety of meanings during the early modern period.[12] It often referred to a familiar spirit or personal *daimon* accompanying individuals in their endeavors, creative and otherwise. This was the sense of the eighteenth-century genre of political satire entitled *Letters of Ingenios from the Court*, which habitually interchanged the terms "genius" or "genie" with *duende* or spirit. *Ingenio* also signified a general concept of reason or intelligence. Confidential assessments of the personal characteristics of local Jesuit novices employed the term as a synonym for intellectual capacity. Superiors classified their charges in three categories of *ingenio*: *buen* (good), *mediano* (medium), or *corto* (little).[13] Moreover, a particular craft could be seen as requiring more "genius" than others. Such at least was the rationale underlying the traditional corporate hierarchy,

---

[12] The best catalogue of early modern usage is Giorgio Tonelli's entry in the *Dictionary of the History of Ideas*, II, 293-297. See also: Rudolf Wittkower, "Genius: Individualism In Art and Artists," in *ibid.*, 297-312; Nitzsche, *Genius Figure*; Panofsky, "Artist, Scientist, Genius"; and Kemp, "From *Mimesis* to *Fantasia*."

[13] A.R.S.I./Arag. 10¹, *Catalogi Triennales*, 1587-1619, 41r.-42r. (1593).

which accorded superiority to trades relying more on the mind than the hand. Thus, as late as 1816, Barcelona's wool and silk dyers defended changing their corporation's name from "guild" to *colegio* by claiming that their profession "requires, thanks to its close contact with the sciences, more *ingenio* than other trades."[14]

Within the Hispanic context, "genius" most frequently denoted a particular inner leaning or inclination. In the eyes of contemporaries, this "disposition"—the strong individualism of which merits emphasis—was determined largely by the vagaries of biological inheritance. External factors like climate or, for the more astrologically inclined, the alignment of the stars were also believed to influence differences in intellectual capacity and personal character. Despite a growing tendency to associate genius specifically with artistic distinction, most early modern writers used the term to refer to a differential psychology of individual disposition. Italian essayists like Antonio Persio, Tommaso Garzoni, and Marco Pellegrini pioneered the systematic exposition of this interpretation of *ingegno*.[15] But the most influential statement of this view came from the pen of a Spanish author, Juan Huarte de San Juan. His *Examination of Men's Wits* (1575) popularized the usage which assigned to each human being a specific "natural" disposition. This "talent" or character was held to be imparted at birth, and determined the conduct of that person for life.[16] Huarte's treatise proved a huge success, going through at least fourteen printings in four languages by 1600. Despite its initial proscription by the Inquisition, copies of the *Examination* were found in many of Barcelona's public and private libraries.

---

[14] Cited in Molas, *Economia i Societat*, 39.

[15] Persio, *Trattato dell'Ingegno*; Garzoni, *Theatro*; Pellegrini, *Fonti dell'Ingegno*. Similar views are found in Bartoli's *L'Uomo di Lettere* (English translation *The Learned Man*, 275-300). See also Raimondi, "Ingegno e Metafora nella Poetica del Tesauro," in his *Letteratura Barocca*, 1-32; and Summers, *Michelangelo*, 58.

[16] Huarte de San Juan, *Examen de Ingenios*, 66-67. Richard Carew published the first English translation in London in 1594. See also Iriarte, *Huarte de San Juan*, and Read, *Juan Huarte de San Juan*.

Its owners included the honored citizen Joaquin Setantí, himself the author of an interesting collection of aphorisms (1617); the physicians Jeroni Tarrassa (1629) and Joan Nadal de Prats (1648); D. Pau Ignasi de Dalmases, the founder of the noble Academy (1718); and the library of the Jesuit school (inventoried 1785).[17] Not surprisingly, numerous Spanish authors tried to follow in his footsteps. For example, Diego de Gurrea, an Aragonese preacher and tutor to the offspring of the Duke of Cardona, argued in a 1627 pedagogical treatise that *ingenios*, while not immutable, were natural endowments distributed by God, who thus indelibly marked the intellectual and moral inclinations of all individuals.[18]

Usage of the term underwent at least two significant transformations during the early modern era. While the older sense of innate character or disposition survived well into the eighteenth century, it was soon overtaken by the refinement specifying "genius" as markedly *superior* intellect and wit. The habit of prefacing *ingenio* with *alto*, *raro*, or *lúcido* was dropped in favor of letting the term stand without modifiers. The writer whose work best reflected this transition was the Aragonese Jesuit Baltasar Gracián (1601-1658). In his hands "genius" shed its earlier neutralism to become synonymous with wit, acumen, and general intellectual preeminence. Moreover, in works such as the *Art of Genius* (1642), Gracián forged an irrevocable association between superior intellect and its particular stylistic manifestation in the form of intricate and complex conceits.[19] Not sur-

---

[17] Cortes, *Els Setantí*, 149; A.H.P.B./José Pedrol, *Manual de Inventarios 1624-35* (29 Aug. 1629); B.C./Ms. 1960, untitled Nadal inventory (12 Aug. 1648); B.C./Ms. 677, untitled catalogue of Dalmases library (undated); A.E.B/Seminari IV, *Inventari de . . . la Biblioteca Pública Episcopal* (1785).

[18] Gurrea, *Arte de Enseñar*, Chapter 8.

[19] Gracián, *Obras Completas*, clxi-clxvii and 1163-1254. To be sure, Pellegrini claimed to be the first to link *ingegno* and *acutezze* (*Fonti dell'Ingegno*, 21); see also Curtius, *European Literature*, 294-301. Gracián and other seventeenth-century writers transposed Huarte's definition of *ingenio* as "inclination" to the term *genio*: see the first chapter of *El Discreto* (1646) entitled "Genio y Ingenio" (*Obras Completas*, 78-81).

prisingly, local Jesuits eagerly appropriated Gracián's innovations for their academic exercises. Beginning in the seventeenth century, Jesuit school celebrations made countless references to *ingenio*, understood now as the effortless combination of superior intellect and highly witty rhetoric. Thus in 1673, for example, the Barcelona *collegium* held a "joust of geniuses" to celebrate the canonization of St. Francis Borgia.[20]

The second shift in usage involved broadening application of the term from individual intelligence to the superior intellectual inclinations of an entire social class—in this instance, the civic elite. The growing tendency of writers to regard *ingenio* as one of the essential "proofs of nobility" demonstrates that the identification was not limited only to certain sectors of the ruling class. The shift in the use of "genius" from reference to the innate character or special intellectual endowment of specific individuals toward a more general, collective association with the upper class reflected a decisive change in the self-image of the urban elite as a whole.

In the long run, however, a more restricted usage of the word triumphed. By the end of the eighteenth century, "genius" usually denoted the creative endowment of uniquely gifted persons instead of social groups.[21] Ironically, emphasis on artistic and literary talent resurrected the term's original, individualistic connotation. Antoni Capmany's *Philosophy of Eloquence* (1777)— one of the most important treatises on rhetoric of the Spanish Enlightenment—illustrates this transition. Capmany's text drew upon both the traditional sense of *ingenio* as innate disposition, as well as the newer, proto-Romantic usage associating "genius" with individual artistic temperaments "both grand and sublime."[22] Fortunately, early modern writers did not lack other means of indicating intellectual distinction. They pressed into service a variety of terms to this end. Especially notable among

---

[20] *Iusta de Ingenios.*
[21] Wittkower, "Genius"; Engell, *Creative Imagination.*
[22] Capmany, *Filosofía de la Eloquencia*, xiv-xv.

these was the imagery of sun and light that made the eighteenth century its own.

The "most obsequious" D. Francesch de Prada spared no pains to depict his fellow members of the Jesuit alumni association in—literally—the most brilliant light possible:

> This resplendent Congregation
> Presided over by the Sun,
> Whose rays animate it and give it life . . .
> With Phoebus rather than Apollo at its head,
> Armed, as are the wise, with pens . . . ,
> For the Sun always seeks the Wisest and most Learned. . . .[23]

And so forth. While the protracted belaboring of solar metaphors plagued numerous contemporary texts, it achieved special intensity in these academic panegyrics. The future lawyer D. Josep Faust de Potau, for example, cast the allegory of his *ingenio*'s "daring" ascent to the "summit of Parnassus" in similar language equating the sun with the ultimate goal of wisdom. At the end of his journey he encountered an august mansion where "all was light, yet nothing fire." This "lustrous dwelling" was none other than the Palace of Apollo—*Apolineo Alcázar*—within whose walls sat the "shining Senate" of the Jesuit order. Presiding over the latter in a "throne of light" was

> The resplendent Prince of Light,
> Living ray of Celestial Fire,
> Scorching volcano of Divine Love,
> Burning sphere of the most holy fire,
> Lustrous Phoebus . . . Captain of the most famous stars . . . ,
> In short, divine Ignatius of Loyola. . . .

[23] Prada, *Increato Divinae Sapientiae*, s.n.

136

> To the teaching of your followers
> We owe the light that illumines [our] *ingenios*. . . .[24]

The "sun of knowledge" was perhaps the simile most frequently used in the academic and religious writings of sixteenth- and seventeenth-century Catalonia. On the one hand, one can trace the pre-history of the vocabulary of "enlightenment" back to classical Antiquity. Metaphors of light and darkness played a central role in the Platonic tradition in particular. But clearly the most important antecedents of this imagery lay in Biblical, and especially Christian, usage. Sor Hipólita de Rocabertí's homely depiction (see Illustration 3) of the Christian youth as a sunflower guided on pilgrimage to the celestial Jerusalem "by our crucified Lord Jesus Christ, the true Sun of Justice" typified the genre.[25] Identification of sun and light with the revealed truth of Christian doctrine provided a firm intellectual grounding for the subsequent transfer of this imagery from divine to profane knowledge. The theologian Josep Romaguera's approving preface to the local Academy's *Royal Dirges* of 1701 rendered quite explicit the orderly devolution of the descriptive language of the sacred to the secular world. "Each wise man," he wrote, "is an Olympus, and his talents a cluster of stars; in his own knowledge he has his lustre, fortune, and guiding light . . . this Academy has thus become a Milky Way composed of a multitude of stars."[26]

The schema of intellectual distinction underpinning such imagery differed from that linked to "genius" in at least one crucial respect. Unlike *ingenio*, with its strong overtones of innate and inalterable character, the "light of knowledge" was viewed as a quality that could be deliberately acquired. Of course, some texts did suggest that the unequal distribution of "lights" among

---

[24] Potau, *Loa*, A2 and A4.
[25] Rocabertí, *Tratados Espirituales*, II, "Palabras de La Autora."
[26] Amat de Planella, *Nenias Reales*, "Aprobación."

Verus χρι cultor nouum heliotropium
Respicit ut Solem planta hæc vaga semp et affert
florem phœbeis persimilem radis
Sic tu iustitiæ Solem meditare frequenter
Huius ut exemplar Corde opere ore feras.

Palabras de la Autora.

COmo las sacras Imagenes mueven mucho, no solo a los simples, sino tambien a los sabios, y

mas

3

Images for the Simple. From Sor Hipólita de Rocabertí,
Tratados Espirituales (1647), II, preface.

human beings had been predetermined by birth.[27] But by far the great majority of usages specified that *luces* could be accumulated through education. Hence the boast of the law teacher Lluís Valencià that his students "have emerged from my instruction so *luzidos* [literally "shining"] that they have been able to obtain and illumine (*illustrar*) university chairs and posts on the bench, state councils, and in the Church." D. Josep Faust de Potau wondered at the power of education to confer "the light through which [our] genius is illumined." Still other forms of creative activity were believed capable of adding to the cumulative store of resplendent knowledge. Thus Josep Mercader in his eulogy of the Count of Peralada praised the latter's "noble exercise" of "investigating the truth hidden away in archives, thus adding many *luces* to the literary sphere."[28]

Not surprisingly, such splendid reflection was, like *ingenio*, restricted almost exclusively to members of the elite. In fact, the urban nobility exhibited an insatiable craving for description in the imagery of sun and light. Its thirst was hardly slaked by the flood of formulaic panegyrics preached at aristocratic funerals, annual meetings of the Jesuit alumni congregation, and the St. George's Day celebrations of the *Bras Militar*. Self-depiction in the guise of Apollo, his son Phaeton, and the Phoenix scored clamorous successes among local notables. Even the terminology used to describe the everyday activities of the aristocracy drew heavily upon the imagery of light. To Pujades, nobles were "lustrous people" (*gent de lustre*); in the eyes of Bosch, aristocrats were "all those who illumine and shine forth (*illustran y resplendeixen*) in nobility, lineage, knowledge, virtue, strength, office, and in other ways."[29] In 1682, the Noble Estate argued that the inclusion of its members in the municipal government of Girona would "confer the noble order's lustre" upon that city, while in

---

[27] For example, Romaguera, *Atheneo de Grandesa*, 59.

[28] Valencià, untitled retirement petition of 1669 in B.C./F. Bon. 2596; Potau, *Loa*, final page; Mercader, *Oración Fúnebre*, 11.

[29] Pujades, *Dietari*, III, 93; Bosch, *Títols*, 579.

the Barcelona Academy D. Agustí de Copons approvingly cited Aristotle's definition of nobility as a *claritas*.[30]

Contemporaries also habitually employed the vocabulary of light to describe patrician *fêtes* and ceremonies. The lawyer Josep Montfar i Sorts dutifully noted reports of a "*lucidíssima* and costly equestrian festival" staged in Paris by the peers of France for Louis XIV. Yet the Barcelona aristocracy was hardly to be out-done, if one were to believe Parets' description of the *luzidas* floats mounted by local nobles during their reception for the Queen of Hungary in 1630.[31] This imagery—also employed with great frequency in contemporary descriptions of religious processions and festivals—was allowed most extensive play in Francesch Tagell's poetic account of a series of private Carnival balls held in 1720 in several noble mansions on the Carrer de Montcada. At the beginning of his description of each party, Tagell praised the countless "lamps, chandeliers, and candles" set out "to illumine everything," especially those aristocrats "who have come to lustre [their] beauty and grace." "This lus-trous salon"; the "brilliant sphere"; the "noble, illustrious, beau-tiful group from whose singular *luz* love forges its darts"—in expressions such as these the author repeatedly wed lavish aris-tocratic display to the vocabulary of brilliance, splendor, and reflection.[32]

Metaphors of illumination continued to be used in the eight-eenth century to set apart the distinctive knowledge and com-portment deemed characteristic of elites throughout Spain. Meanwhile, the vocabulary of light underwent a retrenchment similar to that visited upon the term "genius." The meaning of the term *luces* gradually narrowed to "enlightenment," either in

---

[30] Untitled pamphlet in B.C./F. Bon. 323, 17; A.H.M.B./Ms. B-98, session of 22 July 1700; Dalmases, *Disertación Histórica*, prefaces.

[31] Montfar, *Diario*, in B.U.B./Ms. 397, 27 March 1685; Parets, "Sucesos," vol. 20, 50.

[32] Tagell, *Descripció dels Dotze Celebres Festins* (1720), in B.U.B./Ms. 5, 14v., 18r., 22r., and 24v.

the sense of the European-wide literary movement of that name, or in relation to the crown program of political reform which derived inspiration from *philosophes* and government officials in France and Italy. Thus when the historian Jaume Caresmar referred in the 1780s to a cleric *de algunas luces* (literally "of some lights"), he drew upon the former sense of the literary trends which produced the *Encyclopedia* and other manifestations of the *siècle des lumières*.[33] His praise, however, of the Madrid government's success in "dissipating darkness through the active rays of its *luces*" obviously referred to the royal program of "modernization from above" which sought to adapt to Spanish circumstances many of the slogans and policies of the Physiocrats.[34] Soon only one term could be employed unequivocally to signify the superior knowledge, refined behavior, and cultivation of intellect associated with the upper class. By the end of the eighteenth century, "culture" had triumphed over its rivals.

Late medieval Catalan use of the term *cultura* reflected classical notions of process and breeding. When Andreu Febrer in his fifteenth-century translation of the *Inferno* spoke of land "lying without *cultura*," or when the agronomist Miquel Agustí recommended in 1617 that "if your inheritance consists of uncultivated land, put it to *cultura* and you will make it good," they drew upon older traditions identifying "culture" with agricultural growth.[35] Yet ancient writers had not limited usage of the term and its cognates to a strictly bucolic setting. Rather, they wielded "culture"—originally derived from *colere*, "to tend, till or adorn"—as a highly flexible metaphor for breeding and edu-

---

[33] Galí, *Maldà*, 282.

[34] Cited in Arranz, "Profesionales," I, 10. See also in general Sarrailh, *L'Espagne Éclairée*, II and III.

[35] Febrer, *Infern*, XX, 84; and Agustí, *Llibre de Secrets*, 146v., cited in Alcover, *Diccionari Català-Valencià-Balear*, III, 845.

cation. The property of *cultura* distinguished civilized from barbarian, the polished and domesticated from the unbred and wild. Julius Caesar used the term in this way, for example, in his terse dismissal of the Belgians as lacking the *cultu atque humanitate* of the more Latinized Provençals.[36] Closer to home, the *cultura animi* of Antiquity referred to the active perfection of the individual through formal study. In both its collective and individual applications, *cultura* denoted education and nurture—literally, the "cultivation" that set apart certain human beings from others.[37]

Despite the clear classical precedents for the use of "culture," few examples are found in Catalan literature prior to the early modern era. The most popular medieval Catalan pedagogical text, Lull's *Doctrine for the Young*, forsook "culture" for more Scholastic substantives like *estudi*, *doctrina*, and *sciència*. The earliest local examples of "culture" in the classical sense date from the sixteenth century. Joan Boscà, for instance, occasionally used the words *cultura*, *culterío*, and *culteridad* in his 1534 translation of the *Book of the Courtier*.[38] At the beginning of the following decade, a group of students at the University of Barcelona wrote to the city Councillors protesting the local Dominican onslaught on Erasmian teaching. They asked the magistrates

> not to permit the introduction of such a great barbarity [Dominican control over the chairs of Philosophy], for afterwards no *cultura* or diligence will be able to extirpate these barbarous sophists raised on 'inhumane' letters. . . . It would be a great misfortune for all if, just when God has blessed us to live when letters are being reborn, we should remain subject to ancient ignorance. . . .[39]

[36] *De Bello Gallico*, I, 1.

[37] Marrou, *Education In Antiquity*, 21-34 and 137-146; Williams, *Keywords*, 76.

[38] At one point Boscà substituted for "culture" *buen granjear* (literally, "good acquisition" or "profit"): Morreale, *Castiglione y Boscán*, II, 70.

[39] *Epistolari del Renaixement*, II, 76.

This remarkable defense of Erasmian and humanist education against its monkish opponents employed *cultura* in the sense of "effort" or diligent care. Simultaneously it revived the older tendency to link "culture" with liberal education and humane letters. Association of the "discipline" of *cultura* with upper-class education expanded during the following century. Gilabert's *Discourse* of 1616 contained an interesting paraphrase of a well-known passage from Cicero. In it Gilabert defined the "undisciplined soul" as a "field which, although naturally fertile, only produces thorns if it lacks the proper *cultura*."[40] Here the author deliberately pressed into service a latinate metaphor strongly redolent of agricultural process to advance his plea for more sustained dedication to formal education on the part of the Catalan aristocracy.

Cognates of the term also enjoyed growing popularity, beginning in the sixteenth century. Of special importance in the Hispanic context was the past participle *culto* (literally "cultured" or "cultivated").[41] At least two meanings of this term can be isolated. First, *culto* (or *culterano*) referred to a Baroque literary style marked by a high level of metaphorical and stylistic complexity. Sebastián de Covarrubias, the dean of early modern Spanish lexicographers, sarcastically defined *culto* language as "a belabored manner of speaking 'cultivated' for the pulpit, worthy of the high and divine matters preached there, pleasing to the ear, honest and chaste, neither jarring nor excessive."[42] Early modern Catalans also frequently used the term to denote highly conceited rhetoric. Thus D. Ramon de Salba's preface to the Cervera poem of 1637 showered effusive praise on its author's *culto* turns of phrase. A few years later a Sergeant Josep Doms

---

[40] Gilabert, *Discurso*, 7r. His source was the *Tusculan Disputations*, II, 5, 13.

[41] According to Corominas, the earliest usage of *culto* in Castilian (1377) was as a noun, denoting devotion or a liturgical act: see his *Diccionario Crítico Etimológico*, I, 980.

[42] Covarrubias, *Tesoro*, 386-387. For some lucid remarks on the *culterano* phenomenon, see Russell, *Spain: A Companion*, 316-319.

apologized in the opening pages of his drill manual for the "curt-ness and *poca cultura* of its language." When in 1695 Joan Carles de Vilaplana recommended that his fellow preachers avoid *lacónicos cultos*, he was making obvious reference to oratory deemed too strained and sophisticated for the average congregation. And, as late as 1763, a local theologian approvingly dubbed Milton a *poeta culto*.[43]

The other usage of *culto* derived from the earlier, latinate sense of "culture" as the display of learning and aesthetic refine-ment. As the wrangling over *culterana* poetry died out in the later seventeenth century, *cultura* became firmly—even perma-nently—wedded to the accomplished fact of education and proper "taste." When the editors of a 1703 poetic anthology lauded the "*culta* and erudite" noble Academy of Barcelona, or when in 1753 Mercader praised the singular "erudition and *cultura*" of the Count of Peralada, they forged an unbreakable bond between "culture" and the visible body of acquired knowledge and behavior fostered by elite education.[44] Not surprisingly, the writer who most extensively explored the diverse facets of *cultura* was Gracián. In his *Wit and the Art of Genius* (revised edition, 1648), Gracián punned with at least two meanings of the term. For example, while criticizing the "*culto* style" of the poet Luis de Góngora, he noted that its partisans regarded "artificial" verse the most perfect, "as nature without art has always been *inculta*."[45] And in *The Discreet Man* (1646), Gracián dropped his word-play to offer a positive alternative to the *gongoristas*. In a chapter entitled "Of Culture and Dressing (*Aliño*)," he extolled the civility and decorum of the Greeks and Romans, and called for their imitation by contemporary nobles, who should devote themselves to "gallantry, courtesy, discretion . . . and knowl-

---

[43] Cervera, *Grave Ostentación*, 2v.; Doms, *Orde de Batalla*, introductory epistle; Vilaplana, *Discurso Panegírico*, "aprobación"; Sans, *Sabio Ignorante*, I, 18.

[44] *Armonia del Parnàs*, introduction; Mercader, *Oración Fúnebre*, 20.

[45] *Agudeza y Arte de Ingenio* (Huesca, 1648), Discourse 62 (*Obras Completas*, 506-512).

edge."[46] In these and other texts, Gracián chided the excesses of the *culteranistas*, while urging his compatriots to recover the true "culture" of the ancients.[47] By driving a firm wedge between the two usages of *cultura*, he sped its transition from literary affectation to the conscious display of knowledge and refinement—in a word, from "mannered" to "manners."

Ingenio, luz, cultura—three words united by a shared meaning, each with its own nuances. The firmest tie binding these concepts was common service within the world-view of the learned elite. While a broad range of modifiers—discreet, prudent, grave, serene, *gustoso*, *claro*, curious, *agudo*—were used to describe the manners and comportment of the upper class, this triad won precedence as the leading terms of reference for the self-image of the patriciate.

One notes a clear progression in their usage. Tensions between inherent natural disposition and the attainment of knowledge through education had traditionally marked ruling-class claims to intellectual distinction. The early modern period witnessed a gradual shift away from the fixed ontology of innate "racial" characteristics embedded in the term "genius," toward a more flexible concept of "culture" which allowed greater room for its acquisition. As the pedagogue Diego de Gurrea noted, "proper breeding (*crianza*) has the power to change both nature and race."[48] This opposition closely paralleled contemporary arguments regarding inherent versus acquired nobility. Not surprisingly, opportunities for the acquisition of "culture" increased with the improved social standing of the civic oligarchy and liberal professionals. Conversely, the more acceptance these strata found with the aristocracy, the more likely their argument for a

---

[46] *El Discreto*, chap. 18 (*Obras Completas*, 129).
[47] *Agudeza y Arte de Ingenio*, Discourse 61 (*Obras completas*, 499-504).
[48] Gurrea, *Arte de Enseñar*, 3r.

145

learned nobility would be adopted by all members of the urban ruling class.

The replacement of "genius" by "culture" was hardly the only significant semantic shift of the early modern period. In a remarkably similar fashion, *giudizio*—the innate faculty of discernment linked by writers like Persio to *ingegno*—gave way to *gusto*, or acquired "good taste."[49] Yet few key words have experienced the linguistic success of *cultura*. The preeminence "culture" began to enjoy in the later seventeenth century bore witness to the striking durability of its underlying construct—the distinctive knowledge and behavior distinguishing rulers from ruled.

The Mirror Image of Ignorance

In the eyes of early modern elites, the "lower" classes served a variety of functions. Not least among these was that of an inverse or mirror reflection lending sharper focus to the self-image of the educated patriciate. A remarkably bipolar schema of cultural stratification matched clearly drawn lines of demarcation within the social sphere, as a rigidly symmetrical dichotomy opposed the special knowledge of the elite to the brutish "ignorance" and "superstition" of the *vulgo*. In the eyes of the ruling class, "culture" was not superimposed upon social inequality. Rather, the elite considered it an integral *determinant* of class differences, both informing and justifying their existence. The gradual replacement of the innate psychology of "genius" by a more overt emphasis on the acquisition of knowledge through schooling did not alter the elite's perception of other social classes as intellectually deficient. This distinction was now defined in terms of the "possession" or "lack" of *cultura*. Just as over the centuries a special lexicon had been devised to charac-

---

[49] Curtius, *European Literature*, 297; Klein, *Form and Meaning*, chap. 9.

terize the superior intellect and refined behavior of the nobility, in like manner learned "culture" gave birth to a distinctive vocabulary applied to the "lower" classes. The history of knowledge bore within itself a history of ignorance.

"Now do not imagine, sir, that by vulgar I mean only the common and humble people; for all who are ignorant, even if they are lords or princes, can rightfully be included under the name of vulgar." Thus Don Quijote informed D. Diego de Miranda, the village squire who took time off from his hunting and fishing to consult the six dozen books that gave him "honest entertainment."[50] The "sagacity and good sense" that so delighted the knight errant's travelling companion centered around a concept of "vulgar ignorance" eminently familiar to ruling classes throughout early modern Europe, who inevitably contrasted *gente popular e idiota*—"popular and unlettered folk"— with the "learned nobility." Rather than catalogue the innumerable examples of this usage, I would like briefly to note the principal characteristics of lower-class ignorance as defined by the educated elite.

Traditional opposition between city and country played an important role in the depiction of "vile ignorance." While the Barcelona ruling class claimed precedence, thanks to its "civility" and "urbanity," it predictably stigmatized social inferiors as "rustic" or "rude." When the anonymous author of the menacing *Brief by the Captain of the Christian Army* of peasants besieging the city in 1640 labelled his followers "rural and uncultivated people," or when the evangelist Francesch Baucells directed his proselytizing efforts toward the "ignorant and rustic illiterate," they merely followed longstanding patterns emphasizing the cultural deprivation of the countryside.[51]

---

[50] *Don Quijote*, II, 16. I have used the English translation by J. M. Cohen (Harmondsworth, 1972), 566 and 570.

[51] *Memòrial de lo Capità General del Exèrcit Christià* (1640), in B.C./F. Bon. 6139; Baucells, *Font Mystica*, "aprobación." Equally typical was a rural priest's reference to his parishioners as *persones idiotas: Processo de Fé Contra el Ermitaño de San*

In a similar vein, lower-class "ignorance" was often defined as a lack of familiarity with formal religious dogma. This usage evolved in at least two directions. First, there gradually coalesced a notion of popular "superstition," a term increasingly used to describe the syncretic and apparently pagan religious attitudes and practices of lower classes, both rural and urban. Thus, in the late fifteenth century, the local humanist Jeroni Pau referred to annual Midsummer's Day processions to a spring atop Montjuïch mountain as an "old superstition . . . of plebeian persons, yet to be abolished." More than a century later, Pere Gil, the rector of Barcelona's Jesuit college, drew upon the same association to defend women accused of witchcraft as "rude, simple, with little understanding . . . most of them poor, with little or no knowledge of Christian doctrine." And, in the eighteenth century, writers such as the reforming bishop Gavino Valladares continued to charge the lower classes with habitual misunderstanding or neglect of religious dogma.[52] Yet popular disregard of elite theological conceptions also found another, more sinister interpretation. The "yoke of ignorance" enslaving the lower classes was often viewed, not as passive superstition, but as obstinate heresy. The introduction by Joan Joffreu, a prominent local barrister, to the 1628 reprinting of Pedro Ciruelo's treatise on witchcraft echoed this reading of popular knowledge and conduct. In the prologue, Joffreu made a remarkable confession, repenting of his former leniency as a magistrate in dealing with "heretics and *supersticiosos*." This opening passage set the tone for the interpretation of plebeian superstition as heresy sustained throughout the rest of the book.[53]

Another feature of elite commentaries on popular ignorance was the literalness with which descriptions of the lower classes

---

Bartolomé . . . de Solsona, 12 Oct. 1642 (A.H.M.B./C-XVIII, Clero/Inquisición, leg. 9, s.n.). See also Richter, "*Urbanitas-Rusticitas*," and Ramage, *Urbanitas*.

[52] Pau, *Barcino*, 52; *Memorial de Pedro Gil . . . en Defensa de la Bruxas* (1619) in B.U.B./Ms. 1008; and Valladares, *Promptuari*, "Advertència."

[53] Ciruelo, *Supersticiones*, prologue by Dr. Joan Joffreu.

inverted the terms of noble self-depiction. This tendency was most evident in the obsessive manipulation of images of light and darkness. Identification of ignorance with dark "obscurity" was a common staple of learned characterizations of the plebs.[54] Hence, for example, Gilabert's intriguing reference to the "clouds" of the mechanical arts, whose function was to render even brighter the "sun" of nobility. "It is honorable," he wrote, to possess "knowledge of the liberal arts, and even of the mechanical, for even if some of the latter are vile and infamous, they still through their *verguença* (shame) illumine the other, more noble ones, just as clouds make all the more beautiful the sun's rays shattering the darkness of their servitude. . . ."[55] Contemporary onslaughts on lower-class festive life also echoed this association between popular ignorance and obscurity. Diego Pérez de Valdivia's *Discourse on Masking* attacked the Carnival celebrations of "low and vile persons" as a "time of shadows, an exercise of people who abhor the light." Similarly, the jurist Fructuoso Bisbe Vidal railed against theatregoers as "common and vulgar people" whose taste for "vulgar plays" could only be satisfied in the "dark cave of the Demon." And in a slightly less alarmist tone, the preface to Baucells' *Mystic Fount* spoke of the need for "shining" books of doctrine to "illumine with a hidden and pure light the shadows . . . of the rude, vulgar, and ignorant."[56]

[54] One could cite countless instances of this usage. For example, Shakespeare drew upon this association in: *The Winter's Tale*, IV, 4; *The Tempest*, V, 1; *Twelfth Night*, IV, 2; and *I Henry IV*, I, 2. For the links between darkness and ignorance, see Panofsky and Panofsky, *Pandora's Box*, 39-40 and 149-150.

[55] Gilabert, *Discurso*, 12r. This passage was taken without attribution from Tommaso Garzoni's *Piazza Universale di tutte le Scienze* (Venice, 1589), 30, from which Gilabert pilfered with abandon.

[56] Pérez de Valdivia, *Plática*, prologue and 23v. (originally preached in 1583); Bisbe Vidal, *Tratado de las Comedias*, 2r. and dedication; Baucells, *Font Mystica*, "aprobaciones." Passages such as these drew heavily on the traditional Christian association of theological ignorance and heresy with darkness (see e.g., Ephesians 4:17-18).

A final characteristic of elite views of popular intellectual and moral debility was their frequent recourse to animal imagery to depict the lower classes.[57] Once again one finds in Gilabert a remarkable frank statement of the power of knowledge to separate not just rulers and ruled but, even more fundamentally, men from beasts:

> As David says, what is a man without knowledge but a horse or mule in whom there is no understanding? . . . One reads that one day Diogenes cried out from a high place, Come, men to me. As only popular and unlettered (*ydiota*) people gathered, he said with disdain, I call not for you, but for human beings . . . And Socrates affirmed that there is as much distance between learned and ignorant men as that which exists between men and beasts. . . .[58]

The same identification of ignorance with bestiality is found in Josep Sans's moral treatise *The Ignorant Wise Man* (1763). "If there were no wise men nor knowledge," he claimed, "the world would be a Theatre of Ignorance, with hardly any difference between men and animals; for a man without letters is not a man, but a dead person, without a soul, and equal to the beasts."[59] Other texts elaborated upon the association of ignorance with "brutish" animality. Perhaps the favorite simile was that depicting manual laborers as mules. In his *Microcosmia* (1592), the theologian Marc Antoni Camós likened "apprentices and journeymen of the mechanical arts" to "laborious, patient, suffering . . . *asnos*." Sans echoed the comparison, approvingly citing Pius II's observation that "the ignorant man differs from

---

[57] Hill, "Many-Headed Monster." M. Bakhtin has explored the link between the populace and the "material bodily stratum" in his *Rabelais*.

[58] Gilabert, *Discurso*, 9v. The passage attributed to David is from Psalms 31: 8-9 (Vulgate).

[59] Sans, *Sabio Ignorante*, I, 8.

the mule only in that he walks on two feet, whereas the mule walks on four."[60]

During the heated discussions at the Tarragona provincial synod of 1636 surrounding the issue of the use of Catalan in preaching, a local bishop noted that the more elegant Castilian language was not understood by those who most needed the teachings of Christian doctrine—"children, women, and *ygno-rants*."[61] This phrase concisely evokes the mirror image through which the elite contrasted itself with those scorned as handi-capped by innate mental immaturity or lack of knowledge. In the words of a 1661 Jesuit scholastic oration, "whoever looks at his reflection in a pool sees everything in reverse . . . even so we see high as low, right as left."[62] Many of the features of early modern elite world-views—the passion for order and symmetry, obsession with the imagery of light and brilliance, the simplistic reductionism of their characterizations of subordinate classes— owe much to this tendency to treat the universe as a mirror for upper-class lustre and display. Between the sun of knowledge and the moon of ignorance stood a world approached not di-rectly, but darkly, as through a glass.

Reason and the Language of Control

It is a delicious irony that the self-definition of patricians should rely so crucially upon their social inferiors. The elite's strikingly holistic vision of social hierarchy left no alternative to fixing the contours of its own image by distancing itself from the sphere of the "lower" classes. Prospero obviously could not exist without the physical labors of Caliban. Yet there was more to the prob-

---

[60] Camós, *Microcosmia*, 218-220; A. S. Piccolomini, *Epistola IV*, cited in Sans, *Sabio Ignorante*, I, 8. Richelieu employed this simile in a famous passage in his *Political Testament*, 31. See also La Bruyère, *Oeuvres*, II, 61.

[61] Cited in García Cárcel and Nicolau, "Castella contra Catalunya," 45.

[62] Bru, *Oración*, s.n.

lem than that. Ultimately the master proved incapable of shaping a convincing self-portrait without staring in the mirror at the distorted reflection of his slave.

Up to this point elite systems of cultural classification have been presented solely in terms of their "social" function. In this capacity they served to define the composition and character of the nobility, while distinguishing upper from lower classes. However, the schema of cultural distinction also played a crucial "political" role. By assigning the parts of rulers and ruled to high and low, it furnished a fully articulated ideological justification of contemporary power structures. Social hierarchy and political domination were closely interwoven in a coherent pattern whose vital center was the doctrine of cultural differentiation.

Gilabert's paraphrase of Aristotle's dictum that knowledge confers "power and seigneury" provides a convenient starting-point for discussion of the political dimensions of the ideology of *cultura*. As we have seen, early modern elites opposed the perceived intellectual and educational superiority of the nobility to a generic "lower" sphere characterized by ignorance and mental immaturity. At the base of this dichotomy lay an ontology identifying the plebeian order with animality and the sensual life of the material stratum, in contrast to the more refined, disembodied, and "elevated" nobility. Contested issues of class identity and public authority frequently shaped the confrontation of passion and reason so prevalent a theme in early modern literature and political discourse.[63]

In the eyes of most contemporary writers, passion or "appetite" had been the natural inclination of all men and women *ab initio*. According to Camós, Adam upset the "natural rectitude of man" which knew "no rebellion of the senses against reason, as the flesh obeyed the spirit and the superior presided over the inferior." By "despising and breaking the law of God," man "subjected the spirit to the flesh." Thus "he who was honored

---

[63] Hirschman, *Passions and the Interests*, I; Elias, *Court Society*, 110-114.

as an angel came to be treated as a brutish animal." Other writers also attributed the victory of passion over inherent reason to the Fall. In the words of the barrister Joffreu, thanks to original sin "man's inclination is to covet what is prohibited," to seek a "liberty" that "drowns all understanding." In like manner, Bishop Valladares' late-eighteenth-century catechism linked teaching of Christian doctrine to the "creation of just men and obedient subjects" by "correcting their excessive passion" and instilling through discipline "a certain docility toward the good."[64]

The next step in the argument was an obvious one. According to this ontology, only those in control of their own inclinations could master the passions of others. Men and women incapable of curbing their own appetites became the passive objects of a political authority born of self-discipline and education. The internal control the elite imposed upon itself thus legitimated its rule over the rest of society. In this light, the close association between *cultura* and discipline took on new meaning. Pleas for the education of the aristocracy rested on the belief that only proper schooling could confer the self-control that determined the distribution of power between upper and lower classes. Della Casa spoke for all nobles when he acknowledged that

> However great the power of our natural inclinations may be, they are very often overcome and corrected by the rules of behavior. But we must start early to pit ourselves against them and repel them before they assert themselves and become too strong for us. So far from doing this, most people drift along without control, following wherever their instincts lead them. . . .[65]

---

[64] Camós, *Microcosmia*, 222-223; Ciruelo, *Supersticiones*, prologue; Valladares, *Promptuari*, "Advertència."

[65] Della Casa, *Galateo*, Chapter 25 (Pine-Coffin translation, 57).

The same opposition between reason instilled through *cultura* and the natural indiscipline of the uneducated found expression in Sans's *The Ignorant Wise Man*. The point of departure of his eloquent exhortation to self-control was the familiar equation of passion with the body, and reason with the soul. The author then pleaded for a transfer of "law" and "justice" from the external to the internal sphere. "In this fashion," he argued, one can "contain the injustice of our appetites with the same *luces* of knowledge with which one brakes those inclinations in which sin has taken command. . . . Thus we render the soul subject like a vile serf to the far nobler and most excellent obedience of reason."[66]

The transparently political variables of control and rule stood at the crux of early modern elite views of the relations of different social classes to *cultura*. The theologian Juan Pineda's tripartite division of society into "governors, the governed, and the ungovernable" found a corollary in statements of the patriciate's desire to extend the control exercised over itself to other classes. Small wonder, then, that the "hero of virtue" of elite literature won rule over others by first dominating his own passions. In contrast to *grossers* Turks, subjects rather than masters of their "disordered appetites," the Christian warrior idealized in Joan Pujol's celebration of the battle of Lepanto was distinguished above all by the triumph of inner discipline over his own will.[67]

This construct could be superimposed with ease over a broad range of social relations. For example, association of women with irrationality and unbridled passion did much to reinforce the rigidly masculine character of authority.[68] The criterion of self-control also determined contemporary formulae for tutelage of minors and the insane. Thus the royal decree of 1600

---

[66] Sans, *Sabio Ignorante*, II, 172-173.

[67] Pineda, *Diálogos Familiares*, vol. 161, 76-78; Pujol, *Obra Poètica*, 7-8.

[68] Davis, "Women on Top," in her *Society and Culture*, Chapter 5; Pomata, *In Scienza e Coscienza*.

transferring *cura dementis* of the honored citizen Pere Bernat Codina to a consortium of relatives rested on his being judged "unable to rule and govern himself and his goods." Members of the liberal professions also drew upon this distinction to enhance their position of intellectual and social domination. In his *Treatise on Childbirth*, the physician Josep Torner contrasted the *razón* of medical knowledge to the "passion" and *sentido* (literally "sense," "emotion") of "ignorant" midwives. Similarly, the jurist Vicent Domenech opposed the "reason" inherent in the barrister's ministration of the law to "litigants who, swept along by violent passion, do not recognize any superior authority save the powerful emotions dominating them."[69]

The cultural construct of the schema of reason versus passion found most explicit expression when applied to the "lower" classes. Frank assertions of the innate political incapacity of the "many-headed monster" were a standard feature of early modern elite discourse.[70] Thus in the late fifteenth century Jeroni Pau noted that "some believe that the admission of the populace to municipal government in 1454 caused the ruin of our city. The plebs," he sniffed, "lack all aptitude for governing, because of their inexperience and their inability to agree on anything, because they are always prone to dissension, because they hate the nobility, and finally because they were made to be ruled rather than to rule." In the late 1620s Joffreu lamented the predilection of the ignorant and "superstitious" to throw off "the holy yoke and subjection man owes to God, much like a runaway horse without a bridle loses obedience. . . . From this disloyalty and disobedience are born rebellions against Princes . . . discord, revolts, and civil wars." Less than a decade later the preacher Gaspar Sala warned that unless vagabonds were shut away and lower-class children "indoctrinated in our schools," Barcelona

---

[69] A.C.A./Can., reg. 4886, 106r.; J. Torner, *Tratado de Partos*, undated manuscript (ca. 1720?) in A.H.M.B./Ms. 166; Domenech, *Discurso*, 26.

[70] Hill, "Many-Headed Monster"; Sewell, *Work and Revolution*, 74; Chisick, *Limits to Reform*.

would suffer an "uprising like that Lyon witnessed in 1529." There was clearly a need for strong control by the elite; otherwise, he argued, "the bad customs of the vagabonds and their free way of speaking would be more quickly learned by our children than the instruction in letters and virtue given by their schoolteachers."[71]

The cultural construct distinguishing learned nobility from ignorant lower classes played an important role in justifying existing social hierarchies. To the extent that knowledge was associated with reason, and appetite with popular ignorance, the paradigm also legitimated unequal distribution of political influence. Gilabert quite correctly insisted that learning conferred power. By his time knowledge was seen as an external authority absorbed through a rigorous program of study—of *cultura* in the strict sense of discipline. The upper classes enjoyed the good fortune of being able to acquire the "virtue of ruling" themselves. For those outside this reduced circle, however, control was destined to be exercised from without.

"No social phenomenon can be adequately studied merely in the language and categories of thought in which the people among whom it is found represent it to themselves."[72] Social scientists never hesitate to state the obvious. All the same, I have tried in this chapter to present a systematic reading of some of the language which urban nobles used to mold their own self-image. Study of the social vocabulary of the elite constitutes a necessary prologue to the themes of this book's final chapters: the media of diffusion and forms of expression of ruling-class identity in early modern Barcelona. Genius, light, civility, ignorance, darkness— all were "keywords" of a semantic of cultural distinction tailored

[71] Pau, *Barcino*, 36; Ciruelo, *Supersticiones*, introduction; Sala, *Govern Polítich*, 7r., 8v., and 11r.
[72] Lienhardt, *Social Anthropology*, 123.

to endow the urban patriciate with a sense of common purpose and identity. Its leading premise was the wedding of a static ideal of "culture" to *nobilitas*. Not surprisingly, the new collective vision of the elite found depiction in a wide variety of symbols and metaphors. These were in turn elaborated and disseminated by institutions of socialization and leisure like the Jesuit college and the noble Academy. Within their confines the governors of the city reproduced their values and beliefs, refined their comportment, and celebrated the privilege of defining their own identity.

VII

THE ADVANCEMENT OF

LEARNING

The acquisition of *cultura* required a lengthy apprenticeship, a training designed to extirpate the "ignorance" characterizing all human beings at infancy. Thus education could scarcely be limited to formal indoctrination in the liberal arts. Rather, the patrician appropriated "culture" as a pattern after which he modelled all aspects of behavior. This was nowhere made more apparent than in the various handbooks offering crash courses in gentility and *politesse* to those anxious to imitate the manners of "true nobility." The most widely read of these manuals was Lucas Gracián Dantisco's *The Spanish Galateo*, first published in Tarragona in 1593. In the preface to this adaptation of Della Casa's treatise, the author flatly stated his purpose: to "elevate" the reader to a higher level of prudence, discretion, and courtesy.[1]

Books of manners did much to diffuse the values and comportment of the nobility among members of a wider reading public. The significance of these more informal means of dissem-

---

[1] Gracián Dantisco, *Galateo Español*. The *editio princeps* bore a dedication to the honored citizen Joaquin Setantí. The first Barcelona edition of 1595 was dedicated to Francesch Bonet, a *Diputat Reial* and city Councillor elected honored citizen in 1600. Interestingly, this work headed the list of books owned and read by the noble lawyer D. Josep Faust de Potau; see Amelang, "The Education of Josep Faust De Potau." Other local texts guaranteed their readers instant learning. See for example: Palmireno, *Estudioso Cortesano*, *Vocabulario del Humanista*, and *Latino de Repente*; and Ferrer, *Método y Art Molt Breu*.

inating notions of aristocratic selfhood should not be underestimated.[2] Nevertheless, institutions of communication and sociability bore the brunt of the task of instilling elite ideals and behavior. Having examined the political associations of the Barcelona ruling class, we can now shift our focus to the formal structures charged with reproducing aristocratic identity—the Jesuit *collegium*, and the "Academy of the Distrustful."

Hercules of Eloquence

Little is known of the history of primary and secondary education in early modern Barcelona. During the fifteenth and sixteenth centuries, private "masters of reading and writing" shouldered most of the burden of teaching, offering instruction in the basic skills of literacy and arithmetic.[3] The cathedral chapter and several local monasteries also provided some limited elementary education. The city Council subsidized only one official pedagogue, a *mestre de minyons* who taught reading and writing to poor children under the portico of the university building.[4] Prior to the seventeenth century, in short, most pre-university instruction lay in the hands of private initiative, ranging from lessons taught for pay by impoverished schoolmasters to small circles where working-class women learned to read while spinning and sewing.[5]

Barcelona's educational offerings expanded significantly in

[2] Magendie, *Politesse Mondaine*, II and III; Elias, *History of Manners*.

[3] A.E.B./Gratiarum, "Llicències per a tenir Estudi de Minyons." Persistent research has turned up few sources for the history of education in early modern Barcelona. In particular, the destruction or disappearance of Jesuit documentation following the expulsion of the Society from Spain in the later 1760s hampers study of the organization, extent, and content of elite education. The following account has thus been assembled from widely dispersed sources, and seeks merely to provide a preliminary sketch of general trends.

[4] *Ordinacions de la Universitat de Barcelona*, 63-64.

[5] Azcárate, "Enseñanza Primaria."

the sixteenth and seventeenth centuries. During these years local religious orders organized a variety of schools, each with its own permanent teaching staff. At first, the new, more dynamic orders of the Counter-Reformation took the lead in these foundations. Most notable was the Jesuit "College of Bethlehem," discussed at length below. Also of importance was the episcopal seminary, established by bishop Joan Dimas Loris in 1593 in fulfillment of the pedagogical initiatives of the Council of Trent. In the later seventeenth century, moreover, the traditional religious orders made a concerted effort to catch up. In 1643, the Mercedarians founded the College of Saint Peter Nolasco; in 1652, the Franciscans established the College of Saint Bonaventure in their monastery on the Carrer Ample. Not to be outdone, the Dominican order inaugurated its College of Saints Vincent Ferrer and Raymond Penyafort in 1668. By the mid-eighteenth century, Barcelona housed at least twelve monastic *colegios*, supplemented by a variety of smaller, more informal schools.[6]

Members of the traditional aristocracy often received primary and secondary instruction in more distant institutions like the famed *Escolania* or choir-school of the monastery of Montserrat. This practice—resembling study at the prestigious *colegios mayores* of Castilian universities—was limited on the whole to titled noble families like the Requesens, Erill, Montcada, and Queralt.[7] Prior to the mid-seventeenth century, private tutors taught most aristocrats at home. Perhaps the most famous preceptor was Diego de Gurrea. In 1627 this Aragonese theologian—himself from a noble family—dedicated a pedagogic treatise entitled *The Art of Teaching Sons of Princes and Nobles* to his most illustrious pupil, D. Luis Fernández Ramón Folch de Car-

[6] Jutglar, "Enseñanza en Barcelona"; García Panadés, *Pedagogía Catalana*, I; Soldevila, *Barcelona Sense Universitat*; Coll, "Antiguo Colegio Mayor"; Collell, "Fundación del Colegio."

[7] Albareda, *Història de Montserrat*, 203-210; Saldoni, *Reseña Histórica*; Kagan, *Students and Society*, Chapters 1 and 7.

dona, heir to the family title.[8] Significantly, as late as the closing years of the century the architectural plan for the new urban palace of the powerful Sentmenat family included a "teacher's room" alongside the children's quarters.[9]

Most local patricians apparently combined private tutorials with instruction at formal institutions. Some of our most reliable information on the history of secondary schooling in Barcelona comes from the notes that the future lawyer D. Josep de Potau took from 1700 to 1704. Potau, born in 1685 to a noted judge and a merchant's daughter, probably obtained his early instruction from private tutors at home. He began his formal schooling at the Jesuit *collegium* at the age of ten. After remaining there for five years, he completed its philosophy course and took final examinations. His secondary education now over, Potau undertook further study in mathematics with a "teacher of handwriting and accounting." At the same time he commenced lessons in dancing and "fencing in the Italian style."[10]

What most distinguished the education of Potau from that of earlier aristocrats like Cardona was the time spent at the city's leading secondary school, the Jesuit *Col.legi de Cordelles*. In fact, by the mid-seventeenth century, noble education in Barcelona had become nearly synonymous with this institution.[11] The school derived its name from two contiguous establishments on the *Rambla*: the Jesuit "College" of Bethlehem, and the *Collegium* of Holy Mary and Saint James. Jaume de Cordelles, a local cathedral canon, instituted the latter through a private bequest, and personally drew up its first statutes in 1572. Instruction at the *Col.legi de Cordelles* was originally limited to relatives of its patron. However, his heirs chose not to maintain the founda-

---

[8] Gurrea, *Arte de Enseñar*. Julia Varela analyzes this and other early modern Spanish educational texts in her *Modos de Educación*.

[9] Conde and Tintó, "Projecte d'una Casa."

[10] A.H.M.B./Ms. A-30. Potau later obtained a doctorate in civil and canon law. For a fuller discussion, see my "Education of Joseph Faust de Potau."

[11] Borràs, "Col.legi de Sta. Maria," and his "Col.legi de Nobles."

tion.[12] In 1635, D. Alexandre de Cordelles transferred control over the school to the Jesuits, who in 1662 joined it to their own College of Bethlehem. After the suppression of Barcelona's university in 1714—one of the many measures of reprisal taken against the city by the new Bourbon administration—the *Col.legi* became the leading educational institution in the city, and the only one empowered to teach advanced courses in grammar and philosophy.[13] The Jesuits controlled the school until their expulsion in 1767. In that year it passed into the hands of the local seminary and remained under episcopal control until the nineteenth century.

The Society originally established the *collegium* of Bethlehem in 1544 to provide its novices with primary instruction. Soon thereafter, however, the order began to admit external lay students. In 1576 the school reported the enrollment of at least 140 outsiders; by the end of the century, their number had increased to 160.[14] The dramatic growth of the *collegium* encouraged the Jesuits to expand its offerings to secondary teaching as well. Annual reports to their superiors in Rome soon boasted of a string of successes, like the impressive *fête* of 1616 "attended by learned nobles and the city magistrates."[15] The brief lull experienced during the revolutionary decade of the 1640s—the *Col.legi* housed only 50 students in 1647—served merely as prelude to even greater splendor. The neo-foral period inaugurated the Barcelona Jesuits' true predominance within education. The academic ceremonies staged by the *collegium* symbolized its expanding role in local schooling. The first reference to such "lit-

---

[12] In 1628, the *Col.legi de Cordelles* enrolled only six students: A.R.S.I./Arag. 27[I], Misiones, 221r. I am grateful to Frs. Miquel Batllori, Antoni Borràs, Edmond Lamalle, S.J., and Dr. Nigel Griffin for references and assistance with these documents.

[13] A.S.V./Sac. Cong. Concilio, *Relat. Dioc. ad Liminam*, III A (Barcinon.), 283r. (1717).

[14] A.R.S.I./Arag. 25-I, *Litterae Annuae*, 2v. and 19r. For matriculation figures of other Jesuit colleges in Spain, see Astrain, *Compañía de Jesús*, I, 197.

[15] A.R.S.I./Arag. 25-I, *Litterae Annuae*, 140r.

erary exercises" dates to Philip II's 1585 visit to Barcelona, when the Bethlehem students recited for the king "poetical compositions" and scholastic *disputae*.[16] Similar exercises were staged annually, beginning in the early 1660s. At their conclusion, the college awarded prizes to student eulogies of the school's patrons, which were then published and distributed to a wider audience.[17]

Another token of the Jesuits' increasing importance in local instruction was the growing visibility of its alumni association. The order established Barcelona's Marian Congregation in 1579 as a means of drumming up support among the urban clergy and other "leading citizens."[18] By the 1630s, the brotherhood had expanded to include both matriculated students and former graduates. The Congregation met at least once a year, centering its festivities around the vigil of the Immaculate Conception. As in the case of the Cordelles orations, the published descriptions and texts of sermons preached at these *fêtes* did much to diffuse the prestige of Jesuit education throughout the city. The association also constituted one of the more important institutions of sociability within the local ruling class.

The Jesuit school's expansion in size and importance provoked deep resentment among the more established institutions of education in Barcelona. The 1660s witnessed a bitter dispute between the Jesuits and the local university over the *Collegium*'s right to confer advanced degrees. Following the exchange of numerous pamphlets, theological tracts, and legal briefs, a royal decree of 1662 resolved the disagreement by ordering the university to award Cordelles students degrees without their having

---

[16] A.R.S.I./Arag. 23-II, *Fundaciones*, 270v.

[17] The day-book of the city Councillors first reported their attendance at the *fêtes* in 1663: *Dietari*, XVII, 262. Similarly, episcopal visitations first mention the *col.legi* in 1661 (A.S.V./*Relat. Dioc.*, 175r.). For academic theatre in nearby Aragon, see Figueras, *Teatro Escolar Zaragozano*.

[18] A.R.S.I./Arag. 25-I, *Litterae Annuae*, 8r. See in general Mullan, *Congregazione Mariana*. Unfortunately, I have not been able to locate any of the documents of the Barcelona association.

undergone the minimum three years of study.[19] While the Dominican-dominated university accepted the decision with no little grumbling, from this point onward the Jesuits exercised undisputed control over elite education in Barcelona.

The absence of surviving documentation frustrates precise identification of the social background of Cordelles students. Contemporary references to the school without exception emphasize the aristocratic character of its student body. Writers of the period frequently referred to it as the "Royal and Imperial College of Nobles," in clear imitation of the academy established by the same order in seventeenth-century Madrid.[20] It is indeed highly probable that aristocratic youths no longer receiving elementary instruction from tutors at home enrolled in the *Col.legi*. The cost of matriculation—annual fees totalled £85 in 1662, and £100 a century later—certainly prevented most commoners from studying there.[21] Nevertheless, despite the prominence of nobles within this institution, we should not assume that the student body was composed exclusively of aristocrats. A list of pupils taking part in public exercises in rhetoric and grammar in 1700 reveals the presence of a sizeable minority of commoners. Of the 35 students mentioned, 8 were *nobles*. At least 12 were offspring of gentry and honored citizen families, while the remaining 15 hailed from non-noble and *gaudint* backgrounds.[22] The representation of the latter group—composed largely of sons of lawyers—points to the way in which study at the *Col.legi* served as a means of social promotion for upwardly mobile professionals. Even more significant, however, was its function as an institutional venue for the symbiosis of civic oligarchy and established aristocracy.

[19] Bruniquer, *Rúbriques*, II, 348-349; *Dietari*, XVII, 656-673 (1662-1663); Rubió Borràs, *Motines y Algaradas*.

[20] Borràs, "Col.legi de Nobles," 59; Simón Díaz, *Colegio Imperial de Madrid*.

[21] Borràs, "Col.legi de Nobles," 69; *Constituciones de Cordelles*, 7.

[22] *Magestuosa Poética Fiesta*. An internal memorandum of 1694 indicates that the policy of admitting a broader selection of students had only recently been adopted: Borràs, "Col.legi de Nobles," 54.

It is somewhat easier to identify what was taught at the *Collegium*, in part because its curriculum apparently differed little from that of other Jesuit schools, and partly thanks to the survival of several revealing documents.[23] Of the latter, the most important by far were the Potau notebooks and the rhetorical orations in praise of the school published beginning in the mid-seventeenth century. These sources convey the image of an education oriented not toward any specific professional preparation, but rather toward the diffusion of a general model of gentlemanly knowledge and behavior. The relentless instruction in Latin (and to a lesser extent in Castilian), rather than the vernacular, and the emphasis placed on exercises in theatre, dance, and music were calculated to endow the nobility with a veneer of adornment and studied refinement. Advertisements for the college baldly prized *crianza*, or upbringing, over *estudio*, or devotion to study. In the words of a 1763 prospectus, the Cordelles academy was above all a "school for virtue, discipline (*policía*), and letters," educating young nobles "to the greater glory of God and the utility of the State."[24]

A pronounced environmental psychology underlay the Jesuits' strenuous cultivation of artifice and rhetorical effect. This epistemological point of departure defined education as an acquisitive process whereby children passed from an initial state of total ignorance to the final condition of "erudite, ingenious, subtle, and learned." Josep Sans's succinct paraphrase of Seneca— "human understanding is a barren field, where God casts the seeds of all knowledge so that it may grow and be fruitful through study and *cultura*"—exemplified the equation of primeval human nature with unqualified ignorance.[25] Adaptation of

---

[23] For Jesuit education in general, see: Lukács, *Monumenta Paedagogica*; Herman, *La Pédagogie des Jésuites*; Brizzi, *Formazione della Classe Dirigente*, and his *Ratio Studiorum*; Dainville, *Éducation des Jésuites*; and Salomone's introduction to his edition of the *Ratio Studiorum*.

[24] *Constituciones de Cordelles*, 4 and 16.

[25] Julià, *Oración Fúnebre*, "censura" by S. Escofet; Sans, *Sabio Ignorante*, I, 22-23.

the theory of the mind as *tabula rasa* proved a commonplace of local educational doctrine. Lluís Valencià's view of his mission as a professor—"the teacher frees the student from natural servitude and delivers him from ignorance"—found echo in numerous affirmations of the "congenital ignorance" of children.[26] As noted above, such an approach naturally encouraged belief in the power of education to transform individuals. This widely held opinion confirmed the view of both early modern pedagogues and their students that a proper education could do much to compensate for the stigma of low birth. Not surprisingly, education came to be seen as the vehicle of upward social mobility *par excellence*. The acquisition through schooling of *crianza*, or the good upbringing deemed a necessary quality of the nobility, served to mask the disadvantages of commoner background.[27]

Care was taken not to place excessive emphasis on the "improving" character of education, lest it take on overly democratic overtones—hence the consistent, almost obsessive, association of education with the nobility. D. Miquel de Calderó's speech to the "wise and noble" Marian Congregation offered a typical panegyric of the "triumph of nobility and knowledge" proferred by the *Col.legi*. The distinguished judge drew upon the entire stock of symbols employed in these stereotyped orations in his account of the ascent up Mount Parnassus, with its gallery of "noble exemplars" seeking to imitate the "flight" of the "Imperial Eagle . . . to the resplendent sphere of the Sun." Not to be deterred by the examples of Phaeton and Icarus, and moved by the "noble ardor" and heroic exploits of other members of the Congregation, Calderó mastered his fear and joined in the collective quest for knowledge and virtue. The uphill struggle to the lofty heights of Parnassus; glimpses of the majestic eagle soaring above all earthly prominences; the inability of previous failures to discourage his making the journey; above all, the central role played

---

[26] Moreno, *Claridad de Simples*, dedication; Valencià, retirement petition, s.n.

[27] Amat de Planella, *Nenias Reales*, "Razón de la Obra"; Garau, *Sabio Instruido*, II; Gurrea, *Arte de Enseñar*, 2v.

by the sun's light in symbolizing the final goal of knowledge and accomplished *virtus*—all these topoi formed part of the hackneyed imagery repeatedly drawn on to depict and inspire the experience of new generations of students.[28]

Perhaps the most popular symbol designed to evoke the pupil's admiration was that of the "Erudite Hercules." One could hardly imagine a more vivid tale for emulation than the history of this singularly laborious hero, which ranged from the realistic experience of doubt prior to choosing Virtue over Pleasure to repeated episodes of "arduous enterprise," the overcoming of obstacles, and endless ascents up mountains. Hercules' death through immolation also contained strong christological overtones, and encouraged reference to the sunbird the Phoenix, a favored symbol in late-seventeenth-century Catalonia. Above all, Hercules provided a model for the superiority of eloquence over physical strength, a point Alciati had previously made in his highly influential emblem book. Contemporary sources like the eighteenth-century commonplace book *The Twelve Labors of the Erudite Hercules* echoed the theme of the "strength of Eloquence." The nascent aristocratic Academy of Barcelona also enthusiastically referred in its works to this titan among the "heroes of virtue."[29]

A glance at texts like D. Josep Faust de Potau's Cordelles oration of 1696 reveals yet another dimension of the world-view propagated in local elite schooling: the overwhelming emphasis placed on education as an instrument defining class boundaries. Beginning in the fourth strophe, one finds a highly self-conscious statement of the different response of upper and lower classes to the challenge of knowledge and virtue:

---

[28] Calderó, *Canción Real*.

[29] Alciati, *Emblemata*, nos. 137 and 180; B.U.B./Ms. 1588, *Las Doce Empresas de Hércules Erudito* (s.d.); A.H.M.B./Ms. B-98, session of 10 June 1700. See also: Panofsky, *Hercules am Scheidewege*; Tate, "Mythology in Spanish Historiography"; Morreale, "Salutati's *De Laboribus Herculis*"; Waith, *Herculean Hero*, Chapter 2; Jung, *Hércule dans la Littérature Française*; Galinsky, *Herakles Theme*, Chapter 9; and Vivanti, *Lotta Politica*, Chapter 2.

Vulgar spirits turn coward
When confronted with these heroic enterprises;
Glorious ambitions have no place
In the narrow realm of their breasts.
But he whose debt is to
Exalted and not vulgar birth,
Should not refuse great and difficult tasks;
By being born noble he was born for these.

Only the "daring," supported during their journey by *ingenio*, "high thoughts," and honor (*pundonor*), could brave the ascent up this "inaccessible" and "harsh road."[30] Potau's *Loa*, like all other Cordelles orations, drew upon a vocabulary impregnated with metaphors of ascent and upward movement. Time and again they depicted education as an elevation out of the "common" level, culminating in the establishment of a variety of forms of superiority and distinction: hence the endless references to eagles, the most lofty of birds, soaring above all others; to the lynx, whose sharp vision permitted his seeing farther and with greater clarity than other animals; and especially to the mountain, the "high prominence" nearest the sun, locus of the ceaseless struggle for the splendor and virtue of letters.

The goal of class separation also encouraged the conscious adoption of a visibly elite "style" of comportment. "Mannerly distinction" centered around a diametrical opposition between elite behavior based on the concepts of "gravity" and "good taste," and popular comportment associated with the comic, material, and "indecent."[31] Contemporary texts frankly commended the functional value of elite schooling in distinguishing "high" from "low." Statements of educational intent placed strong emphasis on isolation, separation, and avoidance of "mixture" with others. Such writings habitually opposed noble "courtesy" to the "rude," "unpolished," and "plebeian." Stringent definitions of

---

[30] Potau, *Loa*, A1.
[31] Elias, *History of Manners*; Bakhtin, *Rabelais*.

table manners warned against the "suggestions of vileness" inherent in gluttony. Recreational habits also exposed "good" or "bad upbringing": "decency" and "quiet behavior" indicated noble birth, while passion and violence revealed *baxeza*, or lowly origins.[32] In short, elite education placed unrelenting emphasis on the power of knowledge and comportment to define—and distinguish—nobility. As a result, the cultivation of "external representation" formed an integral part of the socialization of noble youth.

One can obtain a firmer grasp of the underlying principles of elite education by contrasting the Jesuit *col.legi* with another leading elementary school in Barcelona, the episcopal *seminarium*. From its beginning in the 1590's, the seminary enjoyed close ties with the local university and the Dominican order. Inadequate financing obliged the school to matriculate few students during the seventeenth century. However, it expanded rapidly beginning in the early eighteenth century, and by 1736 boasted an enrollment of 42 pupils.[33] Fundamental differences marked the social backgrounds of the two bodies of students. The list of seminary students in 1737 included only one "Don," whereas all 35 Cordelles matriculants in 1762 boasted that honorific distinction.[34] The subject matter taught in the seminary also reflected the lower social standing of its clientele. Its ordinances show far less concern for the *politesse*, etiquette, and social separation prevailing at the Jesuit school. Its curriculum also reveals stronger resistance to the teaching of physical science, in contrast with the Jesuits' well-known fondness for mathematics.[35]

Toward the mid-eighteenth century a reaction set in against

---

[32] *Constituciones de Cordelles*, 31-39.

[33] A.S.V./*Relat. Dioc.*, 43r. (1602) and 36or. (1736).

[34] A.E.B./*Ordinacions del Seminari o Col.legi Episcopal* (1737), 104-105; Borràs, "Col.legi de Nobles," 86-87. As noted above, by that point "don" indicated general social distinction, as opposed to the earlier, more restricted reference to *noblesa*.

[35] A.E.B./*Ordinacions del Seminari*, 1744 additions, unnumbered section entitled "Philosophia."

the sort of education offered at elite institutions like the *Col.legi de Cordelles*. The growing unpopularity of the Jesuits accounted in part for the upsurge in criticism. Moreover, the aims and content of elite education itself came under increasing fire from those critical of its obsessive superficiality. The famed jurist and rector of the University of Cervera, Josep Finestres—himself a Jesuit—dismissed the *Col.legi*'s offerings as "mere confusions and grammatical idiocies."[36] His harsh strictures echoed the complaints of earlier humanists like Pedro Simón Abril, who attacked the abstract and non-utilitarian character of elite schooling.[37] Popular dialogues also lampooned the mannered learning and Scholastic subtleties of local *col.legials*. The *Visit of Gabriel Noodle to Francis Rice* of 1738 satirized the feud between Jesuits and Dominicans, along with the artificial rhetoric and vapid style characterizing both factions.[38] Yet in a certain sense these criticisms missed the point. After all, the very intent of upper-class education was to produce these effects. The inflated rhetorical style, the studied cultivation of latinate erudition and esoteric *enigmata*—these constituted the deliberate ends of elite schooling.[39] The shared experience of schooling endowed the patriciate with a common sense of identity. Such elaborate if abstract preparation also provided a clear test of membership in the local ruling class. As the theologian Josep Romaguera noted in his emblem book of 1681, the true noble could "persuade through external evidence his greatness of heart."[40] It was a lesson both teachers and students learned exceedingly well.

[36] Cited in Galí, *Maldà*, 150.

[37] Maravall, *Poder, Honor, y Elites*, 235.

[38] *Visitas de Gabriel Fideo a Francisco Arroz*.

[39] According to the *Magestuosa Poética Fiesta*, the public exercises of 1700 included the following contests: improvisation in Latin, Castilian, and Catalan in at least 28 metrical forms; replies in Latin to questions on Cicero's *Epistles*, "explaining . . . the plot, genre, year, and Consuls, all with erudition in Roman history"; written and oral examinations on the last six books of the *Aeneid*, the emblems of Alciati, and five books of Horace, "raising doubts and giving solutions through citation of authorities"; ending with a poetry reading in the "pompously adorned Theatre."

[40] Romaguera, *Atheneo de Grandesa*, no. 6.

Distrustful Academicians

On June 3, 1700, sixteen of the "most noble and erudite Catalans" gathered in the magnificient library of the Dalmases palace on the Carrer de Montcada to inaugurate the first amateur academy in the city's history. The constitution unanimously approved that day specified their purpose. As "persons in whom Erudition marches side by side with Nobility," they pledged themselves to the "most arduous undertakings" of "learning" and other "high matters." After some discussion, the members chose the uncharacteristically modest name of the Academy of the *Desconfiats*—literally the "unconfident" or "distrustful." They also adopted for their emblem an allegory of a shipwreck huddled beneath the motto *tuta quia diffidens*—"safe through distrust" (see Illustration 4). The members finally agreed to hold meetings every two weeks to recite speeches on prearranged themes (*assumptos*), and to perform musical compositions. The first regular session of the Academy took place a week later. At least ten meetings followed between June and January of the succeeding year. Since the minutes of most sessions after early 1701 are missing, the bulk of our knowledge of the Academy's activities derives from records of the 1700 meetings and the published works of its members.[41]

In a strict sense, the *Desconfiats* sodality was not the first academy founded in Barcelona. The *Acadèmia* of Saint Thomas Aquinas, established during the 1660s, united local university professors and theologians in a Dominican attempt to rival the prominent Marian Congregation of the Jesuit Cordelles school.[42]

[41] A.H.M.B./Ms. B-98; B.C./Ms. 1004. For the history of the Academy, see: Miret Sans, "Dos Siglos de Vida Académica"; Moliné Brases, "Acadèmia dels Desconfiats"; Carreras Bulbena, "Constitució," and his "Estudis Biogràfics"; Voltes Bou, "Nuevas Noticias"; Comas, *Història de la Literatura Catalana*, IV, 76-103, 123-146, and 645-662; and García Dini, "Pablo Ignacio de Dalmases."

[42] Voltes Bou, "Estatutos."

4
Emblem of the *Acadèmia dels Desconfiats* (18th century).
Engraving by Francesch Gazan.

This association was composed almost exclusively of professional academics and served merely as an adjunct to regular university teaching. It offered none of the opportunities for amateur literary exposition so conspicuous a feature of the *Desconfiats* group. More importantly, its literal "academicism" was far removed from the effortless elitism of true dilettantes. Only the *Desconfiats* could mimic the wedding of nobility and learning increasingly common among elite sodalities throughout late-seventeenth- and eighteenth-century Europe.

The founders of the aristocratic *Acadèmia* did not adopt any local institution as their model. Rather, they turned for inspiration to amateur patrician associations in France and especially Italy. The preface to the collective anthology *Royal Dirges* of 1701 noted that "among all other nations, that which has most distinguished itself in this tasteful sort of studies has been Italy, the most fertile mother of clever and industrious Geniuses, for in almost all her important provinces one finds a variety of Academies."[43] The editor, D. Joan de Amat i Planella, listed some fifty academies serving as models for the Barcelona institution. He predictably included such well-known examples as the *Lincei* of Rome, the Florentine *Crusca*, and the Olympian Academy of Vicenza. Noting with approval state sponsorship of learned societies in France and Tuscany, the author echoed Cristóbal Suárez de Figueroa's lament concerning the absence of similar organizations in Spain, despite the "importance and wit of its geniuses, well-developed in all faculties."[44] The accuracy of the complaint that Spain lacked academies is certainly open to doubt. Beginning in the sixteenth century, academies and especially *tertulias* or salons flourished in Valencia, Seville, Madrid, and Saragossa.[45] Yet the varied fortunes and sporadic existence

[43] Amat de Planella, *Nenias Reales*, "Razón de la Obra."

[44] *Ibid*. The paraphrase is from Suárez de Figueroa's Castilian adaptation of Garzoni's *Piazza Universale*, published as *Plaza Universal* (*verbo* "Academia").

[45] For early modern Spanish literary academies, see: King, *Prosa Novelística*;

of these groups was a far cry from the permanent, even bureau-cratic nature of sister groups like the *Crusca* or the Parisian royal academies. There was thus some justice in the Barcelona founders' view of themselves as filling a gap not just in the cultural life of their own city, but in that of the entire peninsula as well.

A glance at the social background of the Academy's initial membership reveals a group drawn largely from the higher ranks of the Catalan aristocracy. Six of the sixteen founders belonged to families that had been *nobles* for at least three generations. An additional three—the Counts of Darnius and Çavallà and the Marquis of Rubí—hailed from the titled nobility.[46] Four other members belonged to the *noblesa*, although two were sons of fathers ennobled in their lifetimes. The remaining three founders included one *cavaller*, one honored citizen, and one commoner. Membership in the initial group was thus heavily weighted toward the upper levels of the traditional aristocracy, with a minority drawn from the ranks of the lower and/or more recent nobility.

What in particular attracted these individuals to the Academy? Little is known about how nobles entered the group. Several factors apparently influenced the recruitment of members. Not surprisingly, kinship ties linked together many of the founders. At least 3 of the original 16 members belonged to the

---

Sánchez, *Academias Literarias*; Mestre, *Despotismo e Ilustración*, Chapter 2; Brown, *Images and Ideas*, I; Robles, *Academias de Valencia*; and Lleó, *Nueva Roma*, 52-69.

[46] The sixteen founding members were: D. Josep d'Amat i de Planella (made Marquis of Castellbell by Philip V in 1702); D. Llorens de Barutell i de Erill, Count of Erill-Orcau; D. Joan Antoni de Boixadors, Count of Çavallà; Josep Clua i Granyena; D. Agustí Copons i de Copons (named Marquis of Moyà in 1702); D. Pau Ignasi de Dalmases i Ros (invested Marquis of Vilallonga by Archduke Charles in 1710); Martín Díaz de Mayorga; D. Felip de Ferran i Çacirera (named Count of Ferran in 1706); D. Francesch de Josa i de Agulló; D. Francesch Junyent i de Vergós; D. Aleix de Palau i de Aguilar; D. Antoni de Paguera i de Aymerich; D. Joan de Pinós i de Rocabertí; D. Josep de Rius i de Falguera; D. Josep Antoni Rubí i de Boixadors, Marquis of Rubí; and D. Josep Taverner i de Ardena, Count of Darnius.

Boixadors-Rocabertí lineage cluster mentioned above. Moreover, marriage connections reveal several affinal relations among members: between Copons and Paguera, Taverner and Rubí, Dalmases and Rius, Amat and Junyent, and Rius and Taverner. Kinship also affected the admission of the 30 newcomers from June 1700 to March 1703. These included the younger brother and no fewer than 3 brothers-in-law of the Academy's most celebrated member, the antiquarian D. Pau Ignasi de Dalmases (1670-1718); the 2 Pellicer brothers (grandsons of the famed chronicler of Aragon); and the nephew of D. Joan de Pinós i de Rocabertí.

Other ties united the small nucleus of the Academy's founders. For example, common professional backgrounds were much in evidence. Eight of the 46 members were lawyers, while 2 others served in the central government bureaucracy. Another 7—including almost all the non-Catalans—were professional soldiers. The single largest shared occupation was that of the clergy. Fourteen members were ecclesiastics, half of whom were attached to the local cathedral as canons (5) or musicians (2). The rest of the clerical group comprised 4 canons of other churches resident in Barcelona, along with 3 theologians or members of special religious establishments like the Collegiate Church of Saint Anne's.

The venue of the Academy—the Carrer de Montcada—also provided a certain continuity. D. Pau Ignasi de Dalmases originally installed the *Acadèmia* in the mansion recently acquired by his family on that street. He spent a considerable portion of the fortune that his forebears had amassed through the putting-out of cloth in Barcelona's hinterland, converting the medieval buildings into a patrician townhouse redesigned in the latest Baroque style.[47] The Academy continued to meet in the Dalmases palace

---

[47] The sculpted friezes of the Triumph of Neptune and the Rape of Europa on the stairwell of the courtyard of the Dalmases palace rank among the finest examples of secular Baroque sculpture in Catalonia: Martinell, *Arquitectura i Escultura Barròques*, II, nos. 17-18.

after resuming its activities in 1727 following the War of Spanish Succession. With the admission in 1728 of D. Josep de Mora, Marquis of Llió, it began to alternate sessions between the Dalmases residence and the nearby Mora palace. The strong identification between the Carrer de Montcada and the noble Academy was hardly surprising. For centuries the street had attracted wealthy merchants and recently ennobled patricians like the Dalmases and Moras, who sought to enhance their claims to high status by taking up residence in its luxurious palaces. The specific social function of these mansions—their role as a vehicle for the conspicuous exhibition of wealth deemed an essential attribute of the nobility—resided not only in the direct patronage of fine arts, as in the Dalmases courtyard. The Academy afforded yet another opportunity to display the same learned *cultura* increasingly identified with the aristocracy.[48]

Common political affiliations also united most of the academicians. Only a small handful of members supported the Bourbon cause during the War of Spanish Succession. In the meantime, patricians like Dalmases, D. Josep Faust de Potau, Francesch Sans, the Marquis of Rubí, and the Counts of Çavallà and Ferran played major parts within the Habsburg camp, beginning as early as 1700.[49] Although the role of politics in the Academy's activities has received little notice, the shared political allegiance of its members proved crucial in determining not only the composition but also the timing of the group's foundation. Its first meetings took place in the tense atmosphere of political uncertainty surrounding the dynastic succession of Charles II. His death later that year gave rise to the first public manifestation of the Academy's literary endeavors, a collective panegyric of the last Habsburg king published in 1701 under the title *Nenias Reales* (Royal Dirges). Furthermore, the themes for discussion in 1700 betrayed a growing preoccupation with con-

[48] Amelang, "Carrer de Montcada." See also Burke, "Conspicuous Consumption."

[49] *Diccionari Biogràfic dels Catalans*, entries for these individuals.

temporary politics. Amid the normal array of discourses on fine points of classical erudition and moral philosophy, one finds political topics presented under the guise of studies of episodes from Catalan or Imperial history. The meeting of August 30 in particular drew upon such themes in a deliberate attempt to rally support for the Habsburg dynasty. The first discourse thus celebrated James I's heroic defense of his succession at the age of ten against a clique of discontented nobles—a clear allusion to the Austrian Pretender.[50] The second *assumpto*—one of the very few delivered in Catalan—consisted of a eulogy of the famed medieval warrior, Dalmau de Creixell, who died defending his king at the battle of Las Navas de Tolosa (1212).[51] Another grimly prophetic discourse praised the "courage of the citizens of Sagunto, who preferred death and the destruction of their city to subjection to the Carthaginians."[52] The final speech contained the most overtly pro-Habsburg statement, relating the foundation of a holy shrine by a recent Emperor "so celebrated for his piety."[53] Orations like these—ostensibly historical in character, extolling in tandem both traditional Catalan nationalism and the Habsburg dynasty—point to a growing willingness to make at least indirect political statements in favor of the Austrian claimant of the throne. Significantly, the tenth session was also marked by a palpably anti-French tone. After D. Agustí de Copons recalled the sufferings of Barcelona during the French siege of 1697, the Marquis of Rubí unleashed a harangue on the perils

[50] A.H.M.B./Ms. B-98, 30 August 1700. Josa, a canon of the Barcelona cathedral and later a principal "Carlista" who went into exile in Italy in 1713, delivered this speech.

[51] The author of this discourse was D. Felip de Ferran, who served as Catalan ambassador to Holland in 1713. His son D. Josep de Ferran i de Ferran played a leading role in the defense of Barcelona during the following year.

[52] D. Antoni de Paguera, later a prominent Austrophile, delivered this *assumpto*.

[53] The author of this speech—an account of a famous episode of the Austrian Counter-Reformation involving Emperor Ferdinand II—was the Marquis of Rubí, who later served as the Archduke's viceroy in Mallorca and Sardinia, dying in exile in Vienna in 1741.

nations suffered during years of prolonged peace.[54] However, this brief flurry of activism soon died out, and was replaced by a period of relative tranquility. The adverse political climate following the resolution of the succession in favor of Philip V doubtless encouraged the Academy to maintain a low profile until the Barcelona elite aligned itself in favor of Archduke Charles in 1705.[55]

Outside the realm of politics, the *Desconfiats* turned to less historical vocabulary and imagery. A strikingly consistent vision linking membership in the nobility with sustained intellectual activity informed their turgid musings. Time and again the academicians identified themselves with "wisdom," "knowledge," and especially *ingenio*. Thus the group's original charter specified its aims to be dedication to "ingenious occupations." At its first meeting, the "noble youth" seeking entry into the "Parnassus" of the Dalmases palace pleaded for an opportunity to "learn from the subtle and shining *ingenio*" of the Academy. Even more explicit was the *Harmony of Parnassus* (1703), a collective anthology of poems "edited by two *ingenis* of the Barcelona Academy."[56] The deliberately belletristic tone cultivated in these meetings did not forbid appropriation of the stock themes and *personae* of the Cordelles and funeral orations. One finds the same association of nobility with study, accompanied by the fierce onslaught against *ocio* that loomed large as a subject in contemporary sermons and moral treatises. Hence also the appearance of familiar figures like Icarus and Phaeton, Minerva, the Phoenix, and especially the "Hercules of Eloquence."

Members of the Academy took considerable pains to distinguish their privileged knowledge from popular ignorance. Sym-

[54] Carreras Bulbena, "Constitució," 238-239.

[55] Soldevila, *Història de Catalunya*, III, Chapters 33-34. The early arrest of Dalmases provides a likely explanation for the inactivity of the Academy during the Habsburg Interregnum.

[56] A.H.M.B./Ms. B-98, 10 June 1700; Amat de Planella, *Nenias Reales*, "Razón de la Obra"; *Armonia del Parnàs*, title-page.

bolizing the power of education to set nobles apart from plebeian obscurity was an *assumpto* the barrister Josep Pla devoted to popular belief in black magic. This fascinating oration (ca. 1730) lampooned the "vulgarity" of the "false dream" of the witches' sabbath. Its ironic, even burlesque tone issued from the author's desire to ridicule the "superstitious" credulity of the lower orders. At the same time, the poem reveals a dramatic shift in ruling-class attitudes toward magic and the supernatural. What was previously regarded a dangerous form of plebeian knowledge was now belittled as an amusing proof of popular ignorance.[57]

The presence of such themes and symbols in the Academy's literary and musical compositions highlights the fundamental continuity of aristocratic self-image uniting institutions of elite socialization and leisure. The *Acadèmia dels Desconfiats* constituted the most visible embodiment within early modern Barcelona of the ideal of an educated nobility. To be sure, its penchant for literary *jeux d'esprit* distanced it from the deliberately scientific character of many Italian sodalities.[58] And, with the brief exception of the Austrophile years of the first decade of the century, it showed little of the enthusiasm for politics and the discussion of public utility of eighteenth-century French academies.[59] Still, it provided a unique meeting-ground for old and new nobility, bound by a common class identity centering around a shared vision of learned "culture." As a result, the ideals and models it propagated through literature, art, and public discourse contrib-

[57] B.N./Ms. 19,576, 281r.-284v., "Assumpto que Donà la Acadèmia de Bones Lletres al Dr. Josep Pla, Celebra Advocat y Poeta, sobre la Vulgaritat dels Balls de las Bruixas." See also Thomas, *Religion and The Decline of Magic*, Chapters 18 and 22.

[58] Cochrane, *Tradition and Enlightenment*; Vasoli, *Cultura della Corti*, 159-189; *Quaderni Storici*; and *Accademie e Cultura*. For a broad overview of similar groups in Germany and Austria, see Evans, "Learned Societies."

[59] Roche, *Siècle des Lumières*, I, 323-355; Emerson, "Enlightenment and Social Structures"; Chisick, *Limits to Reform*, Chapter 1.

uted significantly to the reproduction of aristocratic identity in the city.

A handful of fundamental principles underlay the emerging ideal of elite *cultura*. First, contemporaries took pains to define "culture" as *acquired* knowledge. While some early modern writers considered proper innate disposition a necessary prerequisite, all agreed that *cultura* was obtained principally through formal education. It was thus a markedly *public* form of knowledge, one that could be openly verified or denied. As a result, "culture" often—though hardly exclusively—found validation through institutional sanctions like university degrees. It also possessed close ties to literacy, in deliberate contrast to the strictly oral or visual means of communication restricted to the lower classes. Finally, elite *cultura* was highly *restrictive* in character—that is, the limits placed on access by outsiders defined it to a crucial extent.

Such constrictions shaped both the content and forms of elite consciousness. For example, emphasis on the public character of ruling-class attitudes and behavior exaggerated its theatricality and sense of display. Moreover, insistence on literate sources of reference encouraged elite preferences for the nonvernacular languages, especially Castilian. It would thus be a mistake to try to reduce aristocratic *cultura* to an expository body of doctrines and beliefs. Equally if not more important were its forms of expression—its choice of literary style and language, and the changing modes of elite comportment in Barcelona's rituals and *fêtes*.

VIII

SIGNS

OF IDENTITY

A Question of Style

"*In* Spanish as in every other language . . . there is a great difference between fine speech and common speech." In his *Discourse on the Castilian Language* (1586), the humanist Ambrosio de Morales reproduced a fundamental tenet of earlier treatises on noble conduct like the *Book of the Courtier* and the *Galateo*.[1] Uniting these arguments was a belief in the power of speech to distinguish the "vulgar" from "noble men of letters." The "civil conversation" of the educated noble evidenced itself not only in the content of his address but also in its form. Both the vocabulary and modes of expression deemed appropriate for elite usage conferred glittering badges of class identity.

That all discourse could be divided into "vulgar" or "learned" proved a durable commonplace of early modern literary commentary. Book prefaces in particular habitually distinguished patterns of address along the lines of social class. The Catalan preacher Francesch Eiximenis began his fourteenth-century *Crestià* with an apology for its "simple and rude (*grossera*) style . . . for although this book can be of service to knowledgeable and learned persons, I nevertheless intend to speak princi-

---

[1] A. de Morales, "Discurso sobre la Lengua Castellana," in Pérez de Oliva, *Diálogo*, 73-74; *Galateo*, Chapter 20; *Book of the Courtier*, 47-57.

pally to simple laymen without great learning." Two centuries later Diego Pérez de Valdivia vowed at the outset of his harangue against Barcelona's Carnival revelry not to treat the matter "in a metaphysical way, for such would be indiscreet, because the common people (*pueblo*) would not understand . . . rather we must talk in a plain style (*llanamente*)." A contemporary Valencian cleric apologized in 1586 for his

> simple style . . . as one must perforce use in dealing with simple Christians. For this reason I beg the learned reader not to seek in this work *curiosidad*, nor ornate style, nor exquisite vocabulary, nor polished Castilian language, for such . . . curious style . . . was never my intent. . . .

Honofre Manescal pursued the opposite effect in a 1611 text. Therein the Barcelona preacher confessed to the "discreet Reader and Lover of fine Learning" his wish to write a book "of conceits so high, of discourse so erudite, and of thoughts so towering, worthy of the good *ingenios* of my nation, so full of . . . great *letrados* and persons learned in all disciplines."[2]

The same framework linking discrete literary styles to different social classes informed the prologue to Rocabertí's *Fatal Omens* of 1646. In this windy passage Rius praised the noble author's

> great erudition, beautifully composed of learned maxims, choice sayings, proper *exempla*, and sound doctrine approved by classical authors, written not in a vulgar style, but rather with the gravity befitting its matter and language. . . .

The opening pages of Josep Romaguera's emblem book, the *Atheneum of Greatness* of 1681, featured a similar dichotomy. In the

---

[2] F. Eiximenis, cited in Carrère, *Barcelona 1380-1462*, II, 185n.; Pérez de Valdivia, *Plática de Máscaras*, prologue; Moreno, *Claridad de Simples*, prologue; Manescal, *Miscelánea de Tratados*, "Al Lector."

eyes of the prominent theologian's panegyrists, his conceited (*conceptuós*) meter and elegant syntax bespoke the "beauty . . . of a delicate genius and the forthright order of his mind." Romaguera himself went on to distinguish the "mechanical comprehension" of "plebeian upstarts" from the "learned (*noticiosa*) intelligence" of "curious and noble men of wisdom."[3] Slightly more restrained in tone was the preface to Francesch Baucells' *Mystic Fount* of 1704. Here the missionary affirmed his intention not to address "rectors and parish priests, who already have enough books, but rather the most vulgar and needy people." He thus resolved not to write "with elegant phrases, nor with high-sounding words, but rather in the vulgar method. . . ."[4]

A common vision unites these passages. Their coherence derives from shared perception of the need to adjust modes of literary presentation to the social background of individual audiences. More significantly, the separation between the learned manner of the elite and the "vulgar" or "rude" style of the lower classes—satirized with disarming irony by Cervantes in the prologue to *Don Quijote*—exercised considerable influence upon the nature of early modern elite discourse itself. Conscious recognition of the power of style to express social distinctions was the product of an era witnessing significant transformations in the composition and functions of the urban ruling class and in public representations of elite identity. Awareness of the social valence of learned "culture" contributed to the flourishing of a highly mannered literary style which drew heavily upon the themes and figurae of classical Antiquity. Sentences like the following typified the wedding of "artificial Gymnastics" and "conceited Cadences" with "most sublime" pedantry:

If a simple little bird scaling spheres towered above the palaces of the stars, wishing to establish its home near

---

[3] Rocabertí, *Presagios Fatales*, "aprobación"; Romaguera, *Atheneo de Grandesa*, "aprobacions" and "Pròlech al Lector."

[4] Baucells, *Font Mystica*, "Lo Autor al Lector."

the rays of the Sun, in order to usurp from the Eagle
the diadem which the latter so justly enjoys as the
Queen of the entire Realm of Flight (*República volante*),
who would be surprised if it fell like the unfortunate
Phaeton into the cold waves of the Eridanus, in the
craggy roughness of the deep valley, as a punishment
for its daring zeal and blind ambition . . . ?[5]

One pities the hapless reader of the rest of this oration by
D. Joan de Sagarriga, Count of Creixell and fervent participant
in the literary world of eighteenth-century Barcelona.

The direct link between social standing and a taste for artifice and erudition also helps explain contemporary interest in
the esoteric and hermetic. The ever-popular emblem books, the
use of hieroglyphics in elite ceremonial, and the *bizarries* Academicians cultivated in their published poetry (which often included acrostics and inverted letter patterns) drew nourishment
from this penchant for the inaccessible (see Illustration 5). The
Janus-like quality of such literary forms found expression in the
laying of an external, literal face directed toward public display
over an internal, deeper level of significance. Only a select few
could penetrate the latter sphere—a veritable Silenus-box of social distinction. Classical allegory and Baroque flourish joined to
erect a "veil of mystery" excluding all but the initiated from the
most recondite and profound meaning.[6]

Public cultivation of erudition and stylistic obscurity was
not in itself sufficient to define class boundaries. Upper-class education also sought to endow students with an *autonomous* capacity for judgment and selection—one that permitted them to de-
tect and confirm patterns of social hierarchy in more personal,

---

[5] Sagarriga, *Dietario*, xxii.

[6] For the vogue of emblem literature, see Klein, *Form and Meaning*, Chapter 1.
Bartoli made the revealing observation that "some Ancients, to conceal from the
eyes of the vulgar the mysteries of their Theology, hid them (as treasure hidden
within the Silenus) under . . . Fables . . . and learned Hieroglyphs" (*The Learned
Man*, 186). For the deliberate pursuit of esoteric knowledge by early modern
elites, see Lowinsky, *Secret Chromatic Art*, Chapter 9.

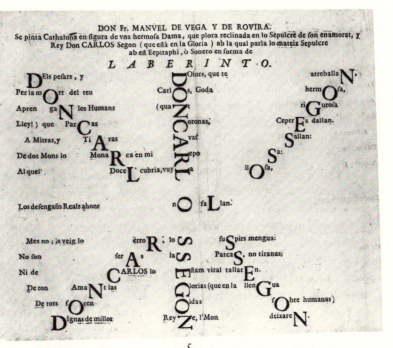

DON Fr. MANVEL DE VEGA Y DE ROVIRA:
Se pinta Cathaluña en figura de vna hermofa Dama, que plora reclinada en lo Sepulcre de fon enamorat, y
Rey Don CARLOS Segon (que eſtà en la Gloria) ab la qual parla lo mateix Sepulcre
ab eſt Eepitaphi , ò Soneto en forma de

L A B E R I N T O.

5

Academic Acrostics. From J. Amat de Planella, ed., *Nenias Reales y Lágrimas Obsequiosas* (1701), s.n.

less ostentatious ways. Indoctrination in the principles of tacit discernment thus involved deliberate promotion of the qualities of "discretion" and "subtlety." An intriguing passage in a 1674 legal treatise developed the opposition between literalness, "common to all the *vulgo*," and *sutileza* (subtlety) of interpretation, which "discovers the ambiguous and hidden, expounding what lays beneath the letter of the law." In dedicating his book to the *noble* D. Jeroni de Pinós, the local cleric Joan Pujol expressed a similar hope: that such a "prudent reader" would "subtly separate the wheat from the chaff" by "going beyond the letter and penetrating the marrow" of the text.[7]

[7] Valencià, *Ilustración*, 7 and 21; Pujol, *Obra Poètica*, 15. Gracián's *El Discreto* (Huesca, 1646) discussed the ways in which one obtained (and subtly displayed) the quality of discretion.

Construction of elite knowledge as recondite, esoteric, requiring interpretation—in short, accessible to only a select few—
also underlay the public ceremonies of the Cordelles school. A
text published in 1696 explained their constant resort to "ingenious devices" and hieroglyphics, which even included competi-
tive exegesis of Alciati's *Emblems*. In that year, the Jesuits
mounted in Barcelona's Plaça del Rei a "vivid hieroglyph" to
celebrate one of Charles II's many restorations to health. A host
of statues, altars, sacred texts, and other pictorial and sculptural
elements adorned this "expressive emblem." "Its coats-of-arms,"
according to a contemporary account, "were made intelligible to
all by means of written poems, thus reserving understanding of
the mute language of their emblems to only the erudite."[8] Opposition between the superficial, literalistic perception of the
masses and the deeper, interpretative faculty restricted to the
elite provided a coherent framework of differential understanding and perception. Ironically, the 1696 text reversed the longstanding identification of visual images with the lower classes.
Early modern writers had long distinguished the written media
of "learned persons" from the exclusively visual and oral means
of communication of the "ignorant, needy, and vulgar." Theologians also dwelt on this dichotomy. While reserving the privilege of reading scripture to the elite, they encouraged popular
devotion through sermons, sacred images, and the collective rec-
itation of prayers.[9] The Jesuit *fête* of 1696 thus provides an interesting twist, as there the strictly visual element (in this case
emblems) proved hardest to decipher.

I am not arguing that all developments in literary style from
the sixteenth to eighteenth centuries originated in a conscious
desire to manipulate learned "culture" as an instrument for defining class boundaries. Relations between text and context are
never that simple, nor so obsessively uni-directional. Moreover,

[8] *Festiva Sagrada*, 9-10. See also Wind, *Pagan Mysteries*.

[9] Soler, *Río del Parayso*, first sermon; Dr. Pere Roig i Morell's preface to Baucells, *Font Mystica*.

early modern elite discourse was scarcely of one mind on the issue of literary artifice and classical allusion. For example, religious reformers like the earlier followers of Erasmus strongly advocated a "plain," vernacular style in devotional rhetoric. Their goal was in fact to lower class barriers, at least in the religious sphere, in order to expand familiarity with the gospel.[10] And while manuals of comportment such as the *Book of the Courtier* and the *Galateo* insisted upon the need to avoid recognizably "popular" forms of speech, they condemned excessive mannerism in equally harsh terms. In the words of Castiglione, the true courtier shuns affectation, an error which stems "from an excessive desire to appear very accomplished." Rather, the educated noble should attempt to "conceal all art, and to make whatever is done or said appear to be without effort."[11]

Early modern Spanish authors engaged in bitter polemics over the highly artificial rhetoric of much contemporary literature, especially poetry. In the late sixteenth century, for instance, Sebastián de Covarrubias ridiculed the "mad excesses" of *culterano* preachers. Writers of the stature of Quevedo and Calderón joined the fray by lambasting the affected style of their opponents.[12] However, the impassioned disputes pitting *culterano* against *conceptista* writers only partly defined the terms of this exchange. Viewed from a more general perspective, the two styles can be seen to share a common emphasis on obscurity, impenetrability, and metaphorical complexity. Once again, Gracián loomed large in this debate. A measured ambivalence permitted him to draw upon and at times blend together both stylistic traditions. At the same time, in works like *The Discreet One* and especially the *Criticón*, he showed considerable sensitivity to

---

[10] Bataillon, *Erasmo y España*, II, 145-151.

[11] *Book of the Courtier*, 43 and 47; Gracián Dantisco, *Galateo Español*, 164-165.

[12] Covarrubias, *Tesoro*, 386; Quevedo citations in Corominas, *Diccionario Crítico Etimológico*, I, 980. The normally staid Calderón satirized *culto* speech in plays like *No Hay Burlas Con el Amor*.

the social and political implications of the elite's choice of literary style and illustrative *figurae*.

Criticism of Baroque "excess"—limited at first to a small minority of writers—increased with the passage of time. Eighteenth-century savants excoriated the "sect of false doctors" who emphasized the superfluous over the useful and prized witty conceits over the "simple style of virtue."[13] Capmany's *Philosophy of Eloquence* (1777) constituted the most sustained attack on literary affectation by an eighteenth-century Catalan author. In his fervent defense of neo-classical aesthetics, Capmany chastised those writers who "make themselves obscure in order to seem profound," and whose "overladen sentences" and "sharp subtleties" contributed to the "puerile attempt to make things appear more ingenious than they are" so that "their delicacy is not perceptible to all."[14] In the eyes of Capmany and fellow sympathizers like Jovellanos, elite *cultura* had erected a "wall of separation" between "those who study and those who work." The duty of enlightened reformers was thus to foster a "plain style" facilitating access to public discourse and *luces* by those sectors of the populace hitherto excluded by "literary pride."[15]

In short, early modern Spanish views on proper literary style were far from uniform. In fact, by the mid-eighteenth century, an interesting reversal had taken place. The ornamentation and artifice originally cultivated to distinguish members of the upper class were now condemned as the vulgar opportunism of *parvenus*. Criticism of such rhetoric by the defenders of "plain style" provides interesting evidence for the earlier ties linking "ingenious" modes of expression with membership in the elite. For example, in the mid-seventeenth century the famed Italian Jesuit Daniello Bartoli attributed the conceits of the "contrivers of crooked labyrinths" to the

[13] The passages are from Bartoli, *Learned Man*; see also Sans, *Sabio Ignorante*, I, 10, 52, 62, and 76.
[14] Capmany, *Filosofía de la Eloquencia*, 41.
[15] Cited in Anes, *Economía e Ilustración*, 202-203.

received opinion among the vulgar, that all Obscurity
is an argument of Wit, and the mark of the loftiness of
a great Understanding . . . that Nature hath given the
stars to the Obscurity of the night, and wisdom to the
Obscurity of wits . . . thus the vulgar, deluded by the
false appearance of truth, always most admire what
they least understand. . . .[16]

Josep Sans also attached considerable importance to the impact
of social pretension upon literary style. In his eyes, the "useless
discussions and levities of *ingenios*" took nourishment from the
fact that "the ignorant *vulgo* does not venerate those who are
really wise, but those who appear to be so through their seri-
ousness, verbosity, eloquence, and other external manifestations
assumed precisely in order to fool the masses. . . ." Social ambitions also explained the saddling of books with pompous titles,
as well as "the passion of collecting books and amassing huge
libraries in order to be taken as wise and erudite. . . ."[17]

That contemporaries attributed rhetorical excess to social
pretension suggests that particular literary styles constituted specific cultural representations of class identity. The premium
placed upon ostentation and adornment coincided with a significant change in the world-view of the urban ruling class. The
public display of "ingenious conceit" so assiduously cultivated in
elite education bore close relation to the emerging self-image of
the learned nobility. To be sure, the notion of a separate elite
cultura set in opposition to popular ignorance hardly disappeared
with the triumph of neo-classical aesthetics. The previous era
had nevertheless witnessed an especially intimate bond between
social change and modes of literary expression. Adoption of a
uniquely complex and artificial rhetoric facilitated the public de-

[16] Bartoli, *The Learned Man*, 343-344. See Raimondi, "Daniello Bartoli e la
'Ricreazione del Savio,' " in his *Letteratura Barocca*, 249-326; and Asor Rosa and
Angelini, *Daniello Bartoli*.

[17] Sans, *Sabio Ignorante*, I, 10, 46, and 62.

piction of nobles as men of "genius" and "discretion." The external projection of this self-image through specific literary styles shaped both the forms and content of aristocratic identity, and marked the boundaries of the world it inhabited.

The Castilianization of Language

Linguistic preference also provided a crucial test of social standing in early modern Barcelona. As early as the sixteenth century, writers like Cristòfol Despuig lamented the increasing use of Castilian by the local ruling class. A generation later the Jesuit Pere Gil claimed that Spanish was understood by all local males save in those towns not located on main travel routes and in the countryside. These and other texts bore witness to the growing use of Castilian by the "principal nobles and gentry" and the corresponding limitation of Catalan to "the common people and . . . women."[18]

Symbolizing the pressures placed on Catalan writers was the switch made by the jurist and historian Jeroni Pujades in the later volumes of his *Chronicle of Catalonia*. After publishing the first tome in Catalan in 1609, Pujades—never one to muffle his strident anti-Castilian sentiments—felt compelled to write the rest of the work in Spanish, "for the sake of universal understanding." His fellow barrister Narcís Peralta, in a protectionist trade pamphlet of 1620, offered the same excuse for writing in Castilian. "Our [Catalan] language is not understood outside the Principality," he argued. The hope for wider circulation of his arguments thus justified abandoning the native tongue. Even loyal defenders of the use of Catalan like Andreu Bosch admitted they were fighting a losing battle. "I must disagree," he wrote,

---

[18] Elliott, *Revolt*, 321; García Cárcel and Nicolau, "Castella contra Catalunya," 44; Pujades, *Dietari*, III, 47-48. For a recent survey of the "language question" in early modern Catalonia, see Modest Prats' prologue to Rossich, *Poètica del Barroc*, vii-xliv.

"with what is commonly said of the Catalan tongue, that it is sterile, curt, and sounds badly, while others like Latin and Castilian . . . are abundant, fertile, and sonorous." Framing the debate in these terms obviously placed the dwindling number of elite users of Catalan on the defensive.[19]

The revolt of 1640-1652 constituted a watershed in the linguistic sphere, as in so many others. The intense pamphleteering for the constitutional cause during that decade proved a "last gasp" for published secular discourse in Catalan. Comparison of the language choice of works penned in the 1640s with the propaganda efforts of the War of Spanish Succession renders the contrast especially clear.[20] The earlier period witnessed not only the publication of numerous political tracts in Catalan, but also the singular initiative of the poet Francesch Fontanella, who attempted to revive imaginative literature in that language. A mere six decades later, virtually all the publications of the Catalan cause were printed in Spanish, as were the works of major Catalan apologists like Narcís Feliu de la Penya. Even D. Pau Ignasi de Dalmases wrote the diary of his ill-fated mission to seek English aid in the final months of the war in Castilian.[21]

Several factors encouraged the Castilianization of the urban elite. First, the higher reaches of the Catalan aristocracy, especially the peerage, had already become effectively Castilianized by the later sixteenth century. Families like the Requesens, Cardona, and Montcada had already emigrated from the Principality. In fact, when D. Francesch de Montcada returned to Barcelona as viceroy in 1580, he chose to address his fellow countrymen in Spanish, not in Catalan.[22] The behavior of the

---

[19] Pujades, *Dietari*, I, 17; Peralta, *Memorial*, dedication. For Bosch, see his *Títols*, 28; and Pons, *Littérature Catalane*, 3-74. For an example of the attack on Catalan as "naturally curt and little polished," see Ros, *Cataluña Desengañada*, 239-243.

[20] Aguiló, *Catálogo*; Andreu, *Catálogo*; *Catálogo de la Colección de Folletos Bonsoms*, I.

[21] A.H.M.B./Ms. A-339.

[22] B.N./Ms. 2338, 54r. See also Elliott, "Provincial Aristocracy," 128.

titled nobility exercised an important exemplary influence upon the rest of the civic elite. In fact, one could characterize the trend of the seventeenth century as an incremental filtering-down to the patriciate of the cultural models emanating from the Castilian court and nobility via the Catalan peerage.[23] The acceleration of this tendency following the revolt of the 1640s represented merely the final stage in a process initiated at least a century earlier.

Language decisions in the field of literary expression also influenced the preferences of Barcelona's elite. The early modern period witnessed a drift on the part of Catalan writers toward the Castilian orbit. The honored citizen Joan Boscà pioneered the transition in the mid-sixteenth century. Service as tutor to Castilian aristocrats like the Albas and the development of close ties to the Spanish writer Garcilaso de la Vega led to the exclusive use of Castilian in his writings.[24] Other Catalan authors quickly followed suit. Guillem de Santcliment, also an honored citizen of Barcelona, had little use for his native language during his many years in the diplomatic service. And Galceran de Albanell, royal tutor and later Archbishop of Granada, similarly abandoned Catalan after taking up crown and ecclesiastic service outside the Principality.

The growing importance of Jesuit education also favored the Castilianization of the local ruling class. At first, the Society adopted a flexible attitude toward the use of the vernacular. Portions of the order's early internal correspondence were written in Catalan, although this practice was discontinued by the end of the sixteenth century. A report from a 1596 visitation of the Barcelona *collegium* also included an interesting defense of the use of Catalan in preaching and, to a certain extent, in education.[25]

---

[23] For an interesting remark on the imitation of court dress in early seventeenth-century Barcelona, see Pujades, *Dietari*, III, 135. For similar developments in France, see Elias, *Court Society*.

[24] Maltby, *Alba*, 8 and 12; Fernández de Heredia, *Obras*, xxvii.

[25] A.R.S.I./Hisp. 139, *Epist. Hispan*, 184r.-v. (26 March 1596). Moreover, the

Its rector, Pere Gil, proved a staunch defender of the local language and used it in several of his published works, such as a 1596 guide for pastoral reform written for the diocese of Barcelona.[26] And as late as the 1690s, Jesuit missionaries preached in Catalan not only in the countryside but also in larger cities like Girona.[27]

Still, by the mid-seventeenth century, Jesuit language usage had swung decidedly in favor of Castilian. Beginning in the neoforal period, the Society—which had adopted a fairly equivocal posture during the revolt of 1640-1652—began to champion the Spanish tongue. All the Cordelles orations, which were published beginning in the 1660s, were delivered in either Castilian or Latin, as were most of the speeches and oral exercises of the annual *poéticas fiestas*. On the few occasions when the use of Catalan was permitted, it was limited strictly to comic literary forms such as "burlesque glosses" and "satires." The Order's strong stand in favor of the Castilian cause in the War of Spanish Succession assured it a leading role in the Castilianization of the Barcelona elite during the eighteenth century. The Cordelles ordinances of 1763 permitted students to speak only Latin and Castilian. Practice in the latter was especially encouraged because, according to these guidelines, Catalans found it difficult to pronounce Spanish correctly![28]

Crucial to the elite's adoption of Castilian was the identification of the Catalan vernacular with the "lower" classes. In this case, as in others, the use of specific cultural norms to indicate social status rested upon the perceived "limitations" of the masses. If the lower classes were restricted to the use of Catalan, those wishing to distinguish themselves as patricians were per-

---

academic exercises staged for Philip II in 1585 included performances in all three local languages—Latin, Spanish, and Catalan: A.R.S.I./Arag. 25-I, *Litterae Annuae*, 13v.

[26] Gil, *Memorial*.

[27] A.R.S.I./Arag. 27-I, *Misiones*, 83r. (11 March 1694).

[28] *Constituciones de Cordelles*, 30. According to this document, misplaced accents posed the greatest problem.

force obliged to use Castilian and/or Latin as well. The ruling class apparently did not always regard familiarity with Catalan as demeaning. However, it firmly associated *exclusive* use of that language with the plebeian order. Hence the continual apologies for the use of Catalan, typified by the remark of a group of physicians who begged forgiveness for writing "in such a vulgar language, which every type of person can understand."[29] The association of Catalan with "lower" matters that characterized Jesuit exercises also found a corollary in the practice of the Academy of the *Desconfiats*. Of the handful of orations delivered in Catalan within this important forum of aristocratic learning, almost all dealt with "burlesque" or "ridiculous" themes.[30] Well might Josep Romaguera complain in 1681 of the universal disregard in which contemporaries held the vernacular. Where in other nations there is praise of the native tongue, here there is naught but disdain: "Just because the language is vulgar does not mean that its style must be vulgar . . . only our nation [Catalonia] despises such glory in its geniuses." Romaguera concluded with a vow to write two more works in Catalan. He further promised that "if I experience the usual disdain, I will bury them in the ground." Apparently this is what happened. His emblem book turned out to be virtually the last work of learned lay discourse published in Catalan until the *renaixença* of the nineteenth century.[31]

Languages made prestigious by their literary weight and/or through association with central political authority triumphed throughout early modern Europe.[32] Linguistic preference consti-

[29] *Advertiments de la Pest*, prologue.

[30] A.H.M.B./Ms. B-98, 23 June 1700. Significantly, the only work that the Academicians published in Catalan was their edition of the Rabelaisian poetry of Vicens Garcia, the "Rector of Vallfogona."

[31] Romaguera, *Atheneo de Grandesa*, "Pròlech al Lector." It is worth noting that the only Catalan quoted in the Count of Creixell's diary (1767-1777) was spoken by apprentices and thieves (Sagarriga, *Dietario*, 102).

[32] Burke, "Languages." See also Brunot, *Histoire de la Langue Française*, II, 27-32; III (1), 180-183; III (2), 719-721; and V (1).

tuted an arena wherein members of local ruling classes could garner additional emblems of social distinction. While the range of language choice did not preclude bilingualism, urban elites almost always reserved participation in native dialects and languages to informal, festive, or private venues. Within the Iberian peninsula, Valencia in particular exemplified the precocious Castilianization of a Catalan-speaking civic elite. As such, it provided an important model for Barcelona. Moreover, the establishment there of a Castilian-speaking court during the early decades of the sixteenth century lent added impetus to elite abandonment of Catalan. Writers like Joan Fernández de Heredia relegated Catalan to comic uses, like the theatrical mimicry of women's gossip.[33] In so doing he merely transferred to the stage the sentiments already expressed by Valencia's ruler Germana de Foix (1488-1538). "Doña Hierónima," she asked her maid-in-waiting, "I would like you always to speak in Catalan, which in your mouth sounds so funny (*gracioso*)."[34] Banished by the civic elite to the lower depths of the burlesque, Catalan had to wait two centuries for its reprieve.

Retreat to the Balcony

The means through which nobles distinguished themselves from commoners were hardly limited to the adoption of separate languages or literary styles. To the contrary, these norms embraced areas as diverse as dress, gestures, bodily comportment, and almost all activities susceptible to public display. One of the most significant developments of the early modern era was the definitive consolidation of a separate "style of life" identified exclu-

[33] See, for example, the short farce "La Vesita" in Fernández de Heredia, *Obras*, 137-160. For the linguistic evolution of Valencia, see: Fuster, *Heretgies, Revoltes i Sermons*, 161-230, and his *Poetas, Moriscos y Curas*, 89-103; and García Cárcel, *Herejía y Sociedad*, 312-320, and his *Germanías de Valencia*, 213-218.

[34] Milán, *Cortesano*, 68.

sively with the governing elite. The creation of this world apart was made especially apparent in the changing nature of aristocratic participation in civic ritual. Urban notables increasingly separated themselves from the traditional festive life of the city. They transposed fulfillment of the social imperative of noble pomp and magnificence from the public sphere to private or semi-private venues like the aristocratic palace. Direct participation in communal ceremonies gave way to observation, as the ruling class abandoned the street in favor of the balconies and inner salons of its mansions.[35]

The contrast between municipal *fêtes* at the beginning and end of the early modern period is instructive. Late medieval Barcelona housed a seemingly endless round of secular and religious rituals. The city garnered special fame for three high points in its festive calendar: Carnival, Holy Week, and Corpus Christi. Barcelona also hosted a variety of public celebrations rooted in the political structures and traditions of its municipal and national governments. Prominent among these were the processions and inaugural ceremonies involving the city Council and the Deputies of the *Generalitat*. Finally, Barcelona was one of the few cities in the peninsula with a longstanding tradition of royal pageantry. The most important regal ceremonies were the king's entries, his swearing of an oath to the national constitution, and the solemn convocation of parliament.[36]

By the eighteenth century a strikingly different pattern had supplanted the earlier ceremonial tradition. Among the many changes was, as one might expect, the disappearance of holidays linked to the municipal Council and the *Generalitat*, which the victorious Castilian government abolished in 1714. Ceremonies

[35] For more extensive discussion of Barcelona's ceremonial life, see my "Public Ceremonies and Private *Fêtes*." For suggestive treatments of elite ceremonial in other European cities, see: Phythian-Adams, "Ceremony and the Citizen"; Bergeron, *English Civic Pageantry*; Burke, *Popular Culture*; Trexler, *Public Life*; Muir, *Civic Ritual*; and Buratti, *Città Rituale*.

[36] Amades, *Carnestoltes*; Duran, *Fiesta del Corpus*; Llompart, "Fiesta del Corpus Christi"; Almerich, *Tradiciones*; Bofarull, "Festejos y Ceremonias."

honoring the new Bourbon monarchs replaced political celebrations like the investiture of the city magistrates and the votive procession commemorating the Catalan victory at Montjuïch (1641). Such entertainments, while public in character, recruited their participants exclusively among local notables or "people of distinction." Precedents for this type of *fête* dated back to the mid-sixteenth century, when the *Bras Militar* and Confraternity of St. George established special holidays reserved to members of the aristocracy. The most famous of these were the annual jousts held in the *Born* square on April 23, the day of the nobility's patron, St. George; and the votive procession of the Invention of the Holy Cross (May 3) when the *Bras* elected its officers.[37] Such displays also harkened back to the tradition of special *encamisades*, or masques that aristocrats put on during the visits of royalty and other dignitaries. A high degree of theatricality pervaded these noble entertainments. The minutes of the St. George tourneys in particular betray a growing awareness of the public attending the *festes*.[38] Contemporary descriptions reflect a remarkable self-consciousness within elite festivities, as in the account of the 1653 Carnival that stated that local "knights promenaded through the streets so that the populace might see them."[39] It is hard to determine both the numbers and identity of the spectators of these semi-public entertainments. Still, the exceptionally detailed descriptions of aristocratic *fêtes* in the diary of the tanner Miquel Parets reveal that members of the "lower" classes enjoyed access not only to the processions but to the masques as well.

Another transformation in the city's festive life was the appearance during the intervening period of public entertainments

[37] A.C.A./Generalitat G-68, *Dietari del Bras Militar*, under those dates. Josep Montfar noted in his *Diario* that both admission and chair rental fees were charged at the *Born* jousts (see under 23 April 1686).

[38] A.C.A./Gen. G-75.

[39] A.H.M.B./Ms. B-44, 89v. For a similar emphasis on the theatrical element in early modern elite culture, see Thompson, "Patrician Society," and his "Eighteenth-Century English Society."

for which admission was charged, and which often involved professional performers. Most important in this regard was the establishment in the 1590s of a permanent professional theatre on the *Rambla*. By the eighteenth century, the *Teatre de Santa Creu* (Theatre of the Holy Cross) also housed the growing local enthusiasm for Italian opera. At the same time, outdoor sports increased in popularity. Bullfighting in particular was regularly scheduled in annual seasons beginning in the mid-eighteenth century. Another innovation dating from these years was the public *sarau*, or indoor celebration, usually scheduled at Shrovetide. The government sponsored these balls in the municipal theatre, or in the *Llotja* or Merchant Consulate opposite the civil administrative offices.[40]

The single most important development affecting elite participation in public life was its retreat to the private sphere of the noble palace. While some notables could be found at public masked balls, by the end of the early modern period aristocratic diversions had shifted to more hermetic and controlled venues. The patricians' withdrawal from the earlier mixed, public festive tradition apparently began in the sixteenth century. The chronology of this trend reveals itself most clearly in the case of Barcelona's Carnival.

The earliest references to separate Carnival festivities involving nobles date to the closing years of the sixteenth century. The Andalusian preacher Diego Pérez de Valdivia chastised those who defended special Carnivals for members of "the equestrian order, who claim that they put them on solely for recreation." A generation later, Thomas Platter's lengthy description of the Barcelona Carnival of 1599 singled out Sunday, February 21, as "the day of the Carnival of the Nobles." In 1604, Pujades remarked that "on March 25, Lard Thursday (*dijous llarder*), the

[40] Curet, *Història del Teatre Català*, 71-92; Subirá, *Opera en los Teatros de Barcelona*, 11-54; Alier, *L'Òpera*, 11-60; Capmany, *Memorias Históricas*, II, 996. While we cannot determine exactly who went to these balls, it seems unlikely that the admission fee excluded any save the poorest of local inhabitants.

viceroy gave a dinner party for the noblewomen of the city, which was a most splendid thing. And all throughout this Carnival there have been mounted *festas*, and never has such invention been seen as that devised by the gentry this year." The resort to a separate Carnival composed exclusively of ruling-class participants continued throughout the seventeenth century. Especially memorable were the celebrations of 1630 and 1633, both of which coincided with the entry into the city of members of the royal family. The municipal elite sponsored equally luxurious entertainments during the revolutionary decade of the 1640s. These lengthy festivities included a *momeria* or masque in 1644 curiously entitled a "The Revolution of the Century," wherein visiting French nobles strutted before an audience of several thousand spectators.[41]

In 1720 the cleric Francesch Tagell penned the most detailed account of an aristocratic Carnival in early modern Barcelona. This unusual work, entitled *Description of Twelve Celebrated Balls*, recounted the highlights of a dozen *saraus* or parties held in various mansions on "the most noble street of the entire city," the Carrer de Montcada. Each of the *fêtes* followed a standard pattern which began with conversation accompanied by the serving of hot chocolate—a new stimulant introduced during the expansion of the colonial trade in the seventeenth century (see Illustration 6). A round of genteel dances brought on the next stage, which professional players hired for the occasion, closed with a short mime or scene from a Castilian *comedia*. After a final cotillion, which included allemandes, minuets, and the Catalan *sardana*, the party concluded with a mock invitation to the *sarau* of the following day, usually held in a neighboring palace. At the end of the last evening, an actor impersonating Carnival himself read aloud a parody of his testament and expressed the wish

[41] Pérez de Valdivia, *Plática de Máscaras*, 43r.; Platter, *Journal*, 225; Pujades, *Dietari*, I, 344; Parets, "Sucesos," vols. 20, 54-96 and 24, 226-245; *Dança Momería*; and *Dietari*, XIV, 557-569.

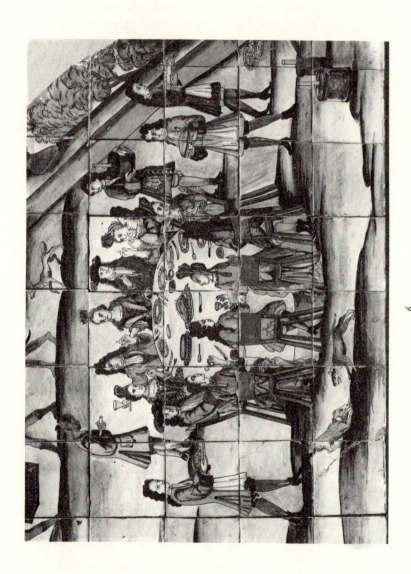

6

Aristocratic dinner. Detail of "La Xocolatada" (early 18th century)

that "everyone so well diverted can now hope to enjoy the coming season of Lent."[42]

By the eighteenth century, noble Carnivals not only included, but rather centered around, fully private entertainments. However, the range of private elite festivities was not limited to the annual Shrovetide cycle. The involution of aristocratic Carnival represented a single strand within a more general trend toward the privatization of ruling-class sociability. Beginning in the later seventeenth century, the *Generalitat* sponsored indoor *saraus* and balls following the jousts of the Confraternity of St. George. Many of the tourneys themselves were now held not in public squares like the *Born*, but in special private enclosures erected in front of the royal palace.[43] Moreover, beginning in the later seventeenth century, one finds abundant references to indoor entertainments like concerts and *tertúlies*, or salons. Amateur plays—which perhaps originated with the viceroy D. Juan de Austria's sponsorship of private representations of *comedias* in the royal palace—also won increasing popularity among nobles during the seventeenth and eighteenth centuries.[44]

The creation of this separate sphere of entertainment was not without its effect upon communal ceremonies involving a broader range of participants. These included not only Carnival, but also patron saint's days, Holy Week, and Corpus Christi. Ironically, an increase in the prior organization of Barcelona's festive life accompanied the withdrawal of the elite. As early as the opening decades of the seventeenth century, professional writers devised scripts for local processions and parades. The structuring of the 1633 Carnival around a program based on the novel *Don Quijote* symbolized the imposition of a fixed schema derived from humanist *cultura*. Sponsors arranged the floats,

[42] F. Tagell, *Obras de la Mussa Catalana Dessocupada*, B.U.B./Ms. 5, 14r. and 73v.

[43] Duran, "L'Estament Militar," 250-252; *Relación Verdadera de las Fiestas de Carnestoliendas*. A typical enclosure of this type is depicted in Illustration 8.

[44] Sagarriga, *Dietario*, 108; Galí, *Maldà*, 238-242; Curet, *Teatres Particulars*.

bearing costumed figures from novels of chivalric romance along with legends in Catalan and Castilian, according to an elaborate predetermined scenario.[45]

Increased regulation of public ceremonies also accompanied the growing resort to written scripts. As these entertainments became more "popular" in character, bureaucratic attempts to control festive life intensified. During the second half of the eighteenth century, fear of repetition of the widespread disturbances of 1766 led to the exercise of severe vigilance over these parades.[46] Measures adopted by the government to improve supervision over the crowd included the suspension of Carnival beginning in 1767, the abolition of Holy Week processions in 1770, and a strict ban on all public gatherings after nightfall. It is also likely that the well-known royal ban on *autos sacramentales*, or eucharistic plays, reflected not just enlightened disdain of these instances of Baroque religiosity, but also fear of the popular license that accompanied their presentation.

Barcelona was not the only city subjected to repressive legislation of this sort. All across Europe, the concern for "decorum" pervading the world-view of the ruling class joined with the central government's fear of political unrest to produce attempts to control the more spontaneous and potentially disruptive festive life of the subaltern classes.[47] In the specific case of Barcelona, while the local elite avoided direct involvement in an expanding range of spectacles and processions, the central gov-

[45] Mas Givanel, *Mascarada Quixotesca*. For a similar manipulation of the Roman Carnival of 1639, see Boiteux, "Carnaval Annexé." For a study of a peculiarly violent contrast between aristocratic and popular festivities, see Le Roy Ladurie, *Carnival in Romans*.

[46] In 1766, riots against the high price of grain broke out in many Spanish cities. See: Vilar, "*Motín de Esquilache*"; Rodríguez, "Spanish Riots of 1766," and her "Riots of 1766"; and Mercader, *Capitans Generals*, 108-109.

[47] Davis, "The Reasons of Misrule," in her *Society and Culture*, chap. 4; Ginzburg, *Cheese and the Worms*, 125-126; Burke, *Popular Culture*, Chapter 8. The actual success the elite enjoyed in its attempt to suppress popular culture is open to doubt; for some judicious remarks on this point, see Beik, "Popular Culture and Elite Repression."

ernment exercised and even increased its control over public *fêtes*. Not surprisingly, one finds a growing emphasis on hierarchy and separation within the celebrations in which the local ruling class continued to participate. As early as the fifteenth century, the Barcelona aristocracy had won for itself a highly privileged corporate position in the Corpus Christi parade. During the eighteenth century, local officials encouraged extension of this hieratic configuration to other pageants. Especially symbolic were the Holy Week penitential processions on Maundy Thursday and Good Friday, in which the nobility marched as a separate body under the banner of the largely aristocratic—and aptly named—Confraternity of Solitude.[48]

Changing patterns of membership in devotional confraternities also reflected the growing distance between Barcelona's ruling class and its social "inferiors." By the eighteenth century, a small number of religious brotherhoods had shed their formerly broad social composition in favor of predominantly aristocratic membership. To be sure, devotional confraternities usually maintained the general principle of inter-class sociability. Marching alongside plebeians was an act of humiliation that penitent nobles willingly suffered. Still, a widening gap separated visibly elite brotherhoods like the Congregations of Good Death, of Sorrows, and of Solitude from the mass fellowships of the Rosary and St. Francis sponsored by the Mendicant orders.[49] Once again, the experience of Barcelona paralleled trends found in much of the rest of Mediterranean Europe, where urban patricians "slowly disengaged themselves from mixing and conversing with the populace."[50]

In short, Barcelona's ruling class retained a certain degree

---

[48] Sagarriga, *Dietario*, 241.

[49] A.H.N./Consejos Suprimidos, leg. 7106, untitled report on Barcelona confraternities (1771); A.S.V./*Relat. Dioc.*, 308v.-309r. (1729); Xaupí, *Recherches*, 505.

[50] Giovan Battista Spinola, cited in Savelli, *Repubblica Oligarchica*, 47. See also Weissman, *Ritual Brotherhood*, chap. 5; Grendi, "Compagnie del SS. Sacramento," and his "Confraternite Liguri"; and Agulhon, *Pénitents et Francs-Maçons*, III.

of involvement in communal festive life throughout the early modern period. Nevertheless, its growing estrangement from a substantial portion of these ceremonies and entertainments proved by far a more significant development. A new vision of elite identity dictated this withdrawal—one which deliberately eschewed the comic, material, and seeming "indecent" imagery and activities of popular festive life.[51] The following description of a marriage celebration, written around 1780 by the "enlightened" bureaucrat J. A. Navarro-Mas, illustrates the diffusion of the new, "serious" style of gravity and "good taste":

> Late in the wedding night, three or four close relatives conduct the bride to her room. Once this is done the groom is informed, who without saying anything to the others who are dancing goes into her room and shuts the door. This is how it is done among serious and distinguished people (*gente seria y principal*). Among the lighthearted (*alegre*) and middling sorts, there is usually a great deal of levity when the groom is put to bed, with a host of persons shouting a thousand things to the bride. The former custom of taking a cup of broth to the couple at midnight, when all the young people entered the room to do and say a thousand foolish things, is rapidly disappearing.[52]

Most remarkable is the narrator's awareness both of differences in patterns of festive behavior along the lines of class, as well as the relatively recent origins of this separation.

These pages on how changes in festive traditions overlay fundamental transformations in contemporary society have drawn largely upon printed accounts and other public documents. Yet more intimate sources like aristocratic journals also

---

[51] Bakhtin, *Rabelais and His World*; Thomas, "Place of Laughter"; Elias, *History of Manners*.

[52] Published in Zamora, *Diario de los Viajes*, 470. See also Stone, *Family, Sex, and Marriage*, 223-224.

reveal the thoroughness with which the elite absorbed and manipulated its schema of "cultural" differentiation between high and low. For example, the personal chronicle D. Joan de Sagarriga, Count of Creixell, wrote from 1767 to 1777 frequently depicted local social structures in the fluid idiom of civic *fêtes*. Creixell took painstaking care to distinguish the social background of the participants in different types of ceremonials. The fundamental division perceived by the author separated the nobility—also characterized as "patricians" or "persons of distinction"—and its ally, the local military establishment, from the *pueblo*, or "people." Not surprisingly, different holidays called forth different combinations of participants—hence the diligence with which Creixell noted that the annual royal birthday celebrations were strictly reserved to the "nobility and garrison," in contrast to more general parades like Corpus Christi, open to "all classes of persons."[53]

Similar concern with the way in which entertainments and rituals were rooted in distinct class backgrounds pervaded the lengthy *Calaix de Sastre* or "Grab-bag" of D. Rafael d'Amat, Baron of Maldà.[54] This exhaustive diary—written from 1783 to 1816 in a lively if woefully corrupt Catalan—bore strong resemblance to Creixell's journal. However, the frequent eruption of the author's spiteful temper and its sheer weight of detail render it far more valuable evidence for the way in which contemporary aristocrats linked *nobilitas* to a style of life radically distinct from that of the masses.[55] Maldà gave over his day-to-day schedule to

---

[53] Sagarriga, *Dietario*, 17, 94, and 271.

[54] The 53 volumes of this diary are found in A.H.M.B./Mss. A-201 to 254. I take most of the references cited here from Alexandre Galí's indispensable anthology with commentary, *Maldà*.

[55] It is revealing that such strong emphasis on a separate style of life is found in an aristocrat who often shared fairly close proximity to the "lower" classes. Maldà frequently cited artisan acquaintances in his diary (Galí, *Maldà*, 73); the old goat even found "peasant and artisan girls" (*pagesetes y menestrales*) more attractive than noblewomen (*ibid.*, 109). In many respects he exemplifies the "pa-

an endless round of *tertúlies*, salons, *xocolotades*, and other soirées with fellow aristocrats both within and in the immediate environs of the city (see Illustration 7). The diversions he so enthusiastically pursued were studiously unacademic in character, and serve to remind us of the way in which the separate *cultura* of the elite was at no point seen as exclusively erudite or even bookish. As with Creixell, a marked tendency toward social separation along cultural lines pervaded Maldà's thinking. The crucial determinant in his schema of classification was *gusto*, or "taste." The author—a passionate devotee of music and thus invariably in attendance at all local performances—employed the concept of taste to distinguish members of the elite from the lower classes present within the mixed sphere of public concerts. A "person of class"—an expression Maldà frequently used—differed from one "without class" through possession of *buen gusto*. "Music," he wrote, "calms us, and makes us enjoy a placid sweetness . . . the upper crust (*primers personatges*), the greatest men in arms and letters, show good taste in this diversion; he who doesn't take pleasure in it is a rude mistanthrope. . . ."[56] It is revealing that, like Creixell, the otherwise gregarious Maldà loathed places like the theatre, where one had to mix "with the popular crowd." Both authors showed a marked preference for the more private sphere of salons and intimate concerts over public *saraus* and Carnival balls, where all was "noise" and "confusion of persons."[57]

Urban ceremonial and display provided a backdrop for the consolidation of aristocratic identity in at least two respects. First, noble entertainments functioned as theatres of integration for the local elite. Shared participation in exclusively aristocratic *fêtes* contributed vitally to the formation of a unified, cohesive upper class. Second, public and private sociability defined and expressed the dominant class's vision of hierarchy—a world-view

---

ternalist" tradition so important a part of the eighteenth-century social equation delineated by E. P. Thompson.

[56] Alier, "Vida Musical," 52.

[57] Galí, *Maldà*, 98-102 and 205.

Aristocratic *Tertúlia*. Detail of "La Xocolatada" (early 18th century), Museu de Ceràmica, Barcelona.

positing clear cultural distinctions between different social classes. It goes without saying that the elite's manipulation of symbolic language hardly exhausted the full range of the lexicon's social meanings. At no point did the ruling class enjoy untrammeled authority over the city's ritual time and space. Thus elite disassociation from the "demeaning" Carnival of the plebs could also be read as the subaltern classes' conquest of a contested *fête*. In fact, popular rituals and sociability displayed admirable resilience in the face of increased regulation of public ceremonies, first by the local ruling class and then by the central government. In Mediterranean Europe at least, Lent scored few lasting triumphs over Carnival. Hence the basic wisdom of the elite tactic of withdrawal, which was far preferable to an uncertain war of attrition over deeply engrained popular festive traditions.

As the trumpets of prudence sounded retreat, the symbolic and practical importance of the balcony took on new meaning. The balcony fulfilled the architectural requirements of the aristocracy's new attitude of distance from the street and other areas of promiscuous and uncontrolled contact with the "lower" classes. It provided a unique vantage-point from which the ruling class could observe and be observed. At the same time, it preserved the requisite of separation, and lent direct spatial configuration to the hierarchy of high and low. When poets like the Valencian notary Andreu Pineda exhorted contemporaries to avoid popular street celebrations by "watching jousts, bullfights, and tourneys from your terrace," many patricians took this advice quite seriously.[58] Beginning in the late sixteenth century, one finds numerous references to local dignitaries and notables observing public events from balconies or window tribunes (see Illustration 8). A rather crass example can be found in the registers of the *Bras Militar*, which note a Barcelonan's decision to

[58] *Escriu Andreu Martí Pineda.*

8

Silversmiths' *Fête* at the Royal Palace with Don Juan de Austria in Attendance (1677).
Engraving by Francesch Via.

add a balcony to his house immediately following his ennoblement as an honored citizen.[59]

In the climactic final pages of *Don Quijote*, the mad knight entered Barcelona on Midsummer's Day, always an occasion of high merriment and festive play. There he found hospitality in the palace of one D. Antonio Moreno, a "rich and intelligent gentleman." D. Antonio invited his celebrated guest to "show himself on a balcony giving onto one of the principal streets of the city, in sight of the populace."[60] In so doing he repeated the challenge extended to all nobles—to exhibit themselves to their fellows and to the lower classes, while maintaining sufficient distance from the latter. There, on the balcony, lay the security nurtured by distinction, and the power born of vigilance. For Don Quijote these qualities were but illusions, laid bare without pity shortly thereafter. For the ruling class of Barcelona, however, the immediate future held no such dramatic reproach.

[59] Pujades, *Dietari*, III, 218; Montfar, *Diario*, 7 April 1686; A.C.A./Gen. G-69, *Dietari del Bras Militar*, III, 18 Jan. 1683.

[60] *Don Quijote*, II, 62.

IX

CONCLUSION

The Barcelona elite cast *cultura* in a variety of roles, and, like all accomplished thespians, it changed costumes with ease. In the guise of formal education, "culture" was pressed into service to convert economic resources into professional identity, social prestige, and political influence. The ruling class also used it as a mythic schema to define and justify hierarchies of wealth, status, and power, thus laying the foundations for a new vision of aristocratic selfhood. Finally, patricians wielded *cultura* to delineate class boundaries within the larger pageant of urban society, much as a stage-manager would assign parts, hand out scripts, and block out the players' every move until the final curtain. Or such, at least, was their intention.

In the preceding pages I have placed overriding emphasis on the elite's manipulation of "culture" as a test separating high and low. In my view, this approach does justice to the remarkably instrumental way in which urban notables appropriated the concept to forge their collective identity. I have moreover argued that a notion of cultural distinction gradually won epistemological primacy in the elite's perception of contemporary social relations. *Cultura* did more than to envelop traditional inequalities in a new semantic. While providing a compelling *mythos* for the whole of the body social, it formed the core of a novel class consciousness.

To some the uncompromising dichotomy between "high" and "low" depicted above may seem overdrawn. Yet this starkly reductionist schema accurately reflects how the Barcelona ruling class construed the society over which it claimed power and pre-eminence. I was struck time and again during the course of my readings by the lack of mediating vision within the world-view of the privileged. Theirs was a universe admitting few ambiguities. No shaded lines blurred the boundaries of their mental maps.

Tracing the origins and chronology of the expanding role of *cultura* in the elite's articulation of social boundaries is a daunting task. Few historical records invite precise dating of the language of a collective world-view. It is nevertheless clear that the "rise" of the liberal professionals did much to bind the urban elite to learning and formal education. The conceptual schema separating high and low on the basis of the relative acquisition of *cultura* was in the first instance an ideology of upwardly mobile sectors within urban society. This proved most evident in the case of barristers' arguments for the noble status of their profession. Equally patent assertions of the power of "culture" to confer high social standing colored the biography of newly ennobled patricians like D. Pau Ignasi de Dalmases. An extensive program of artistic and literary patronage capped the rapid elevation of his family from provincial obscurity to the center of the Barcelona elite. As we have seen, Dalmases' projects included remodelling a lavish palace on the Carrer de Montcada, long the preferred residential quarter of the city's mercantile *nouveaux riches*. He moreover accompanied this renovation with the flood of scholarly activity that culminated in the founding of the *Desconfiats* Academy in his own library—a collection graced by numerous genealogies, noble chronicles, and heraldic treatises.[1]

It would nevertheless be a fundamental mistake to reduce

---

[1] "Biblioteca Dalmases." Unfortunately, the terseness of local notarial records has frustrated study of aristocratic ownership of books. Many early modern inventories give full titles only for the professional libraries of lawyers and physicians. It is not unusual to find a nobleman's library summarily described as "one hundred fifteen small and large history books by diverse authors" (1694 inventory of D. Josep Pons de Çacosta i Castellví, in A.H.P.B./Vicente Gavarro menor, *Lib. Invent. Almon. 1689-1706*, no. 19).

the functions of learned "culture" to an apologia for the upwardly ascendent. Mechanistic interpretations of this sort fail to
account for a far more significant pattern of change—the coalescence of a new, unified ruling class. The adoption by all urban
notables of an ideal of *cultura* depended ultimately on the transformation of the existing nobility. After all, the leading role in
local literary and artistic patronage was assumed by the peerage,
a group whose social standing could hardly be impugned. Titled
aristocrats like the Cardona, Requesens, Montcada, Rocabertí,
and Pinós proved the most assiduous Catalan supporters of
learning and the fine arts both within the Principality and beyond its confines. At the same time, individual members of these
families contributed significantly to the literary corpus of the
Siglo de Oro.[2] These were obviously not parvenus making their
way up in society through the visible display of "culture."
Rather, one finds more fitting analogues among the characters of
works like *The Book of the Courtier*, which depicted nobles groping
about for new public roles in the wake of the dramatic changes
of the later Middle Ages. The authorship in 1671 of a treatise
on military geometry by D. Pedro Antonio Ramón Folch de
Cardona—the last direct male descendant of his lineage—symbolized the new route taken by these aristocrats. The contrast
between the mastery of intricate mathematical formulae shown
in this work and the well-known anecdotes of the rude and unlettered Cardona nobles of the thirteenth century reveals this
family's degree of adaptability.[3] Theirs was clearly a change en-
suring that all other things would remain the same.

History provided the ground of learning most frequently
cultivated by both old and new notables. There lawyers and
peers met on equal footing, with the professional demands on

[2] See, for example, Rubió Balaguer, *Cardona*.

[3] Cardona, *Geometría Militar*. The inventory of the magnificent library he do-
nated to the monastery of Poblet is found in B.P.T./Ms. 220. Valls Taverner
remarked the proverbial ignorance of Cardona's medieval forebears in his "Abogados," 306-309. Other references to the lack of letters among fifteenth-century
Spanish nobles are found in Russell, "Arms versus Letters."

the former matching in intensity the personal and familial interests (and vanities) of the latter. The noble chroniclers D. Ramon
Dalmau de Rocabertí, his distant cousin D. Diego de Rocabertí,
and D. Francesch de Montcada shared a common devotion to
historical erudition with jurists like Jeroni Pujades and Diego
Montfar i Sorts.⁴ Yet, in citing these particular examples, I do
not wish to imply that there were no "cultivated" aristocrats in
Catalonia prior to the seventeenth century. The careers of sixteenth-century nobles like the jurist Antoni Agustí, the *militar*
Francesch Calça, and of the honored citizens Joan Boscà, Guillem de Santcliment, and Galceran Albanell clearly belie any
such interpretation.⁵ Nor would I affirm that all subsequent urban nobles followed in the footsteps of such learned individuals.
To the contrary, I have tried to show that although the topoi of
formal education figured prominently in expressions of aristocratic *cultura*, nobles did not articulate their sense of identity
exclusively through the language of erudition. Their collective
world-view also found expression in a distinctive style of life
which embraced spheres as diverse as language, speech, gestures, leisure habits, and festive behavior. Few early modern
Barcelonan nobles resembled Signor Pococurante, the weary
Venetian aristocrat whose asphyxiating erudition and refinement

---

⁴ Ramon Dalmau's *Discurso Apologético* of 1647 displayed an impressive range
of legal and historical erudition, particularly in Latin and Italian. He also au-
thored a history of the *Casa de los Condes de Peralada* (Madrid, 1651). D. Diego de
Rocabertí edited his rhymed *Epítome Histórico* in 1626; two years later he compiled a lengthy family history (*Genealogía de la Casa de Rocabertí*, ms. in the Biblioteca del Palau de Peralada). D. Francesch de Montcada, Marquis of Aytona,
won acclaim for his Sallustian *Expedición de los Catalanes* of 1623. Diego Montfar
i Sorts, an honored citizen of Barcelona and author of numerous works on Catalan history, owned a personal library of over one thousand books: B.N./Ms.
9342, *Oratio Cujus Auctor fuit Salvator Bofill Rhetoricae Barcinonae Cathedraticus*
(1612), 10r. Pujades, the official chronicler of the Principality, edited the first
part of his chronicle of Catalonia in 1609. Interestingly, the few owners of historical books found in Carme Batlle's survey of fifteenth-century Barcelona libraries were almost all members of the urban elite (Batlle, "Bibliotecas").

⁵ Zulueta, *Don Antonio Agustín*; Calça, *De Catalonia*; San Clemente (Sant Cli-
ment), *Correspondencia Inédita*; and the entries in the *Gran Enciclopèdia Catalana*
under these names.

Voltaire satirized so brilliantly.[6] More typical were the examples of Creixell and Maldà—enthusiastic participants in aristocratic rituals and entertainments, seldom prone to displays of bookish learning, yet ever mindful of the ways in which their existence had been effectively walled off from the customs and beliefs of the "lower" orders.

The neo-foral period in particular witnessed the extension of *cultura* from the preserve of isolated individuals to the ruling class as a whole. The political stability beginning in this era—interrupted only briefly during the first two decades of the following century—encouraged a decisive shift in the attitudes and behavior of the local ruling class. Growing aristocratic exclusivism accompanied the urban elite's waning enthusiasm for politics. Meanwhile, increased theatricality on the part of an upper class retreating into the confines of its palaces compensated for and ultimately contributed to the atrophy of traditional communal celebrations.

Later centuries would enhance and even transform the public functions of elite "culture." The channels of access to the ruling class through education would undergo expansion, while the turn to romanticism led attitudes toward certain hitherto-denigrated qualities like "passion" to suffer a reversal during the nineteenth century. Nevertheless, the overall schema of cultural distinction has persisted to the present day as a mythic explanation for the existence of political and social inequality. In searching for the origins of this familiar structure of domination, we might well consider the tale told herein. In the words of Prospero: "What seest thou else in the dark backward and abysm of time? If thou rememb'rest aught ere thou cam'st here, how thou cam'st here thou mayst."

---

[6] *Candide*, Chapter 25. One is reminded of Casanova's ironic aside: "I also met at Gorice a Count Coronimi, who was known in learned circles as the author of some Latin treatises on diplomacy. Nobody read his books, but everyone agreed he was a very learned man" (*Memoirs*, VI, 576).

THE PLACE OF
BARCELONA

Two perspectives offered themselves to travellers approaching early modern Barcelona. Foreign visitors often had their first glimpse of the city as they entered its port. Others journeying along the inland roads paused on the slopes of Montjuïch, the prominence to the southwest towering over the royal highway to Castile. Both of the vantage-points revealed a city enclosed, even turned upon itself by tall and majestic walls. The nearby mountains and hills seemed to isolate Barcelona from the peninsula. In like manner, the broad expanse of water beyond its seawall evoked a sense of separation from the rest of the world. Such prospects were, of course, highly distorting. Barcelona maintained close ties not only with the surrounding countryside but also with cities throughout the Mediterranean. Still, we would do well to pause and consider Barcelona's place within the larger European context. By re-examining the city within a wider framework, a clearer image comes into focus. We see immediately that the historical developments treated in this book are to a certain degree familiar to all students of the period. Neither the "rise of oligarchy" nor the "redefinition of nobility" should prove much of a revelation to historians used to treasonous bourgeois or aristocrats in crisis. Still relatively unexplored, however, is the range of modes of oligarchical control prevailing in European cities during the early modern era—hence the value of case-studies of individual polities. When inserted within the broader context of comparative urban history, the specific experience of Barcelona can illumine the evolution of social, economic, and political structures throughout the continent.

At least two distinct types of civic rule can be identified in early modern Europe. First, both chronologically and conceptually, lies the route taken by the pioneer of oligarchical control, Venice. There a *serrata*—literally, a "closing-off"—dramatically curtailed access to its ruling class. Beginning in the late thirteenth century, commoners were formally denied participation in local government. A closed, hereditary patriciate devised a series of intricate institutional formulae to ensure its exclusive rule over the polity. Future absorption of newcomers into this unitary "old nobility" occurred only rarely. Even then such dilution did little to alter the composition of the city's ruling class or to disturb its proverbial stability.[1]

The experience of Venice's most powerful rival, Genoa, offers some illustrative points of comparison. The uncertain institutional definition of its elite prior to the seventeenth century contrasted sharply with the high degree of articulation marking the Venetian patriciate. To be sure, both cities reserved their governance to members of the nobility. The Genoese regime further imitated Venice by excluding commoners from high office in 1528, and by barring liberal professionals from the civic aristocracy. Yet Genoa's inability to achieve consensus on the public definition of *nobilitas*—and thus of membership in the ruling class—led to chronic instability. Two contending groups of nobles, the *vecchi* and *nuovi*, vied for political preeminence. Failure to integrate aspiring newcomers into the patriciate erupted into overt constitutional crisis in the mid-1570s. Persistent division within the governing class thus permitted the artisans and

---

[1] Useful summaries of Venetian civic institutions are found in Finlay, *Politics in Renaissance Venice*, Chapters 1-3; Bertelli, *Potere Oligarchico*; and Muir, *Civic Ritual*, I. My analysis of class relations in early modern cities owes much to Brian Pullan's suggestive *Rich and Poor in Renaissance Venice*.

merchants excluded in the *serrata* of 1528 a dramatic if brief re-entry into the political arena. A compromise was finally reached by which the newer nobles forsook their temporary alliance with the *popolo* for promises of fuller integration into the urban aristocracy. The path to more regular ennoblement was also cleared of some of its obstacles. As a result, a more generic "class of power" emerged, determined to avoid repetition of factional strife within the governing elite.[2]

This tale of two cities reveals a balance of conditions influencing the common link between stability and elite hegemony. Venice achieved a high degree of stasis after establishing a sharply defined hereditary nobility, closing off access to its ruling class, and excluding the "lower" classes from participation in politics. Genoa, on the other hand, while similarly denying political rights to merchants and artisans, nevertheless fell victim to turmoil because of its nobility's very lack of definition. Ultimate resolution of the question of the admission of newcomers finally permitted the urban elite a taste of the *pax civitatis* enjoyed by its venerable rival. In the long run, the Venetian and Genoese patriciates achieved the common goal of stability by firmly excluding the subaltern classes from municipal government. Moreover, elite hegemony had external as well as internal consequences, in that both *serrate* generated sufficient political unity to preserve the cities' independence from larger territorial states until the Napoleonic era.

The Barcelona regime exemplifies an alternative approach to forging political and social stasis. There the full integration of old and new nobles, the opening of institutional channels for the regular absorption of commoners into the elite, and the continued, even augmented, political representation of a significant proportion of the "lower" classes preserved the civic peace. Barcelona achieved its impressive stability in the aftermath of the

---

[2] Grendi, "Esempio di Arcaismo Politico," and "Capitazioni e Nobiltà Genovese." For the 1570s crisis, in particular, see Savelli, *Repubblica Oligarchica.*

218

revolutionary turmoil of the late fourteenth and fifteenth centuries. As we have seen, the reforms of 1490-1510 ended the unrest by merging the citizen oligarchy with the local gentry to produce a new, unified ruling class. By redefining its membership to include all urban notables, and by inventing new patterns of institutional articulation, Barcelona's elite deliberately turned its back upon the divisions and rivalries that had previously undermined its authority. Another important aspect of its recomposition was the creation of well-defined channels of social mobility. The new regime did not close off entry to the ruling class. Rather, the Barcelona elite neutralized longstanding social tensions by finding open, visible means for the gradual promotion of commoners into its ranks. Thus, by providing substantial opportunities for individual mobility, the reforms expanded the breadth of aristocratic identity while discouraging cleavages and factionalism within the governing class.

Also contributing to the success of this formula was the concession of significant—if strictly delimited—political rights to citizens outside the ruling class. As in the case of the recomposition of the urban elite, political reform resulted from a shrewd and objective appraisal of recent history. Both the monarch and his supporters recognized that the exclusionary policies of the oligarchy had been the leading cause of lower-class discontent. In stark contrast to the honored citizens' earlier monopoly over civic authority, individual merchants and master artisans now shared well-defined public roles within a limited condominium of power and prestige. The imposition of a more broadly based system of office-holding within the reformed polity nevertheless merely spread the burden of responsibility without diluting the principle—and practice—of elite hegemony.

The expansion of artisan representation in 1641 through the addition of a sixth permanent *menestral* Councillor highlights the uniqueness of Barcelona within the peninsular context.[3] Few cit-

---

[3] I discuss the political controversy surrounding the creation of the Sixth

ies outside the Principality allowed tenure of high office by merchants and craftsmen. To the contrary: beginning in the later Middle Ages, most Iberian towns deliberately excluded the middle and lower classes from their governments. After 1321, only honored citizens and gentlemen could hope to become *jurats* in Valencia. Saragossa formally excluded the few merchants and guild masters still serving as magistrates in 1561. Artisans had even poorer luck in Castile, where urban oligarchies and royal officials reserved seats on city councils to a hereditary caste of *regidores*, most of noble extraction. As a consequence, upward mobility from the lower ranks—even through the familiar channel of the liberal professions—was far less in evidence.[4]

Barcelona's unique position among Iberian cities, however, does not mean that it lacked analogues elsewhere in Europe. The political representation of artisans and merchants also characterized the *Kleinstädte* or "home towns" of the Empire and Switzerland. There municipal governments still accorded substantial voice to craft corporations and other spokesmen for the "middling classes."[5] Their "freedom and good government" delighted closet republicans like Montaigne, who took "infinite pleasure" in seeing the local innkeeper "return from a meeting of the town Council, held in a very magnificent gilded palace, where he had been presiding, to serve his guests at the table."[6] Guild repre-

---

Councillor in my "Oligarquia Ciutadana," 16-19. The Municipal History Museum of Barcelona contains an anonymous portrait of the shoemaker Joseph Torner, Sixth Councillor in 1671 and 1676. Its present unrestored condition prevented its reproduction in this book.

[4] Lapeyre, "Organisation Municipale de Valence," 128-129; Falcón Pérez, *Organización Municipal*, 271; Redondo Veintemillas, *Corporaciones de Artesanos*, 152; and Lunenfeld, "Governing the Cities" (although cf. González Alonso, "Sociedad Urbana"). One apparent exception to this rule was Lisbon, where a special *juiz do povo* represented popular interests (Hanson, *Economy and Society*, 51-55).

[5] Walker, *German Home Towns*, I; Soliday, *Community in Conflict*; Berengo, "Città del Antico Regime," 666-680; and Howell, "Late Medieval and Early Modern City," 12. (Yet cf. Friedrichs, *Urban Society*, 170-179, for the virtual elimination of craftsmen from the Nördlingen city Council during the seventeenth century).

[6] *Montaigne's Travel Journal*, 13. The town he visited was Mulhouse, in the canton of Basel.

sentation also persisted in certain Dutch cities like Leiden, where the tenacious defense of corporate privilege offset declining productivity in urban cloth industries.[7] The special achievement of cities like Barcelona was thus to reshape and fortify their ruling classes within polities that still accorded significant political rights and privileges to citizens outside the elite.

The persistent strength of corporate social and economic structures contributed to political anachronism as well. Not surprisingly, the Barcelona model—what we could label "qualified oligarchy" or "incomplete elitism"—prospered most in towns and cities enjoying a fair measure of civic autonomy. "Corporatist" politics proved much more vulnerable in cities like Florence, which by the sixteenth century had succumbed to the ruthless attentions of modernizing central states.[8] The weakness (or absence) of crown authority in areas like Catalonia, the Empire, and Switzerland allowed their "archaic" civic structures to find shelter under the sturdy umbrella of local constitutionalism. In the Catalan case, the tendency toward effective municipal independence was especially apparent in the matter of royal taxation. During the seventeenth century, Catalan town-dwellers paid far less in crown assessments than their counterparts in Castile. In fact, most royal officials showed reluctance to tamper with longstanding institutional arrangements like the *de facto* autonomy enjoyed by Catalan cities. These and other features distinguished Barcelona from municipalities within centralized states like France, Castile, and Tuscany, where fewer safeguards protected urban corporations from royal interference.[9]

In sum: the reforms of 1490-1510 set the stage for the emergence of a cohesive yet relatively open urban elite. While the merger of Barcelona's oligarchy with the traditional aristocracy

[7] DuPlessis and Howell, "Reconsidering the Early Modern Urban Economy."

[8] Najemy, *Corporatism and Consensus*.

[9] See, for example, Benedict, *Rouen*, 31-45; and Brown, *Shadow of Florence*, 177. Significantly, officials of the Council of Aragon in Madrid regarded cities with popular representation as "most difficult" because of their greater likelihood to vote against tax levies: Gil Pujol, "Cortes de Aragón de 1626," 97-98.

was, by Iberian standards, rather precocious, it did not lack precedents elsewhere, especially among city-states in northern Italy.[10] Moreover, a compromise was reached by which merchants and craftsmen won continued representation in high office as well as on intermediate and lower bodies like the Council of the Hundred. This seeming "archaism" marked the outer limits to the social and cultural separation examined in the course of this book.

Only a large measure of self-assurance enabled Barcelona's patricians to respect the rules of such a game. Much more needs to be known about charity, criminal justice, and the administration of the city's food supply, as well as the elite's attitudes toward poverty and other social problems, before we can identify the precise sources of local stability. For the moment, the ease of access to the governing class and the emergence of a well-defined patrician identity appear to be the principal causes—and consequences—of elite hegemony. Thanks to them, no proud Coriolanus, too absolute a noble to plead in the marketplace, threatened Barcelona. Rather, the city's peace rested on the prudent restraints its ruling class placed upon prerogative. Perhaps the confidence born of this firm grip on power best explains why, atop the lofty citadel of the elite's world-view, doubting words were rarely spoken.

[10] Berengo, "Città Italiana."

BIBLIOGRAPHY

Only works cited in this book are included here; a more systematic list of sources and bibliography by subject can be found in Amelang, "Honored Citizens," 425-460. Place of publication is Barcelona unless otherwise noted.

ABBREVIATIONS

A.H.R.	*American Historical Review* (Bloomington)
A.S.T.	*Analecta Sacra Tarraconensia*
B.R.A.B.L.B.	*Boletín de la Real Academia de Buenas Letras de Barcelona*
E.H.D.A.P.	*Estudis Històrics i Documents dels Arxius de Protocols*
J.I.H.	*Journal of Interdisciplinary History* (Cambridge, Ma.)
J.M.H.	*Journal of Modern History* (Chicago)
P.P.	*Past and Present* (Oxford)
Q.S.	*Quaderni Storici* (Ancona-Bologna)
Vicens	*Homenaje a Jaime Vicens Vives* (1965-1967), 2 vols.

Primary Sources

Advertiments . . . Govern Polítich . . . de la Pest (1652)

Alciati, A., *Emblemata* (1531?). Spanish translation *Emblemas*, trans. B. Daza, ed. M. Montero Vallejo (Madrid, 1975)

Amargòs, A., *Relació de la Solemne Professó . . . per la Canonització de St. Ramon de Penyafort* (1601)

Amat de Planella, J., ed., *Nenias Reales y Lágrimas Obsequiosas* (1701)

Amigant, J. de, *Discurso . . . del Privilegio del Noble* (1670)

Armonia del Parnàs (1703)

Avilés, J. de, *Ciencia Heroyca* (1725), 2 vols.

Bartoli, D., *L'Uomo di Lettere Difeso* (Rome, 1645). English edition *The Learned Man Defended and Reformed*, trans. T. Salusbury (London, 1660).

Baucells, F., *Font Mystica* (1704)

Bisbe Vidal, F., *Tratado de las Comedias* (1618)

Boscà [Boscán], J., *Los Cuatro Libros del Cortesano*, ed. A. M. Fabié (Madrid, 1873)

Bosch, A., *Summari Índex o Epitome dels Títols de Honor de Cathalunya, Rosselló, y Cerdanya* (Perpignan, 1628)

Botero, G., *The Reason of State*, ed. D. P. Waley (New Haven, 1956)

Bru, I. de, *Oración . . . Colegio de Cordelles* (1661)

Bruniquer, E. G., *Rúbriques . . . Ceremonial dels Magnìfics Consellers y Regiment de la Ciutat de Barcelona* (1912-1916), 5 vols.

Calça, F., *De Catalonia* (1588)

Calderó, M. de, *Canción Real a la Sabia y Noble Congregación . . . de María* (1699)

Camós i de Requesens, M. A., *Microcosmia y Gobierno Universal del Hombre Christiano* (1592), 2 vols.

Capmany, A. de, *Filosofía de la Eloquencia* (Madrid, 1777)

———, *Memorias Históricas sobre la Antigua Ciudad de Barcelona*, ed. E. Giralt and C. Batlle (1961-63), 3 vols.

Cartas del Emperador Carlos V a la Ciudad de Barcelona, ed. P. Voltes Bou (1958)

Casanova, J., *Memoirs*, trans. and ed. H. Machen (New York, 1961), 12 vols.

Ciruelo, P., *Tratado en el Qual se Reprueban Todas las Supersticiones y Hechizerías* (1628)

Coluccio Salutati, *De Nobilitate Legum et Medicinae*, ed. E. Garin (Florence, 1947)

Constitutions y Altres Drets de Cathalunya (1704)

Constituciones del Imperial y Real Seminario de Nobles de Barcelona . . . de Cordelles (1763)

Les Corts Generals de Pau Claris, ed. B. de Rubí (1976)

Covarrubias, S. de, *Tesoro de la Lengua Castellana o Española*, ed. M. de Riquer (1943; reprint of 1611 edition, with additions from 1674)

Dalmases, P. I. de, *Disertación Histórica . . . la Patria de Paulo Orosio* (1702)

Dalmau, J., *Memorial sobre lo Mayor Dret Han de Pagar les Mercaderies que serà de Forasters* (1620)

Dança Momería, Hecha por los Cavalleros Franceses . . . Intitulada la Revolución del Siglo (1644)

Della Casa, G., *Galateo*, trans. R.S. Pine-Coffin (Harmondsworth, 1958)

Domenech, V., *Discurso sobre las Obligaciones del Abogado* (1779)

Doms, M., *Orde de Batalla o Breu Compendi Militar* (1643)

Dromendari, J., *Arbol Genealógico . . . de Rocabertí* (Genoa, 1676)

Epistolari del Renaixement, ed. M. Cahner (Valencia, 1978), 2 vols.

Escriu Andreu Martí Pineda a son Gran Amich Novament Casat (Valencia, s.d., mid-16th century)

Feliu de la Penya, N., *Político Discurso . . . El Sobrado Trato y Uso de Algunas Ropas Estrangeras* (1681)

——, *Fénix de Cataluña: Compendio de sus Antiguas Grandezas* (1683) [published under the name of "Martín Piles, Mercader"]

Fernández de Heredia, J., *Obras*, ed. R. Ferreres (Madrid, 1955)

Ferrer, M., *Método y Art Molt Breu en Romans i Molt Clar per a Aprendrer La Gramàtica de la Llengua Llatina* (Lleida, 1578)

Festiva Sagrada . . . Colegio de Belén (1696)

[Folch de] Cardona, P.A.R., *Geometría Militar* (Naples, 1671)

Fontanella, J. P., *Tractactus de Pactis Nuptialibus* (1612)

——, *Sacri Regii Senatus Cathaloniae Decisiones* (Lyon, 1668²)

Fossa, F., *Mémoire . . . sur la Prétendue Noblesse des Bourgeois Majeurs de Perpignan et de Barcelone* (Toulouse, 1777)

Garau, F., *El Sabio Instruido en la Gracia* (1688)

Garzoni, T., *Theatro de' Vari e Diversi Cervelli Mondani* (Venice, 1583)

Garzoni, T., *Plaza Universal de Todas Ciencias y Artes*, ed. C. Suárez de Figueroa (Perpignan, 1630)

Gil, P., *Memorial de Manaments y Advertències* (1598) [published under the name of J. D. Loris, Bishop of Barcelona]

Gilabert, F. de, *Discurso sobre la Fuente de la Verdadera Nobleza* (Lleida, 1616)

Gracián, B., *Obras Completas*, ed. A. del Hoyo (Madrid, 1960)

Gracián Dantisco, L., *El Galateo Español*, ed. M. Morreale (Madrid, 1967)

Guicciardini, F., *Diario del Viaggio in Spagna*, ed. P. Guicciardini (Florence, 1932)

Gurrea, D. de, *Arte de Enseñar Hijos de Príncipes y Señores* (Lleida, 1627)

Huarte de San Juan, J., *Examen de Ingenios*, ed. E. Torre (Madrid, 1976)

Iusta de Ingenios. Certamen que Propone el Colegio de Belén de la Compañía de Jesús (1673)

Jorba, D. H. de, *Descripción de las Excelencias de la muy Insigne Ciudad de Barcelona* (1589)

Julià, N., *Oración Fúnebre . . . Doña Catalina Antonia Folch de Cardona* (Girona, 1698)

La Bruyère, J. de, *Oeuvres*, ed. G. Servois (Paris, 1878-1912), 5 vols.

Llull, R., *Doctrina Pueril*, ed. G. Schib (1972)

Lope de Vega, F. C., *Obras* (Madrid, 1930), 13 vols.

Loyseau, C., *Traité des Ordres et Simples Dignitez*, in his *Oeuvres* (Lyon, 1701), separate pagination

Madramany y Calatayud, M., *Tratado de la Nobleza de la Corona de Aragón* (Valencia, 1788)

Magarola, J. M. de, *El Abogado Perfecto* (1789)

Magestuosa Poética Fiesta . . . Palestra Literaria de . . . Barcelona (1700)

Memorias de la Real Academia de Buenas Letras de Barcelona, I (1756)

Mendo, A., *De Iure Academico* (Salamanca, 1665)

Mercader, J. *Oración Fúnebre . . . por la Real Academia de Buenas*

Letras . . . a la Memoria de su Presidente el . . . Conde de Peralada (1755)

Milán, L., *El Cortesano* (Madrid, 1874)

Miracle, P., *Llanto de los Hombres . . . Oración Fúnebre . . . D. Francisco de Moncada, Conde de Osona* (1699)

Montaigne's Travel Journal, ed. D. M. Frame (San Francisco, 1983)

Moncada, F. de, *Expedición de los Catalanes y Aragoneses Contra Turcos y Griegos* (1623)

Moreno, C., *Libro . . . Intitulado Claridad de Simples* (1586)

Muratori, L. A., *Opere*, ed. G. Falco and F. Forti (Milan-Naples, s.d.), 2 vols.

Muzio, G., *Il Gentiluomo . . . Tre Dialoghi* (Venice, 1571)

Núñez de Velasco, F., *Diálogos de Contención entre la Milicia y la Ciencia* (Valladolid, 1614)

Ordinacions de la Universitat de Barcelona (1596)

Ordinacions y Statuts del Bras Militar (1605)

Palmireno, L., *El Estudioso Cortesano* (Valencia, 1573)

———, *Vocabulario del Humanista* (1575²)

———, *El Latino de Repente* (1615)

Parer de Jaume Damians (1630)

Parets, M., "De los Muchos Sucesos Dignos de Memoria que Han Ocurrido en Barcelona y Otros Lugares de Cataluña," ed. C. Parpal Marqués, *Memorial Histórico Español*, vols. 20-25 (1888-1893)

Pau, J., *Barcino*, ed. J. M. Casas Homs (1957)

Pellegrini, M., *Fonti dell'Ingegno* (Bologna, 1650)

"La Península a Principios del S. XVII," ed. L. Sánchez Costa, *Revue Hispanique*, 35, 1915, 474–487 (edition of B.N./Ms. Q-44, *Floresta Española*)

Peralta, N., *Memorial en Favor de la Ordinación del Consejo de Ciento* (1620)

Pérez de Oliva, F., *Diálogo de la Dignidad del Hombre*, ed. J. L. Abellán (1967)

Pérez de Valdivia, D., *Plática . . . de Máscaras* (1618²)

Persio, A., *Trattato dell'Ingegno dell'Huomo* (Venice, 1576)

Pineda, J., *Diálogos Familiares de la Agricultura Christiana*, ed. J. Messeguer Fernández, in the *Biblioteca de Autores Españoles*, vols. 161-163 and 169-170 (1963-1964)

Platter, T., *Journal of a Younger Brother*, trans. S. Jennett (London, 1963)

Poggio Bracciolini, *Opera* (Basel, 1538; facsimile reprint Turin, 1964)

Potau, P. D., *Oración Fúnebre . . . D. Fernando Joaquín Fajardo de Requesens y Zúñiga, Marqués de los Vélez* (1694)

Pujades, J., *Dietari*, ed. J. M. Casas Homs (1975-1976), 4 vols.

————, *Coronica Universal del Principat de Cathalunya* (1609)

Pujol, J., *Obra Poètica*, ed. K. H. Anton (1970)

Quijano, G., *Vicio de las Tertulias* (1785)

Ratio Studiorum, ed. M. Salomone (Milan, 1979)

Reglas de Buena Crianza Civil y Christiana (1767)

Relación Verdadera de las Fiestas de Carnestoliendas en Agradecimiento de Verse a la Obediencia de Su Magestad Católica Reducida (1653)

Richelieu, A. du P., *Political Testament*, trans. H. B. Hill (Madison, 1968)

Ripoll, A. A. de, *Additiones ad Praxum Ludovici Paguera* (1648)

Rocabertí, D. de, *Epítome Histórico Compendiosíssimo . . . Las Cosas Más Notables Acaecidas en el Mundo desde su Principio . . .* (Palma de Mallorca, 1626)

Rocabertí, J. de, *Sermón Fúnebre . . . Doña María Teresa de Fajardo Requesens Zúñiga* (1715)

Rocabertí, H. de, *Tratados Espirituales* (1647), 2 vols.

Rocabertí, R. D. de, *Presagios Fatales del Mando Francés en Cataluña* (Saragossa, 1646)

————, *Discurso Apologético en Favor del Marqués de Aytona* (s.l., s.d.; Saragossa, 1647?)

Romaguera, J., *Atheneo de Grandesa Sobre Eminencia Culturas: Catalana Facundia ab Emblemas Illustrada* (1681)

Ros, A., *Cataluña Desengañada* (Naples, 1646)

Saavedra Fajardo, D. de, *Emblemas Políticas* (Munich, 1640)

Sagarriga, J. de, Count of Creixell, *Dietario de Barcelona 1767-77*, ed. C. Parpal Marqués (1907)

Sala, G., *Govern Polítich de la Ciutat de Barcelona* (1636)

San Clemente [Santcliment], G. de, *Correspondencia Inédita*, ed. Marquis of Ayerbe (Saragossa, 1892)

Sobrecasas, F., *Oración Fúnebre . . . D. Juan de Boxadors* (1676)

Soler, A., *Río del Parayso* (1629)

Soler, F., *Discurs ab lo Qual Entén Provar que no Convè nis pot en Casa de la Ciutat de Barcelona Admetre en son Regiment los qui tenen Nom de Don* (1621)

Tiraqueau, A., *Commentarii de Nobilitate* (Paris, 1543)

Tractats de Cavalleria, ed. P. Bohigas (1947)

Tristany, A., *Discurs de les Contrafactions . . . dels Mercaders Matriculats de Barcelona* (1650)

Valencià, L., *Illustración a la Constitución VII* (1674)

Valladares, G. de, *Promptuari de la Doctrina Christiana* (1786)

Vilaplana, A. de, *Tractatus de Brachio Militari* (1684²)

Vilaplana, J. C. de, *Discurso Panegírico . . . Santo Tomás de Aquino* (s.d.; 1695?)

Villena, E. de, *Los Doze Trabajos de Hércules*, ed. M. Morreale (Madrid, 1958)

Visitas de Gabriel Fideo a Francisco Arroz (1738)

Xammar, J. P., *Civilis Doctrina Civitatis Barchinonae* (1644)

(Abbé) Xaupí, *Recherches Historiques sur la Noblesse des Citoyens Honorés de Perpignan et de Barcelone* (Paris, 1763)

Secondary Sources

Accademie e Cultura: Aspetti Storici tra '600 e '700 (Florence, 1979)

Aguiló, M., *Catálogo de Obras en Lengua Catalana Impresas Desde 1474 Hasta 1860* (Madrid, 1923)

Agulhon, M., *Pénitents et Franc-Maçons de l'Ancienne Provence* (Paris, 1968)

Agulhon, M., *La Vie Sociale en Provence Intérieure au Lendemain de la Révolution* (Paris, 1970)

Ainaud, J., Gudiol, J., and Verrié, F.-P., *Catálogo Monumental de España: La Ciudad de Barcelona* (Madrid, 1947), 2 vols.

Alatri, P., "La Formazione della Élite nella Francia d'Ancien Régime," *Studi Storici*, 20, 1979, 59-74

Albareda, A. M., *Història de Montserrat*, ed. J. Massot Muntaner (Montserrat, 1972⁵)

Alcover, S. et al., *Diccionari Català-Valencià-Balear* (Palma de Mallorca, 1930-1968), 10 vols.

Alier, R., "La Vida Musical de Barcelona Vista a Través del *Calaix de Sastre* del Baró de Maldà," *Serra d'Or*, Feb. 1978, 51-55

———, *L'Òpera* (1979)

Almerich, L., *Tradiciones, Fiestas y Costumbres Populares en Barcelona* (1944)

Alós, J. M. de, "Disputa Sobre la Nobleza de los Ciudadanos Honrados de Barcelona," *Revista de Historia y Genealogía Española*, 2ª época, 4 (20), 1930, 186-200

Amades, J., *El Carnestoltes a Barcelona fins el S. XVIIIᵉ* (1934)

Amelang, J. S., "El Carrer de Montcada: Canvi Social i Cultura Popular a la Barcelona Moderna," *L'Avenç*, 18, 1979, 56-62

———, "Honored Citizens and Shameful Poor: Social and Cultural Change in Barcelona 1510-1714," Ph.D. dissertation, Princeton University, 1981

———, "The Purchase of Nobility in Castile 1552-1700: A Comment," *Journal of European Economic History*, 11, 1982, 219-226

———, "L'Oligarquia Ciutadana a la Barcelona Moderna: Una Aproximació Comparativa," *Recerques*, 13, 1983, 7-25

———, "Barristers and Judges in Early Modern Barcelona: The Rise of a Legal Elite," *A.H.R.*, 89, 1984, 1264-1284

———, "Public Ceremonies and Private *Fêtes*: Social Segregation and Aristocratic Culture in Early Modern Barcelona," in

G.W. McDonogh, ed., *Conflict in Catalonia: Images of Urban Society* (Gainesville, forthcoming)

———, "The Education of Joseph Faust de Potau," *Bulletin of Hispanic Studies* (forthcoming)

Amich, J., *Historia del Puerto de Barcelona* (1956)

Andreu, J., *Catálogo de una Colección de Impresos Referentes a Cataluña: S. XVI-XVII* (1902)

Anes, G., *Economía e Ilustración en la España del S. XVIII* (1969)

Arranz, M., "Los Profesionales de la Construcción en la Barcelona del S. XVIII," Ph.D. dissertation, University of Barcelona, 1979, 4 vols.

———, and Grau, R., "Problemas de Inmigración y Asimilación en la Barcelona del S. XVIII," *Revista de Geografía*, 4, 1970, 71-80

Arriaza, A., "Nobility in Renaissance Castile: The Formation of a Juristic Structure of Nobiliary Ideology," Ph.D. dissertation, University of Iowa, 1980

Asor Rosa, A., and Angelini, F., *Daniello Bartoli e i Prosatori Barocchi* (Rome-Bari, 1977)

Astraín, A., *Historia de la Compañía de Jesús en la Asistencia de España* (Madrid, 1902-1909), 7 vols.

Azcárate Ristori, I. de, "La Enseñanza Primaria en Barcelona: Educación de la Mujer," *Cuadernos de Arqueología e Historia de la Ciudad*, 10, 1969, 177-192

Bakhtin, M., *Rabelais and His World*, trans. H. Iswolsky (Cambridge, Ma., 1968)

Baron, H., *The Crisis of the Early Italian Renaissance* (Princeton, 1966)

Barraquer, C., *Las Casas de Religiosos en Cataluña Durante el Primer Tercio del S. XIX* (1906), 2 vols.

Bassegoda, B., *Santa Maria del Mar* (1927), 2 vols.

Bataillon, M., *Erasmo y España: Estudios Sobre la Historia Espiritual del S. XVI*, trans. A. Alatorre (Mexico, 1950)

Batlle, C., *La Crisis Social y Económica de Barcelona a Mediados del S. XV* (1973), 2 vols.

Batlle, C., "Las Bibliotecas de los Ciudadanos de Barcelona en el S. XV," in *Livre et Lecture en Espagne et France Sous l'Ancien Régime* (Paris, 1981), 15-34.

Bauman, Z., "Marxism and the Contemporary Theory of Culture," *Coexistence*, 5, 1968, 161-171

Beik, W., "Popular Culture and Elite Repression in Early Modern Europe," *J.I.H.*, 13, 1980, 97-103

Benedict, P., *Rouen During the Wars of Religion* (Cambridge, 1981)

Bennassar, B., *Valladolid au Siècle d'Or* (Paris-Hague, 1967)

Benveniste, E., "Civilisation: Contribution à l'Histoire du Mot," in *Eventail de l'Histoire Vivante* (Paris, 1953), I, 47-54

Berengo, M., *Nobili e Mercanti Nella Lucca del '500* (Turin, 1965)

———, "La Città del Antico Regime," *Q.S.*, 12, 1974, 661-692

———, "Città Italiana e Città Europea: Spunti Comparativi," in *La Demografia Storica Delle Città Italiane* (Bologna, 1982), 3-19

Bergeron, D. M., *English Civic Pageantry 1558-1642* (Columbia, S.C., 1971)

Bertelli, S., *Il Potere Oligarchico Nello Stato-Città Medievale* (Florence, 1978)

"La Biblioteca Dalmases," *Butlletí de la Biblioteca de Catalunya*, 3, 1916, 28-57

Bitton, D., *The French Nobility in Crisis 1560-1640* (Stanford, 1969)

Bofarull i de Sartorio, M., "Festejos y Ceremonias Públicas Celebradas en Barcelona . . . ," *Memorias de la Real Academia de Buenas Letras de Barcelona*, 2, 1856, 251-268

———, *Gremios y Cofradías de la Antigua Corona de Aragón*, in the *Colección de Documentos Inéditos del Archivo de la Corona de Aragón*, vols. 40-41 (1876)

Boiteux, M., "Carnaval Annexé: Essai de Lecture d'une Fête Romaine," *Annales E.S.C.*, 32, 1977, 356-380

Bonnassie, P., *La Organización del Trabajo en Barcelona a Fines del S. XV* (1975)

Borelli, G., "Il Problema dei Patriziati Urbani in Italia nell'Età Moderna," *Economia e Storia*, 25, 1978, 123-130

Borràs, A., "El Col.legi de Sta. Maria i de St. Jaume, dit Vulgarment de Cordelles," *A.S.T.*, 37, 1964, 399-461

———, "El Col.legi de Nobles de Barcelona durant el S. XVIII," in A. Manent et al, eds., *Contribució a l'Història de l'Església Catalana* (Montserrat, 1983), 51-89

Braudel, F. *The Mediterranean and the Mediterranean World in the Age of Philip II*, trans. S. Reynolds (New York, 1972), 2 vols.

Brejon, J., *André Tiraqueau* (Paris, 1957)

Brizzi, G. P., *La Formazione Della Classe Dirigente nel '600-'700* (Bologna, 1976)

———, ed., *La 'Ratio Studiorum': Modelli Culturali e Pratiche Educative dei Gesuiti in Italia tra '500 e '600* (Rome, 1981)

Brown, J., *Images and Ideas in Seventeenth-Century Spanish Painting* (Princeton, 1978)

Brown, J. C., *In the Shadow of Florence: Provincial Society in Renaissance Pescia* (Oxford, 1982)

Brunner, O., *Adeliges Landleben und Europäischer Geist* (Salzburg, 1949). Italian edition *Vita Nobiliare e Cultura Europea*, trans. G. Panzieri (Bologna, 1972)

Brunot, F., *Histoire de la Langue Française des Origines à Nos Jours* (Paris, 1966-72²), 13 vols.

Buratti, F. et al., *La Città Rituale: La Città e lo Stato di Milano nell' Epoca dei Borromeo* (Milan, 1982)

Burke, P., *Venice and Amsterdam: A Study of Seventeenth-Century Elites* (London, 1974)

———, *Popular Culture in Early Modern Europe* (New York, 1978)

———, "Languages and Anti-Languages in Early Modern Italy," *History Workshop*, 11, 1981, 24-32

———, "Conspicuous Consumption in Seventeenth-Century Italy," *Kwartalnik Historii Kultury Materialnej*, 1, 1982, 43-56

Cabestany, J.-F., "Aportación a la Nómina de los Ciudadanos

Honrados de Barcelona," *Documentos y Estudios del Instituto Municipal de Historia*, 10, 1962, 9-61

Canales, E., "Sobre Producció a la Comarca de La Selva: Les Torres de Cartellà 1616-1859," *Estudis d'Història Agrària*, 1, 1978, 154-178

Carreras Bulbena, J. R., "Constitució i Actes Conservades en l'Acadèmia Desconfiada," *B.R.A.B.L.B.*, 10, 1922, 225ff.

————, "Estudis Biogràfichs d'Alguns Benemèrits Patricis," *ibid.*, 23, 1927, 179ff.

Carreras Candi, F., *Geografia General de Catalunya: La Ciutat de Barcelona* (1916)

Carrère, C., *Barcelona 1380-1462: Un Centre Econòmic en Época de Crisi*, trans. H. Grau de Duran (1977-1978), 2 vols.

Casas Homs, J. M., "Les *Llaors* de Barcelona i Pere Joan Comes," *Cuadernos de Arqueologia e Historia de la Ciudad*, 10, 1967, 247-260

Casey, J., *The Kingdom of Valencia in the Seventeenth Century* (Cambridge, 1979)

Catálogo de la Colección de Folletos Bonsoms (1959-1962)

Chisick, H., *The Limits of Reform in the Enlightenment: Attitudes Toward the Education of the Lower Classes in Eighteenth-Century France* (Princeton, 1981)

Chojnacki, S., "Dowries and Kinsmen in Early Renaissance Venice," *J.I.H.*, 4, 1975, 571-600

Cipolla, C. M., "The Decline of Italy," *Economic History Review*, second series, 5, 1952-1953, 178-187

Clanchy, M. T., *From Memory to Written Record: England 1066-1307* (Cambridge, Ma., 1979)

Clark, P., "Migration in England During the late Seventeenth and Early Eighteenth Centuries," *P.P.*, 83, 1979, 57-90

Clements, R.J., *Picta Poesis: Literary and Humanistic Theory in Renaissance Emblem Books* (Rome, 1960)

Cochrane, E., *Tradition and Enlightenment in the Tuscan Academies 1690-1800* (Chicago, 1981)

Codina, J., *El Delta de Llobregat i Barcelona: Géneres i Formes de Vida dels S. XVI al XX* (1971)

Coll, J. M. "El Antiguo Mayor de S. Vicente Ferrer y S. Ramón de Peñafort de Barcelona," *A.S.T.*, 31, 1958, 139-146

Collell, A., "Fundación del Colegio de S. Vicente y de S. Raimundo de Barcelona," *ibid.*, 32, 1959, 309-330

Comas, A., *Història de la Literatura Catalana*, IV (1964)

Conde, R. and Tintó, M., "Projecte d'una Casa per als Sentmenat fet per Josep de Xuriguera," *Quaderns d'Arqueologia e Història de la Ciutat*, 18, 1980, 171-174

di Corcia, J., "Bourg, Bourgeois, Bourgeoisie de Paris from the Eleventh to the Eighteenth Centuries," *J.M.H.*, 50, 1978, 207-233

Corominas, J., and Pascual, J. A., *Diccionario Crítico Etimológico de la Lengua Castellana* (Madrid, 1980-), 4 vols. to date

Cortes, C., *Els Setantí* (1973)

Coveney, P. J., ed., *France in Crisis 1620-75* (London, 1977)

Curet, F., *Teatres Particulars a Barcelona en el S. XVIIIe* (1935)

——, *Història del Teatre Català* (1967)

Curtius, E. R., *European Literature and the Latin Middle Ages* (Princeton, 1973)

Dainville, F. de, *L'Éducation des Jésuites 16e-18e S.* (Paris, 1978)

Dantí, J., "La Revolta dels Gorretes a Catalunya, 1687-1689," *Estudis d'Història Agrària*, 3, 1979, 79-99

Davis, N. Z., *Society and Culture in Early Modern France* (Stanford, 1975)

Deacon, P., "El Cortejo y Nicolás Fernández de Moratín," *Boletín de la Biblioteca Menéndez y Pelayo*, 55, 1979, 85-93

Dewald, J., *The Formation of a Provincial Nobility: The Magistrates of the Parlement of Rouen 1499-1610* (Princeton, 1980)

Diccionari Biogràfic dels Catalans (1966-1970), 4 vols.

Dictionary of the History of Ideas, ed. P.P. Wiener (New York, 1968-1973), 4 vols.

Diefendorf, B. B., *Paris City Councillors in the Sixteenth Century: The Politics of Patrimony* (Princeton, 1982)

Domínguez Ortiz, A., *Las Clases Privilegiadas en la España del Antiguo Régimen* (Madrid, 1973)

Duby G., *The Chivalrous Society*, trans. C. Postan (Berkeley, 1977)

———, *The Three Orders: Feudal Society Imagined*, trans. A. Goldhammer (Chicago, 1980)

Dufourcq, C.-E., *L'Espagne Catalane et le Maghrib aux 13ᵉ et 14³ S.* (Paris, 1966)

DuPlessis, R. S. and Howell, M. C., "Reconsidering the Early Modern Urban Economy: The Cases of Leiden and Lille," *P.P.*, 94, 1982, 49-84

Duran Sanpere, A., *La Fiesta del Corpus* (1943)

———, *Barcelona i la Seva Història* (1973), 3 vols.

Elias, N., *The Civilizing Process I. A History of Manners*, trans. E. Jephcott (New York, 1978)

———, *The Court Society*, trans. E. Jephcott (New York, 1984)

Elliott, J. H., *The Revolt of the Catalans: A Study in the Decline of Spain, 1598-1640* (Cambridge, 1963)

———, "A Provincial Aristocracy: The Catalan Ruling Class in the Sixteenth and Seventeenth Centuries," *Vicens* (1967), II, 125-141

Emerson, R., "The Enlightenment and Social Structures," in P. Fritz and D. Williams, eds., *The City and Society in the Eighteenth Century* (Toronto, 1973), 99-124

Engell, J., *The Creative Imagination: Enlightenment to Romanticism* (Cambridge, Ma., 1982)

Evans, R.J.W., "Learned Societies in Germany in the Seventeenth Century," *European Studies Review*, 7, 1977, 129-151

Falcón Pérez, M. I., *Organización Municipal de Zaragoza en el S. XV* (Saragossa, 1978)

Fayard, J., *Les Membres du Conseil de Castille à l'Époque Moderne 1621-1746* (Geneva, 1979)

Febvre, L., "Civilization: Evolution of a Word and a Group of Ideas," in his *A New Kind of History and other Essays*, ed. P. Burke (New York, 1973), 219-257.

Figueres Martí, M. A., *Teatro Escolar Zaragozano: Las Escuelas Pías en el S. XVIII* (Saragossa, 1981)

Finlay, R., *Politics in Renaissance Venice* (New Brunswick, 1980)

Fluvià, A. de, "Las Categorías Nobiliarias y las Pruebas de Nobleza en el Principado de Cataluña," *Hidalguía*, 9, 1961, 661-668

————, "Títulos Nobiliarios Concedidos a Familias Catalanas," *Documentos y Estudios del Instituto Municipal de Historia*, 16, 1966, 7-55

Font Llagostera, M., "El Problema Triguero en Barcelona en la Epoca de Carlos V," *tesi de llicenciatura*, University of Barcelona, 1964

Fontana, J., "Sobre el Comercio Exterior de Barcelona a Mediados del S. XVII," *Estudios de Historia Moderna*, 5, 1955, 199-219

Friedrichs, C. R., *Urban Society in an Age of War: Nördlingen 1580-1720* (Princeton, 1979)

Fuster, J., *Heretgies, Revoltes i Sermons* (1968)

————, *Poetas, Moriscos y Curas* (Madrid, 1969)

Galasso, G., *Economia e Società Nella Calabria del '500* (Milan, 1975)

Galera, M., Roca, F., and Tarragó, S., *Atlas de Barcelona* (1982²)

Galí, A., *Rafael d'Amat, Baró de Maldà: L'Escriptor, L'Ambient* (1954)

Galinsky, G. K., *The Herakles Theme: The Adaptations of the Hero in Literature* (Oxford, 1972)

Gallego, J., *Visión y Símbolos en la Pintura Española del Siglo de Oro* (Madrid, 1984)

García Camarero, E. and E., eds., *La Polémica de la Ciencia Española* (Madrid, 1970)

García Cárcel, R., *Herejía y Sociedad en el S. XVI: La Inquisición en Valencia 1530-1609* (1980)

————, *Las Germanías de Valencia* (1981²)

————, and Nicolau, H., "Castella contra Catalunya: La Batalla Lingüística al S. XVII," *L'Avenç*, 22, 1979, 42-47

García Dini, E., "Pablo Ignacio de Dalmases y la Academia de los Desconfiados de Barcelona," *Miscelanea di Studi Spanici*, 1969-70, 199-260

García Panadés, J., *La Pedagogía Catalana del Antiguo Régimen* (1977)

Garin, E., *Prosatori Latini del '400* (Milan, s.d.)

———, *La Disputa delle Arti nel '400* (Florence, 1947)

———, *L'Educazione in Europa 1400-1600* (Bari, 1976²)

Giesey, R., "Rules of Inheritance and Strategies of Mobility in Pre-Revolutionary France," *A.H.R.*, 82, 1977, 271-289

Gil Pujol, X., "Las Cortes de Aragón de 1626," unpublished ms. of Ph.D. dissertation, 1984

Ginzburg, C., "High and Low: The Theme of Forbidden Knowledge in the Sixteenth and Seventeenth Centuries," *P.P.*, 73, 1976, 28-41

———, *The Cheese and the Worms: The Cosmos of a Sixteenth-Century Miller*, trans. J. and A. Tedeschi (Harmondsworth, 1982)

Giralt, E., "La Colonia Mercantil Francesa de Barcelona a Mediados del S. XVII," *Estudios de Historia Moderna*, 6, 1956, 215-278

———, "El Comercio Marítimo de Barcelona 1630-65: Hombres, Técnicas y Direcciones de Tráfico," Ph.D. dissertation, University of Barcelona, 1957

Giunta, F., *Aragonesi e Catalani nel Mediterraneo* (Palermo, 1953-1959), 2 vols.

Godelier, M., "Work and Its Representations: A Research Proposal," *History Workshop*, 10, 1982, 164-174

González Alonso, B., "Sociedad Urbana y Gobierno Municipal en Castilla 1450-1600," in his *Sobre el Estado y la Administración de la Corona de Castilla en el Antiguo Régimen* (Madrid, 1981), 57-84

Goody, J. R., ed., *Literacy in Traditional Societies* (Cambridge, 1968)

Goubert, P., *The Ancien Régime: French Society 1600-1750*, trans. S. Cox (New York, 1973)

Gran Enciclopèdia Catalana (1969-1980), 13 vols.

Grendi, E., "Le Compagnie del SS. Sacramento a Genova," *Annali della Facoltà di Giurisprudenza, Università di Genova*, 4, 1965, 454-480

——, "Un Esempio di Arcaismo Politico: Le Conventicole Nobiliare a Genova e la Riforma del 1528," *Rivista Storica Italiana*, 77, 1966, 948-968

——, "Capitazioni e Nobiltà Genovese in Età Moderna," *Q.S.*, 26, 1974, 403-444

——, "Le Confraternite Liguri in Età Moderna," in *La Liguria delle Casacce* (Genoa, 1982), 19-42

Gutiérrez, J., "Armas, Letras y Estoicismo en una Vida Española," *Dieciocho*, 2, 1979, 61-89

Hamscher, A. N., *The Parlement of Paris After the Fronde 1653-73* (Pittsburgh, 1976)

Hanson, C. A., *Economy and Society in Baroque Portugal 1668-1703* (Minneapolis, 1981)

Herman, J. B., *La Pédagogie des Jésuites au 16ᵉ S.* (Louvain, 1914)

Herrero Salgado, F., *Aportación Bibliográfica a la Oratoria Sagrada Española* (Madrid, 1971)

Hexter, J. H., "The Education of the Aristocracy in the Renaissance," in his *Reappraisals in History* (New York, 1969), 45-70

Hill, C., "The Many-Headed Monster in Later Tudor and Early Stuart Political Thinking," in C. H. Carter, ed., *From the Renaissance to the Reformation* (New York, 1965), 296-324

Hirschman, A. O., *The Passions and the Interests: Political Arguments for Capitalism Before its Triumph* (Princeton, 1977)

Hogden, M. T., *Early Anthropology in the Sixteenth and Seventeenth Centuries* (Philadelphia, 1964)

Holmes, G., *The Florentine Enlightenment 1400-1450* (New York, 1969)

——, "The Emergence of an Urban Ideology at Florence c. 1250-1450," *Transactions of the Royal Historical Society*, fifth series, 23, 1973, 111-134

Howell, M. C., "The Late Medieval and Early Modern City," *Trends in History*, 2, 1981, 5-17

Huizinga, J., *The Waning of the Middle Ages*, trans. F. Hopman (New York, 1954)

Huppert, G., "The Idea of Civilization in the Sixteenth Century," in A. Molho and J. Tedeschi, eds., *Renaissance Studies in Honor of Hans Baron* (Dekalb, 1971), 759-769

Huseman, W., "François de la Noue, la Dignité de l'Homme, et l'Institution des Enfants Nobles," *Bibliothèque d'Humanisme et de Renaissance*, 42, 1980, 7-26

Iglésies, J., *Estadístiques de Població de Catalunya: El Primer Vicenni del S. XVIII* (1974), 3 vols.

Iriarte, M. de, *El Doctor Huarte de San Juan y su Examen de Ingenios: Contribución a la Historia de la Psicología Diferencial* (Madrid, 1948)

Jouanna, A., *Ordre Social: Mythes et Hiérarchies dans la France du 16ᵉ S.* (Paris, 1977)

Jung, M. R., *Hércule dans la Littérature Française au 16ᵉ S.* (Geneva, 1966)

Junyent, E., "La Noblesa Vigatana en 1666," *Ausa*, 71-72, 1972, 41-42

Jutglar, A., "Notas para el Estudio de la Enseñanza en Barcelona hasta 1900," *Documentos y Estudios del Instituto Municipal de Historia*, 16, 1966, 283-419

Kagan, R. L., *Students and Society in Early Modern Spain* (Baltimore, 1974)

Kamen, H., "A Forgotten Insurrection of the Seventeenth Century: The Catalan Peasant Rising of 1688," *J.M.H.*, 49, 1977, 210-30

———, *Spain in the Later Seventeenth Century, 1665-1700* (London, 1980)

Kemp, M., "From *Mimesis* to *Fantasia*: The '400 Vocabulary of Creation, Inspiration, and Genius in the Creative Arts," *Viator*, 8, 1977, 347-397

King, W. F., *Prosa Novelística y Academias Literarias en el S. XVII*, trans. M. D. López (Madrid, 1963)

Klein, R., *Form and Meaning: Writings on the Renaissance and Modern Art*, trans. M. Jay and L. Wieseltier (Princeton, 1979)

Kroeber, A. L. and Kluckhorn, C., *Culture: A Critical Review of Concepts and Definitions* (New York, s.d.)

Kuhn, T. S., "Mathematical versus Experimental Traditions in the Development of Physical Science," *J.I.H.*, 7, 1976, 1-31

Labatut, J.-P., *Les Noblesses Européenes de la Fin du 15ᵉ S. à la Fin du 18ᵉ S.* (Paris, 1978)

Lalinde Abadía, J., *La Institución Virreinal en Cataluña* (1964)

Lapeyre, H., "L'Organisation Municipale de la Ville de Valence (Espagne) aux 16ᵉ et 17ᵉ S.," *Villes de l'Europe Mediterranéanne et de l'Europe Occidentale du Moyen Age au 19ᵉ S.* (Nice, 1969), 127-137

Leach, C. S., ed., *Memoirs of the Polish Baroque: The Writings of Jan Chryzostom Pasek* (Berkeley, 1976)

Le Roy Ladurie, E., *Carnival in Romans*, trans. M. Feeney (New York, 1979)

Liehr, R. *Sozialgeschichte Spanischer Adelskorpörationen: Die Maestranzas de Caballería 1670-1808* (Wiesbaden, 1981)

Lienhardt, G., *Social Anthropology* (Oxford, 1966)

Litchfield, R. B., "Demographic Characteristics of Florentine Patrician Families, Sixteenth to Nineteenth Centuries," *Journal of Economic History*, 29, 1969, 191-205

Lleó, V., *Nueva Roma: Mitología y Humanismo en el Renacimiento Sevillano* (Seville, 1979)

Llompart, G., "La Fiesta del Corpus Christi y Representaciones en Barcelona y Mallorca S. XIV-XVIII," *A.S.T.*, 28, 1955, 25-45

Lovejoy, A., *Essays in the History of Ideas* (Baltimore, 1948)

Lowinsky, E. F., *The Secret Chromatic Art of the Netherlands Motet*, trans. C. Buchman (New York, 1946)

241

Lukács, L., ed., *Monumenta Paedagogica Societatis Iesu* (Rome, 1965-1981), 4 vols.

Lunenfeld, M. L., "Governing the Cities of Isabella the Catholic: The *Corregidores*, Governors, and Assistants of Castile 1476-1504," *Journal of Urban History*, 9, 1982, 31-55

Madurell Marimon, J. M., *El Antiguo Comercio con las Islas Canarias y las Indias de Nueva España 1498-1638* (Madrid, 1961)

Magendie, M., *La Politesse Mondaine et les Thèories de l'Honnêteté en France, au 17e S., de 1600 à 1660* (Paris, s.d.)

Maltby, W. S., *Alba: A Biography of Fernando Alvarez de Toledo, Third Duke of Alba, 1507-1582* (Berkeley, 1983)

Maluquer Viladot, J., *Derecho Civil Especial de Barcelona y su Término* (1889)

Maravall, J. A., *Poder, Honor y Elites en el S. XVII* (Madrid, 1979)

Marrara, D., "Nobiltà Civica e Patriziato: Una Distinzione Terminologica nel Pensiero di Alcuni Autori Italiani nell'Età Moderna," *Annali della Scuola Normale Superiore di Pisa: Lettere e Filosofia*, third series, 10, 1980, 219-232

Marrou, H. I., *A History of Education in Antiquity*, trans. G. Lamb (New York, 1964)

Martín Gaite, C., *Usos Amorosos del Dieciocho Español* (Madrid, 1981)

Martinell, C., *Arquitectura i Escultura Barròques a Catalunya* (1961), 2 vols.

Martínez Shaw, C., "El Comercio Marítimo de Barcelona 1675-1712: Aproximación a Partir de las Escrituras de Seguros," *E.H.D.A.P.*, 6, 1978, 287-310

———, "Construcción Naval y Capital Mercantil: Mataró 1690-1709," *ibid.*, 8, 1980, 223-236

Mas, J., *Notícies Històriques del Bisbat de Barcelona* (1906), 14 vols.

Mas Givanel, J., *Una Mascarada Quixotesca Celebrada a Barcelona l'any 1633* (1915)

Maspons, F., *Nostre Dret Familiar* (1907)

Melis, F., *Mercaderes Italianos en España S. XIV-XVI* (Seville, 1976)

Mercader, J., *El Fin de la Insaculación Fernandina* (1963)
———, *Els Capitans Generals: S. XVIII* (1980²)
Mestre, A., *Despotismo e Ilustración en España* (1976)
Miret Sans, J., "Dos Siglos de Vida Académica," *B.R.A.B.L.B.*, 17, 1917, 11-32
Molas Ribalta, P., *Los Gremios Barceloneses del S. XVIII* (Madrid, 1970)
———, *Economia i Societat al S. XVIII* (1975)
———, *Comerç i Estructura Social a Catalunya i València als S. XVII i XVIII* (1977)
Moliné Brases, E., "La Acadèmia dels Desconfiats," *B.R.A.B.L.B.*, 17, 1917, 1-11
Mondolfo, R., "The Greek Attitude to Manual Labor," *P.P.*, 6, 1954, 1-5
———, *En los Orígenes de la Filosofía de la Cultura* (Buenos Aires, 1960²)
Montoto Valero, M. de, "La Cofradía de S. Jorge de la Ciudad de Gerona," *Hidalguía*, 11, 1963, 593-598
Morales Roca, F., "Privilegios Nobiliarios del Principado de Cataluña. Dinastía de Borbón 1700-1838," *Hidalguía*, 23, 1975 and 24, 1976
———, "Gobierno Intruso de Luis XIII y Luis XIV 1641-51," *ibid.*, 24, 1976 and 25, 1977
———, "Gobierno Intruso del Archiduque D. Carlos 1704-1714," *ibid.*, 25, 1978
———, "Dinastía de Austria. Reinado de Carlos II 1665-1700," *ibid.*, 27, 1979 and 28, 1980
Moravia, S., *La Scienza dell'Uomo nel '700* (Rome-Bari, 1978)
Morreale, M., "Coluccio Salutati's *De Laboribus Herculis* (1406) and Enrique de Villena's *Doze Trabajos de Hércules*," *Studies in Philology*, 51, 1954, 95-106
———, *Castiglione y Boscán: El Ideal Cortesano en el Renacimiento Español* (Madrid, 1959)
Morrill, J. S., "French Absolutism as Limited Monarchy," *The Historical Journal*, 21, 1978, 961-972

Mousnier, R., *Social Hierarchies 1450 to the Present*, trans. P. Evans and ed. M. Clark (New York, 1973)

——, *The Institutions of France under the Absolute Monarchy 1598-1789*, trans. B. Pearce (Chicago, 1979)

Muir, E., *Civic Ritual in Renaissance Venice* (Princeton, 1981)

Mullan, P. E., *La Congregazione Mariana Studiata nei Documenti* (Rome, 1911)

Nadal Farreres, J., *Dos Segles d'Oscuritat: XVI i XVII* (1979)

Nadal Oller, J., "La Contribution des Historiens Catalans à l'Histoire de la Démographie Générale," *Population*, 16, 1961, 91-101

——, *La Población Española: S. XVI-XX* (1976[4])

——, and Giralt, E., *La Population Catalane de 1553 à 1717: L'Immigration Française et les Autres Facteurs de son Développement* (Paris, 1960)

——, "Barcelona en 1717-18: Un Modelo de Sociedad Pre-Industrial," *Homenaje a D. Ramón Carande* (Madrid, 1963), II, 277-305

Nader, H., "Noble Income in Sixteenth-Century Castile: The Case of the Marquises of Mondéjar 1480-1580," *Economic History Review*, second series, 30, 1977, 411-428

Najemy, J. M., *Corporatism and Consensus in Florentine Electoral Politics 1280-1400* (Chapel Hill, 1982)

Niccoli, O., *I Sacerdoti, I Guerrieri, I Contadini: Storia di un'Immagine della Società* (Turin, 1979)

Nitzsche, J. C., *The Genius Figure in Antiquity and the Middle Ages* (New York, 1975)

Ocerín, E. de, "Cofradías Nobles de Valladolid," *Hidalguía*, 24, 1976, 369-378

Otte, E., "Los Comienzos del Comercio Catalán con América," *Vicens* (1967), II, 459-480

Palacio, J. M. de, "Contribución al Estudio de los Burgueses y Ciudadanos Honrados de Cataluña," *Hidalguía*, 5, 1957, 305ff.

Panofsky, E., *Hercules am Scheidewege* (Leipzig, 1930)

————, "Artist, Scientist, Genius: Notes on the Renaissance-Dämmerung," in W. F. Ferguson et al., *The Renaissance: Six Essays* (New York, 1962)

Panofsky, D., and Panofsky, E., *Pandora's Box* (Princeton, 1962²)

Payne, H. C., "Elite versus Popular Mentality in the Eighteenth Century," *Studies in the Eighteenth Century*, 8, 1979, 3-32

Pedlow, G. W., "Marriage, Family Size, and Inheritance among Hessian Nobles 1650-1900," *Journal of Family History*, 7, 1982, 333-352

Peláez, M. J., *Catalunya Després de la Guerra Civil del S. XV* (1980²)

Phillips, C. R., *Ciudad Real 1500-1750* (Cambridge, Ma., 1979)

Phythian-Adams, C., "Ceremony and the Citizen: The Communal Year in Coventry 1450-1550," in P. Clark, ed., *The Early Modern Town* (London, 1976), 106-128

Plantada, J., "El Concejo Catalán," *Hidalguía*, 17, 1969, 563-576

Pomata, G., *In Scienza e Coscienza: Donna e Potere nella Società Borghese* (Florence, 1979)

Pons, J.-S., *La Littérature Catalane en Roussillon au 17ᵉ et au 18ᵉ Siècle* (Toulouse-Paris, 1929)

Pullan, B., *Rich and Poor in Renaissance Venice: The Social Institutions of a Catholic State, to 1620* (Cambridge, Ma., 1971)

————, "The Occupations and Investments of the Venetian Nobility in the Middle and Late Sixteenth Century," in J. R. Hale, ed., *Renaissance Venice* (Totowa, N.J., 1973), 379-407

Q.S., 23, 1973 and 48, 1981—issues on early modern academies

Ràfols, J. F., *Pere Blay i l'Arquitectura del Renaixement a Catalunya* (1934)

Raimondi, E., *Letteratura Barocca: Studi sul '600 Italiano* (Florence, 1961)

Ramage, E. S., *Urbanitas: Ancient Sophistication and Refinement* (Norman, Ok., 1973)

Rapp, R. T., "The Unmaking of the Mediterranean Trade Hegemony: International Trade Rivalry and the Commercial Revolution," *Journal of Economic History*, 35, 1975, 499-525

Read, M., *Juan Huarte de San Juan* (Boston, 1981)

Redondo Veintemillas, G., *Las Corporaciones de Artesanos de Zaragoza en el S. XVII* (Saragossa, 1982)

Reglà, J., *Els Virreis de Catalunya* (1956)

———, "Notas Sobre la Política Municipal de Fernando el Católico en la Corona de Aragón," *Vicens* (1967), II, 521-532

———, *Historia de Cataluña* (Madrid, 1974)

Retali, Z., *Il Galateo di Giovanni Della Casa: Storia e Fortuna* (Pisa, 1896)

Riba García, C., *El Consejo Supremo de Aragón en el Reinado de Felipe II* (Valencia, 1914)

Richter, M., *Giovanni Della Casa in Francia nel S. XVI* (Rome, 1966)

———, "*Urbanitas-Rusticitas*: Linguistic Aspects of a Medieval Dichotomy," *Studies in Church History*, 16, 1979, 149-156

Riu, M., "Banking and Society in Late Medieval and Early Modern Aragon," in *The Dawn of Modern Banking* (New Haven, 1977), 131-167

Robles, L., *Las Academias de Valencia* (Valencia, 1979)

Roche, D., *Le Siècle des Lumières en Province: Académies et Académiciens Provinciaux 1680-1789* (Paris, 1978), 2 vols.

Rodríguez, L., "The Spanish Riots of 1766," *P.P.*, 59, 1973, 117-146

———, "The Riots of 1766 in Madrid," *European Studies Review*, 3, 1973, 223-242

Romano, R., "Tra XVI e XVII Secolo: Una Crisi Economica 1619-22," *Rivista Storica Italiana*, 74, 1962, 480-531

Ros Torner, A., *La Ribera de Barcelona* (1973)

Rossi, P., *Philosophy, Technology, and the Arts in the Early Modern Era*, trans. S. Attanasio (New York, 1970)

Rossich, A., *Una Poètica del Barroc: El Parnàs Català* (Girona, 1979)

Rubió Balaguer, J., *Els Cardona i les Lletres* (1957)

Rubió Borràs, M., *Motines y Algaradas de Estudiantes de Barcelona y Cervera* (1914)

Ruiz, T. F., "The Transformation of the Castilian Municipalities: The Case of Burgos 1248-1350," *P.P.*, 77, 1977, 3-32

Ruiz Martín, F., "Joan y Pau Saurí: Negociantes Catalanes que Intervienen en las Empresas Imperiales de Felipe II," in *Homenaje a Juan Reglà Campistol* (Valencia, 1975), I, 457-477

Russell, P. E., "Arms versus Letters: Toward a Definition of Spanish Fifteenth-Century Humanism," in A. R. Lewis, ed., *Aspects of the Renaissance* (Austin, 1967), 47-58

———, ed., *Spain: A Companion to Spanish Studies* (London, 1973)

Russo, V., "Cavalliers e Clercs," *Filologia Romanza*, 6, 1959, 305-332

Ryan, M. T., "Assimilating New Worlds in the Sixteenth and Seventeenth Centuries," *Comparative Studies in Society and History*, 23, 1981, 519-538

Saldoni, B., *Reseña Histórica de la Escolanía o Colegio de Música de . . . Montserrat* (Madrid, 1856)

Sales, N., "La Desaparición del Soldado Gentilhombre," in her *Sobre Esclavos, Reclutas y Mercaderes de Quintos* (1974), 7-56

Salmon, J.H.M., "Storm over the Noblesse," *J.M.H.*, 53, 1981, 242-257

Salvador, F. de, "El Real Cuerpo de la Nobleza, Antiguo Brazo Militar del Principado de Cataluña y Condados de Rosellón y de Cerdaña," *Hidalguía*, 5, 1957, 369-376

Sánchez, J., *Academias Literarias del Siglo de Oro Español* (Madrid, 1961)

Sánchez Pérez, A., *La Literatura Emblemática Española: S. XVI y XVII* (Madrid, 1977)

Sanpere Miquel, S., *Topografía Antigua de Barcelona: Rodalía de Corbera* (1890-1892), 2 vols.

Sarrailh, J., *L'Espagne Éclairée de la Seconde Moitié du 18ᵉ S.* (Paris, 1954)

Savelli, R., *La Repubblica Oligarchica: Legislazione, Istituzioni e Ceti a Genova nel '500* (Milan, 1981)

Sayous, A., *Els Mètodes Comercials a la Barcelona Moderna*, trans. A. García Sanz and G. Feliu Montfort (1975)

Schalk, E., "The Appearance and Reality of Nobility in France During the Wars of Religion," *J.M.H.*, 48, 1976, 19-31

Schnapper, B., *Les Rentes au 16ᵉ S.: Histoire d'Instrument de Crédit* (Paris, 1957)

Serra Puig, E., "La Societat Rural Catalana del S. XVII: Sentmenat, un Exemple Local del Vallès Occidental 1590-1729," Ph.D. dissertation, University of Barcelona, 1978

———, "Consideracions Entorn de la Producció i la Productivitat Agràries de la Catalunya del S. XVII," *Estudis d'Història Agrària*, 1, 1978, 120-153

———, "El Règim Feudal Català Abans i Després de la Sentència Arbitral de Guadalupe," *Recerques*, 10, 1980, 17-32

———, and Garrabou, R., "L'Agricoltura Catalana nei S. XVI-XX," *Studi Storici*, 21, 1980, 339-362

Sewell, Jr. W. H., "*État, Corps*, and *Ordre*: Some Notes on the Social Vocabulary of the French Old Regime," in H. U. Wehler, ed., *Sozialgeschichte Heute: Festschrift für Hans Rosenberg* (Göttingen, 1974), 49-88

———, *Work and Revolution in France: The Language of Labor from the Old Regime to 1848* (Cambridge, 1980)

Sharlin, A., "Natural Decrease in Early Modern Cities: A Reconsideration," *P.P.*, 79, 1978, 84-93

———, "From the Study of Social Mobility to the Study of Society," *American Journal of Sociology*, 85, 1979, 338-360

Simón Díaz, J., *Historia del Colegio Imperial de Madrid* (Madrid, 1952), 2 vols.

Skinner, Q., *The Foundations of Modern Political Thought* (Cambridge, 1978), 2 vols.

Smith, H. O., *Preaching in the Spanish Golden Age* (Oxford, 1978)

Smith, R. S., "Barcelona Bills of Mortality and Population 1457-1590," *Journal of Political Economy*, 44, 1936, 84-93

———, *The Spanish Guild Merchant: A History of the Consulado 1250-1700* (Durham, N.C., 1940)

Solà-Morales, J. M. de, *La Création de Noblesse Patricienne par Certains Conseils Municipaux de Catalogne* (Perpignan, s.d.)

Soldevila, F. de, *Barcelona Sense Universitat* (1938)
———, *Història de Catalunya* (1962-1963²), 3 vols.
Soliday, G. L., *A Community in Conflict: Frankfurt Society in the Seventeenth and Early Eighteenth Centuries* (Hanover, N.H., 1974)
Stone, L., "The Educational Revolution in England 1560-1640," *P.P.*, 28, 1964, 41-80
———, *The Crisis of the Aristocracy 1558-1641* (Oxford, 1965)
———, "Social Mobility in England 1500-1700," *P.P.*, 33, 1966, 16-55
———, *The Family, Sex, and Marriage in England 1500-1800* (New York, abridged edition 1979)
Strauss, G., *Nuremberg in the Sixteenth Century: City Politics and Life Between Middle Ages and Modern Times* (Bloomington, 1976²)
Subirá, J., *La Opera en los Teatros de Barcelona* (1946)
Summers, D., *Michelangelo and the Language of Art* (Princeton, 1981)
Tate, R. B., "Mythology in Spanish Historiography of the Middle Ages and the Renaissance," *Hispanic Review*, 22, 1954, 1-18
Taylor, G. V., "Non-Capitalist Wealth and the Origins of the French Revolution," *A.H.R.*, 72, 1966, 469-496
Tenenti, A., *Piracy and the Decline of Venice 1580-1615*, trans. J. and B. Pullan (Berkeley, 1967)
Thirsk, J., "Younger Sons in the Seventeenth Century," *History*, 54, 1969, 358-377
Thomas, K., *Religion and the Decline of Magic* (New York, 1971)
———, "The Place of Laughter in Tudor and Stuart England," *The London Times Literary Supplement*, Jan. 21, 1977, 77-81
Thompson, E. P., "Patrician Society, Plebeian Culture," *Journal of Social History*, 7, 1974, 382-405
———, "Eighteenth-Century English Society: Class Struggle without Class?", *Social History*, 3, 1978, 133-166

Thompson, I.A.A., "The Purchase of Nobility in Castile 1552-1700," *Journal of European Economic History*, 8, 1979, 313-360

Thorndike, L., "Medicine versus Law in Late Medieval and Medicean Florence," *Romanic Review*, 17, 1926, 8-31

Tintó, M., *Els Gremis a la Barcelona Medieval* (1978)

Torras Bages, J., *En Rocabertí i En Bossuet* (1898)

Torras Ribé, J. M., *Els Municipis Catalans de l'Antic Règim 1454-1808* (1983)

Tournier, M., "Le Vocabulaire de la Révolution: Pour un Inventaire Systématique des Textes," *Annales Historiques de la Révolution Française*, 195, 1969, 109-124

Treppo, M. del, *Els Mercaders Catalans i l'Expansió de la Corona Catalano-Aragonesa al S. XV*, trans. J. Riera Sans (1976)

Trexler, R. C., *Public Life in Renaissance Florence* (New York, 1980)

Turner, R. V., "The *Miles Literatus* in Twelfth- and Thirteenth-Century England: How Rare a Phenomenon?" *A.H.R.*, 83, 1978, 928-947

Ullman, B., *The Humanism of Coluccio Salutati* (Padua, 1963)

Usher, A. P., *The Early History of Deposit Banking in Mediterranean Europe* (Cambridge, Ma., 1943)

Vale, J. T., *Warfare and Aristocratic Culture in England, France, and Burgundy at the End of the Middle Ages* (Athens, Ga., 1981)

Valls Taverner, F., "Los Abogados en Cataluña Durante la Edad Media," in his *Obras. Vol. II. Estudios Histórico-Jurídicos* (Madrid-Barcelona, 1954), 281-318

Varela, J. *Modos de Educación en la España de la Contrarreforma* (Madrid, 1983)

Vasoli, C., *La Cultura Delle Corti* (Bologna, 1980)

Vázquez de Prada, V., "Aportación al Estudio de la Siderurgía Catalana S. XVI-XVII," *Homenaje a Juan Reglà Campistol* (Valencia, 1975), I, 665-673

Vicens Vives, J., *Ferran II i la Ciutat de Barcelona 1479-1516* (1936), 3 vols.

Vidal Pla, J., *Guerra dels Segadors i Crisi Social: Els Exiliats Filipistes 1640-52* (1984)

Vila, P., "Orígens i Evolució de la Rambla," *Miscelánea Barcelonensia*, 4 (11), 1965, 59-74

Vilar, P., *La Catalogne dans l'Espagne Moderne* (Paris, 1962), 3 vols.

——, *Assaigs Sobre la Catalunya del S. XVIII*, trans. E. Duran (1973)

——, "*Motín de Esquilache* et Crises d'Ancien Régime," *Historia Ibérica*, 1, 1973, 11-33

Villari, R., "La Città e la Cultura," *Studi Storici*, 23, 1982, 753-756

Viñas Cusí, F., *La Glànola a Barcelona: Estudi d'una de les Epidèmies 1651-54* (1901)

Vivanti, C., "Alle Origini dell'Idea di Civiltà: Le Scoperte Geografiche e gli Scritti di Henri de la Popelinière," *Rivista Storica Italiana*, 74, 1962, 227-249

——, *Lotta Politica e Pace Religiosa in Francia fra '500 e '600* (Turin, 1974)

Voltes Bou, P., "Nuevas Noticias de D. Pablo Ignacio de Dalmases y Ros y su Tiempo," *B.R.A.B.L.B.*, 26, 1954-56, 95-136

——, "Estatutos Aprobados por la Academia de Santo Tomás de Aquino de Barcelona en 1711," *A.S.T.*, 34, 1961, 341-360

Vovelle, M. and Roche, D., "Bourgeois, Rentiers and Property Owners: Elements for Defining a Social Category at the End of the Eighteenth Century," in J. Kaplow, ed., *New Perspectives on the French Revolution* (New York, 1965), 25-46

Waith, E. W., *The Herculean Hero in Marlowe, Chapman, Shakespeare, and Dryden* (New York, 1962)

Walker, M., *German Home Towns: Community, Estate, and General Estate 1648-1871* (Ithaca, 1971)

Watson, W. B., "Catalans in the Markets of Northern Europe During the Fifteenth Century," *Vicens* (1967), II, 785-810

Weintraub, K. J., *Visions of Culture* (Chicago, 1966)

Weissman, R., *Ritual Brotherhood in Renaissance Florence* (New York, 1982)

Westrich, S. A., *The Ormée of Bordeaux: A Revolution During the Fronde* (Baltimore, 1972)

Williams, R., *Culture and Society 1780-1950* (New York, 1958)

——, *Keywords: A Vocabulary of Culture and Society* (Oxford, 1976)

Wind, E., *Pagan Mysteries in the Renaissance* (New York, 1968)

Wood, J. B., *The Nobility of the Élection of Bayeux 1463-1666: Continuity Through Change* (Princeton, 1980)

Woodward, W. H., *Studies in Education During the Age of the Renaissance 1400-1600* (New York, 1967)

Woolf, S. J., "Venice and the Terraferma: Problems of the Change from Commercial to Landed Activities," in B. Pullan, ed., *Crisis and Change in the Venetian Economy in the Sixteenth and Seventeenth Centuries* (London, 1968), 175-203

Wright, L. P., "The Military Orders in Sixteenth and Seventeenth-Century Spanish Society: The Institutional Embodiment of a Historical Tradition," *P.P.*, 43, 1969, 34-70

Wrightson, K., "Two Concepts of Order: Justices, Constables, and Jurymen in Seventeenth-Century England," in J. Brewer and J. Styles, eds., *An Ungovernable People: The English and Their Law in the Seventeenth and Eighteenth Centuries* (New Brunswick, 1983), 21-46

Zanetti, D., *La Demografia del Patriziato Milanese nei S. XVII, XVIII, XIX* (Pavia, 1972)

Zulueta, F. de, *Don Antonio Agustín* (Glasgow, 1939)

INDEX

JAMES S. AMELANG
is Assistant Professor of History at the
University of Florida

Library of Congress Cataloging-in-Publication Data

Amelang, James S., 1952-
Honored citizens of Barcelona.

Bibliography: p.
Includes index.
1. Social classes—Spain—Barcelona—History.   2. Elite (Social
sciences—Spain—Barcelona—History)   3. Social history—
Modern, 1500-   . I. Title.
HN590.Z9S613   1986   305.5'0946'72   85-43205
ISBN 0-691-05461-4